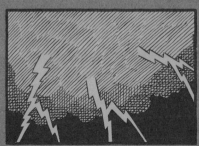

paying for it

a comic-strip memoir about being a john

CHESTER BROWN

DRAWN & QUARTERLY
montreal

Also by Chester Brown:
ED THE HAPPY CLOWN (1989)
THE PLAYBOY (1992)
I NEVER LIKED YOU (1994)
THE LITTLE MAN (1998)
LOUIS RIEL (2003)

Drawn & Quarterly
Post Office Box 48056
Montreal, Quebec
Canada H2V 4S8
www.drawnandquarterly.com

First hardcover edition: May 2011.
Printed in Singapore.
10 9 8 7 6 5 4 3 2 1

Library and Archives Canada Cataloguing in Publication
Brown, Chester, 1960-
          Paying For It / Chester Brown.
ISBN 978-1-77046-048-5
          I. Title.
PN6733.B76P39 2011   741.5'971   C2010-908156-0

Drawn & Quarterly acknowledges the financial contribution of the Government of
Canada through the Canada Book Fund and the Canada Council for the Arts for our
publishing activities and for support of this edition.

Distributed in the USA by:
Farrar, Straus and Giroux
18 West 18th Street
New York, NY 10011
Orders: 888.330.8477

Distributed in Canada by:
Raincoast Books
2440 Viking Way
Richmond, BC V6V 1N2
Orders: 800.663.5714

For Joe Matt.

He's a good friend
and a character
in the following pages,
but it's also appropriate
to dedicate this book to him
because
his autobiographical
comic-strips
were and are
an inspiration
for me.

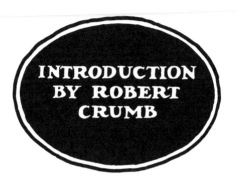

INTRODUCTION BY ROBERT CRUMB

Chester Brown is not of this planet. He is probably the result of one of those alien abductions where they stick a needle in a human woman's abdomen and impregnate her. He is a very advanced human. You can tell by looking at the photo of him. PAYING FOR IT is a very enlightening book, as well as being entertaining: he is a very skillful artist in that way. I'm sure to many people he's a dry, emotionless person. Notice how, throughout the book, his facial expression is always the same. His mouth is a slit. He never shows his teeth, never grins, never grimaces. The opposite of my portrayals of myself. Chester Brown's neutrality in the world is, in my estimation, quite admirable. As Jesus said, "Be as passers-by."

His arguments for the case in favor of unregulated prostitution seem entirely cogent to me. Whose business is it if a woman wants to charge for sex? His presentation of all the usual arguments against prostitution and his rebuttal to them is very effective. He shows that the anti-prostitution arguments are all based on either the old retrograde religious morality or knee-jerk liberal, half-baked assumptions about prostitution. All the smart hookers I've known roll their eyes in despair at the liberal do-gooders' attempts to

v

"reform" them. Not that I've ever had sex with a prostitute myself. I've always been too timid to try it, and also, my sexuality is too quirky and odd. It needs a special type of woman to accept the way I am, or like the way I am. In that regard, Chester Brown's sexual desires seem quite "normal," "MOR" (middle of the road). It's great the way he shows, through the years, how he became a real connoisseur in the world of professional sex workers. All the intelligent men I've known who patronized prostitutes became connoisseurs in this way. Some were married, some were bachelors. Didn't make any difference.

The idea of men paying for sex is repellant to the average woman, a threat to home, family and, yes, the ideal of romantic love. The average woman must believe all the negative stories and ideas about prostitution. But as Chester points out, surely there is as much sordid behavior among married couples as there is in the world of prostitution. And then too, so many of the problems that plague prostitutes are the result of society's scorn for them, to the extent that, as the book shows, many of them have to keep their "work" a secret, even from their friends. I had a female friend who, one night at dinner, confessed that she had done "escort" work for years, unbeknownst to her friends, and I observed that everyone thought of her a bit differently after that. Women thought less of her, I noticed, as if she'd confessed to having been involved in some sort of criminal activity. Men, some of them, then considered her a loose woman, fair game for casual sexual come-ons. It turned out, in fact, that she was a highly sexual woman who did have many casual affairs with men. But you can never tell a book by its cover, on the surface she was a shy, modest, self-effacing woman. You never would've suspected that she'd ever been a professional sex worker. Eventually, she moved out of the area. Almost all her female acquaintances increasingly shunned her as a "slut" and a home-wrecker, though she seemed the nicest and sweetest person, conscientious, hardworking. It was sad, actually. Later, we learned that she became a surrogate child-bearer for some wealthy couple. Dunno what became of her after that.

Well, enough. PAYING FOR IT is a great comic book, maybe Chester Brown's best work to date.

R. Crumb
February 2011

FOREWORD

I live in Toronto, so I was originally going to begin this foreword by explaining Canada's prostitution laws, but a recent court ruling has left the fate of those laws uncertain. They may or may not be changing. This is what the legal situation was like during the years covered by this memoir: "Outcall" prostitution was legal -- that is, sex-workers were allowed to go to a john's home or hotel room. "Incall" prostitution was illegal -- sex-workers were not allowed to work out of a specific location. They couldn't work in brothels, or out of their homes, or rent apartments to work in. When the police raided an incall location, anyone found in there could be arrested -- prostitutes and non-prostitutes. In order to discourage street-walkers, there was also a law forbidding prostitution-related solicitation in public.

In this book I record every time I paid for sex up to the end of 2003 and every prostitute I've had sex with since then.

Quite a few of the sex-workers I spent time with opened up to me and told me about their families, their childhoods, their boyfriends, and other aspects of their lives. I wish I had the freedom to include that material in the following pages -- it would have brought the women to life as full human beings and made this a better book. I'm assuming that all of them want to keep

FOREWORD

secret the sex-for-money part of their lives, so I refrained from putting in personal details that could potentially reveal their identities if a particular friend, family member, lover, or acquaintance were to read this memoir. When I show them giving details about their lives, the details are either trivial or about matters related to their work -- the latter being what you presumably wouldn't tell family and friends who didn't know you were a prostitute. The opinions I have the sex-workers putting forth are pretty common. Any of the more idiosyncratic views they expressed to me, I've omitted. It's a shame -- I felt genuine affection for many of these women and really wish that this narrative gave a better sense of their personalities.

The names the prostitutes went by were all fake, of course, but I've changed those names because even they could be potentially revealing. For example, a woman might choose as her work-name the name of a famous actress she resembles, or the name of a favourite fictional character.

Allowing for some degree of cartoon exaggeration, I've drawn their bodies accurately, or as accurately as my memory allows. I have altered aspects of their bodies if they could potentially reveal an identity -- for instance, I didn't draw any of the tattoos or unusual piercings that some of them had. I've often changed their hair-styles, particularly if the hair was arranged in a distinctive way. While you'd never know it from my drawings, some of these working-girls _did_ have blond hair. (Whether or not they were natural blondes is a different matter.) I saw women of various ethnic backgrounds, but I'm choosing to not indicate who was white, or black, or had another skin colour.

While I've recounted the incidents and conversations that make up this graphic novel in a manner that's reasonably faithful to my memories, you should keep in mind that memory is not precise. I would often remember the gist of a conversation I had with a friend but not where or when it happened or what we were doing at the time. I kept a record of when I saw the prostitutes, so I can vouch for the accuracy of those dates.

I'm going to save most of my thank-yous for the afterword, but up-front here I do want to thank The Canada Council For The Arts for generously assisting me financially while I wrote and drew this work.

Chester
Brown

December 2010

paying for
it

CHAPTER 1

MY LAST GIRLFRIEND

JUNE 1996:

Can we talk?

Sure.

I love you as much as ever, and I'm sure I'm always going to love you, but... I think I'm falling in love with someone else.

1

CHAPTER 1

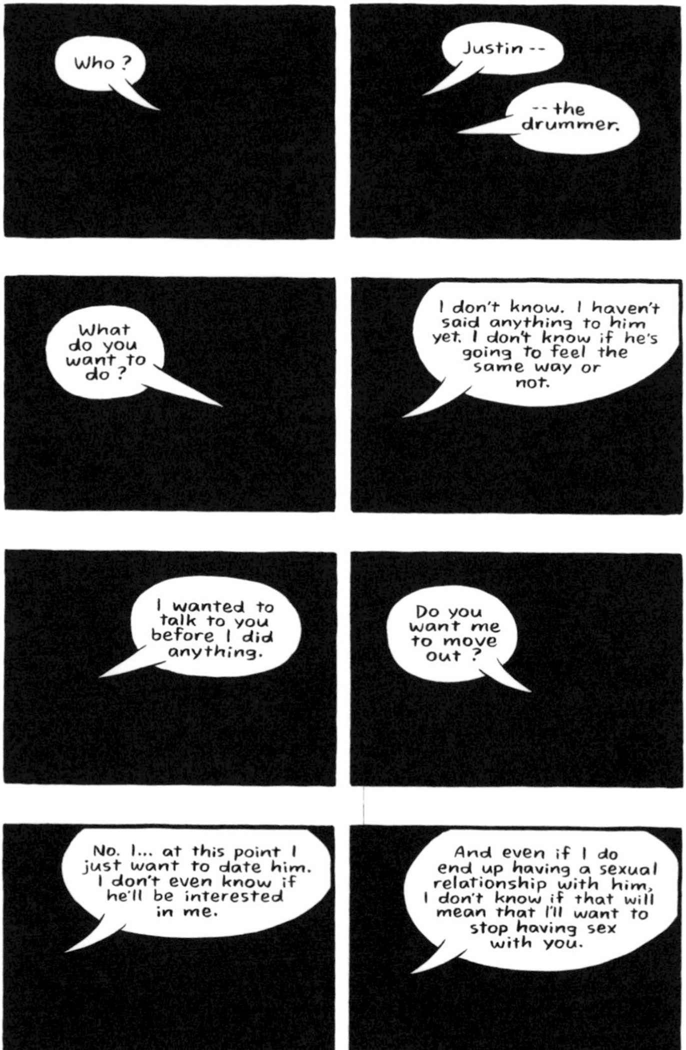

Who?
Justin --
-- the drummer.
What do you want to do?
I don't know. I haven't said anything to him yet. I don't know if he's going to feel the same way or not.
I wanted to talk to you before I did anything.
Do you want me to move out?
No. I... at this point I just want to date him. I don't even know if he'll be interested in me.
And even if I do end up having a sexual relationship with him, I don't know if that will mean that I'll want to stop having sex with you.

MY LAST GIRLFRIEND

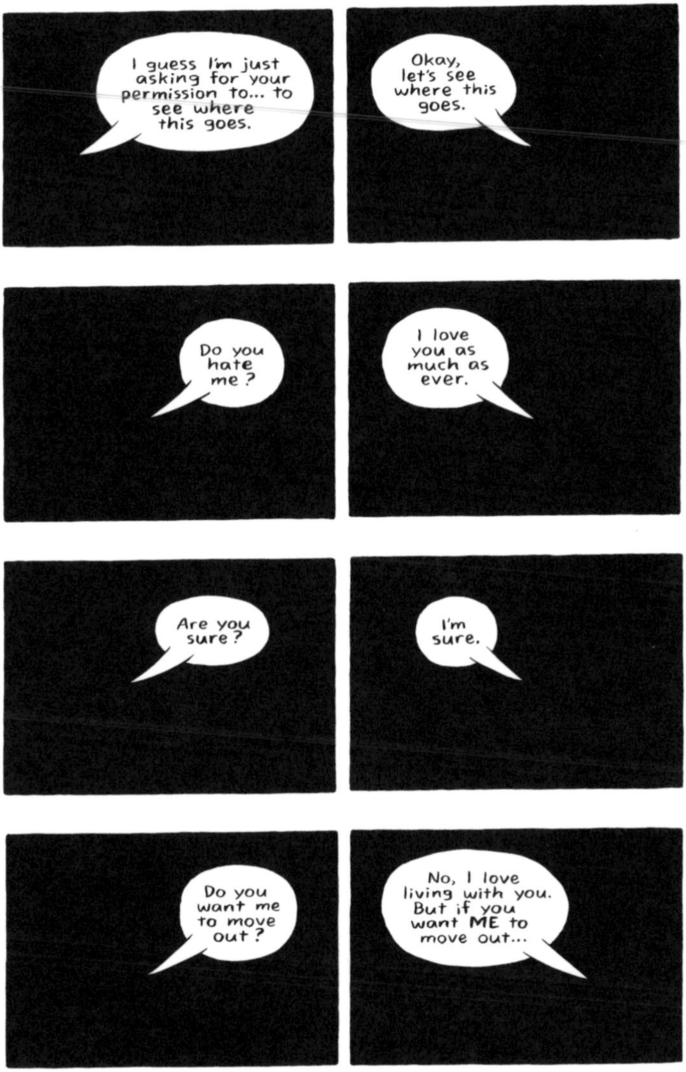
I guess I'm just asking for your permission to... to see where this goes.
Okay, let's see where this goes.
Do you hate me?
I love you as much as ever.
Are you sure?
I'm sure.
Do you want me to move out?
No, I love living with you. But if you want ME to move out...

CHAPTER 1

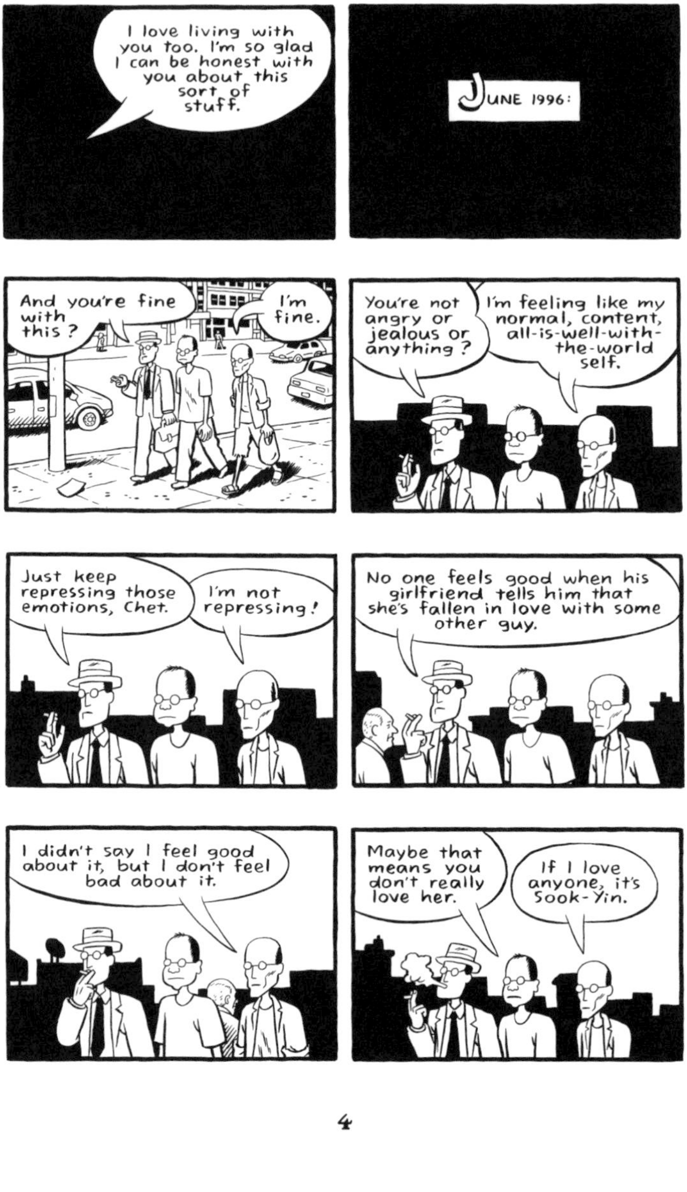
I love living with you too. I'm so glad I can be honest with you about this sort of stuff.
JUNE 1996:
And you're fine with this?
I'm fine.
You're not angry or jealous or anything?
I'm feeling like my normal, content, all-is-well-with-the-world self.
Just keep repressing those emotions, Chet.
I'm not repressing!
No one feels good when his girlfriend tells him that she's fallen in love with some other guy.
I didn't say I feel good about it, but I don't feel bad about it.
Maybe that means you don't really love her.
If I love anyone, it's Sook-Yin.

MY LAST GIRLFRIEND

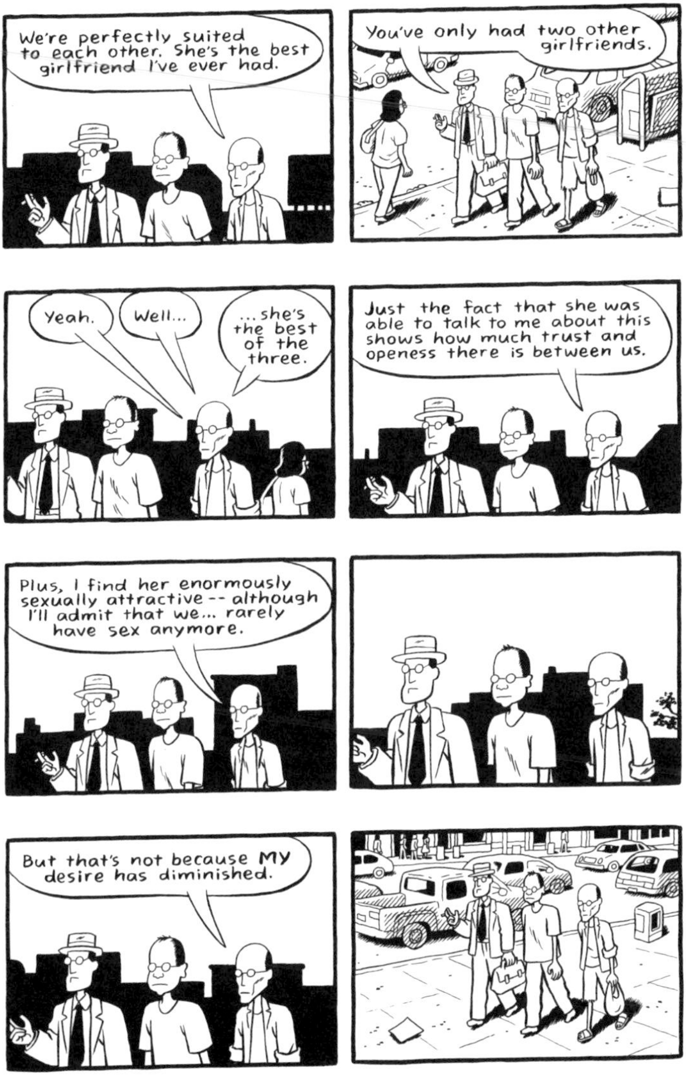
We're perfectly suited to each other. She's the best girlfriend I've ever had.
You've only had two other girlfriends.
Yeah.
Well...
...she's the best of the three.
Just the fact that she was able to talk to me about this shows how much trust and openess there is between us.
Plus, I find her enormously sexually attractive -- although I'll admit that we... rarely have sex anymore.
But that's not because MY desire has diminished.

CHAPTER 1

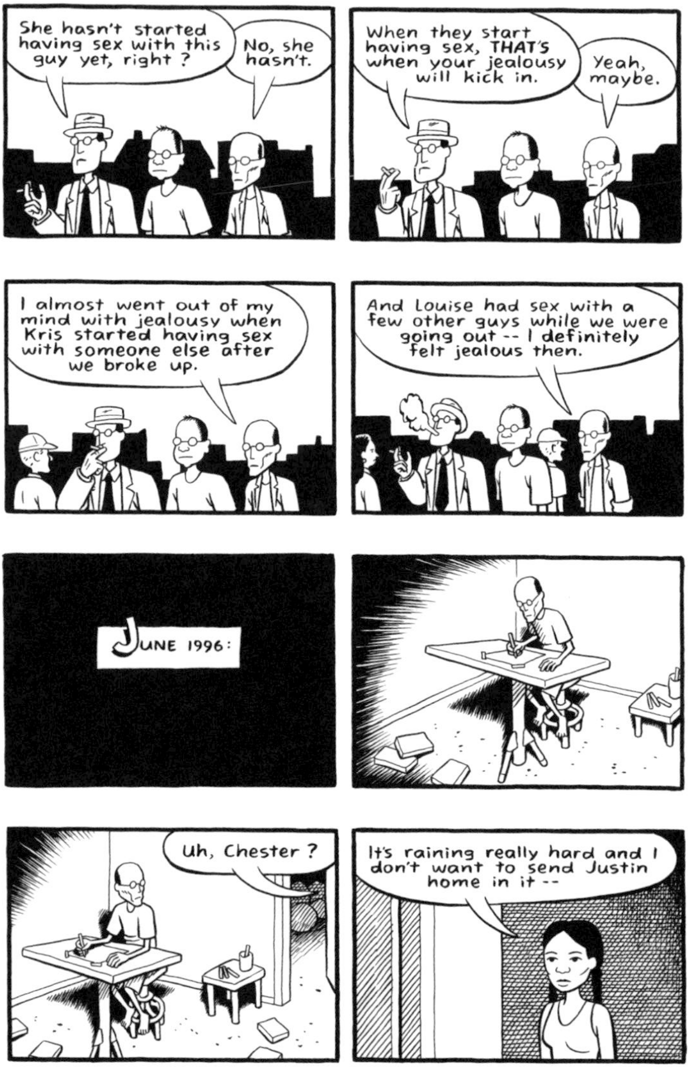
She hasn't started having sex with this guy yet, right?
No, she hasn't.
When they start having sex, THAT'S when your jealousy will kick in.
Yeah, maybe.
I almost went out of my mind with jealousy when Kris started having sex with someone else after we broke up.
And Louise had sex with a few other guys while we were going out -- I definitely felt jealous then.
JUNE 1996:
Uh, Chester?
It's raining really hard and I don't want to send Justin home in it --

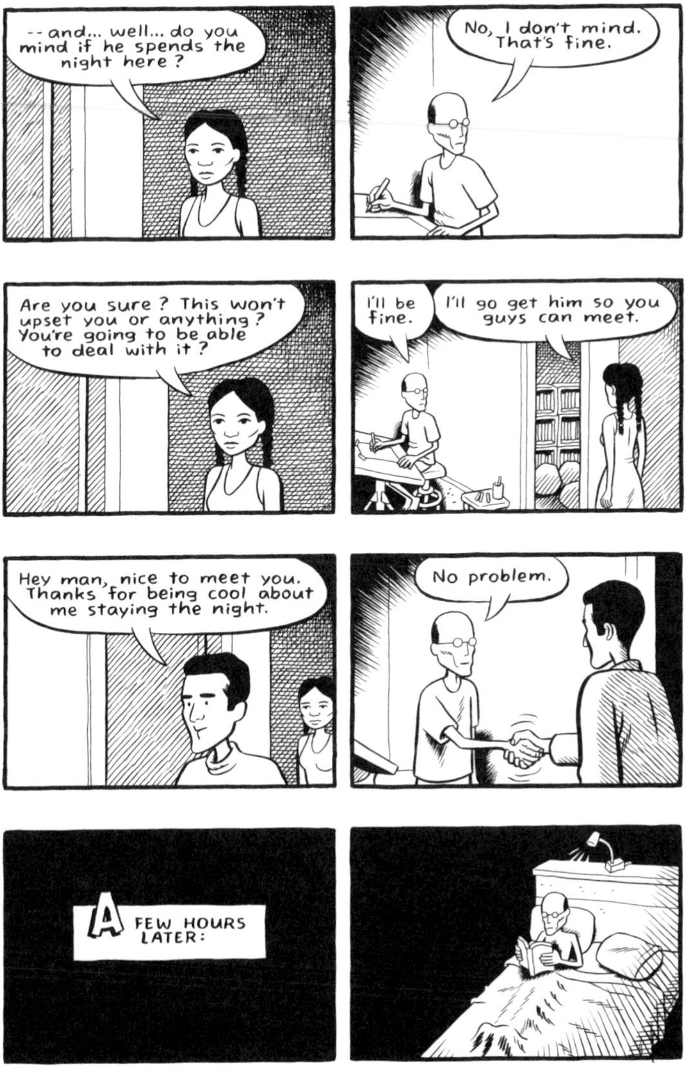
--and... well... do you mind if he spends the night here?
No, I don't mind. That's fine.
Are you sure? This won't upset you or anything? You're going to be able to deal with it?
I'll be fine.
I'll go get him so you guys can meet.
Hey man, nice to meet you. Thanks for being cool about me staying the night.
No problem.
A FEW HOURS LATER:

CHAPTER 1

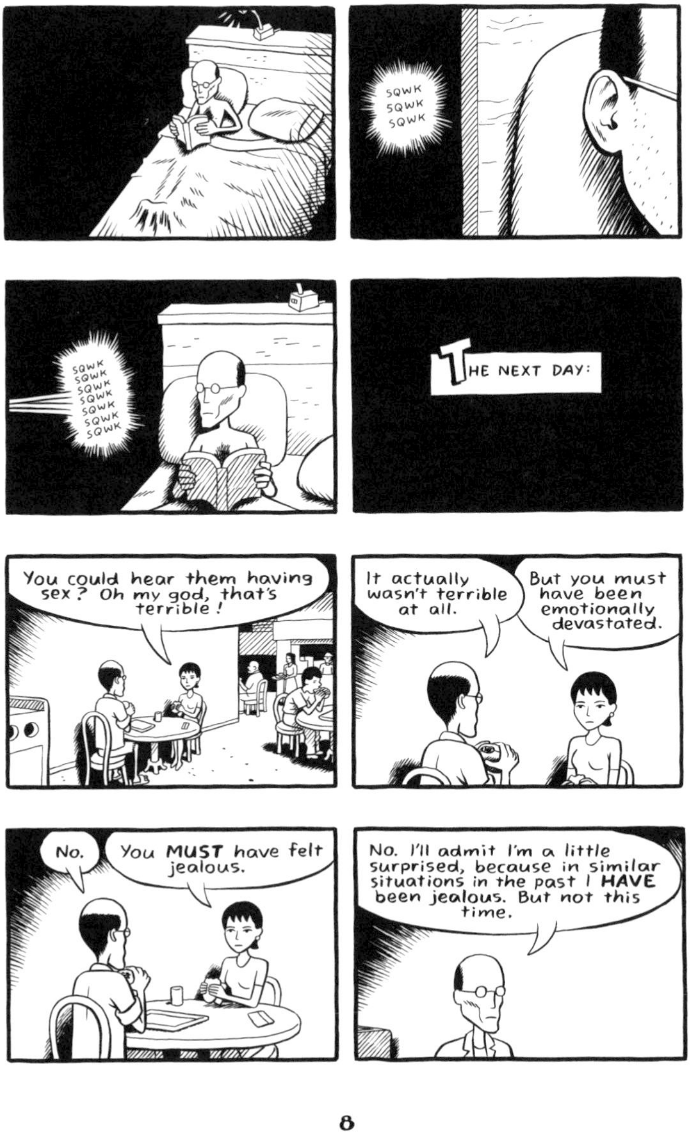
SQWK
SQWK
SQWK
SQWK
SQWK
SQWK
SQWK
SQWK
SQWK
SQWK
THE NEXT DAY:
You could hear them having sex? Oh my god, that's terrible!
It actually wasn't terrible at all.
But you must have been emotionally devastated.
No.
You MUST have felt jealous.
No. I'll admit I'm a little surprised, because in similar situations in the past I HAVE been jealous. But not this time.

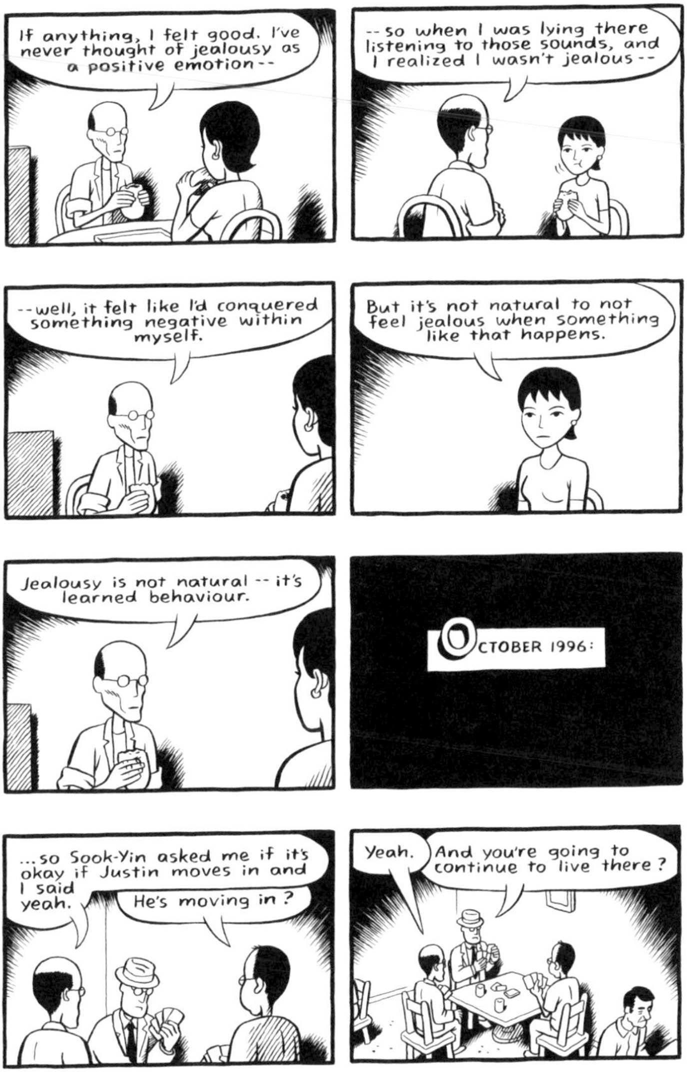
If anything, I felt good. I've never thought of jealousy as a positive emotion--
--so when I was lying there listening to those sounds, and I realized I wasn't jealous--
--well, it felt like I'd conquered something negative within myself.
But it's not natural to not feel jealous when something like that happens.
Jealousy is not natural -- it's learned behaviour.
OCTOBER 1996:
...so Sook-Yin asked me if it's okay if Justin moves in and I said yeah.
He's moving in?
Yeah.
And you're going to continue to live there?

CHAPTER 1

Yeah.
The three of you living in one apartment?
It's a big place -- it has two bedrooms. And my share of the rent will go down.
You're a glutton for punishment.
What punishment? I'm not in any way suffering, and I'll be saving money.
You're repressing. On a subconscious level you're suffering.
Freudian nonsense. If I'm not CONSCIOUSLY suffering, then I'm not suffering.
The fact that you're denying that you're suffering proves that you're suffering.
Oh brother. There's no winning against that argument.
When this whole Justin thing started, didn't Sook-Yin bring up the possibility that you two might continue to have a sexual relationship?
Yeah.
Has that happened?

MY LAST GIRLFRIEND

No, and I'm pretty sure that, sexually, things are completely over between us.
MARCH 1997:
I CAN'T BELIEVE HOW SELFISH YOU ARE!
I'M SELFISH? I'M SELFISH?
YOU'RE NOT EVEN TRYING TO
SHUT UP! JUST SHUT UP!
APRIL 1997:
Living all together in the same apartment is actually great. I get to hear all of their arguments.
I'm becoming more and more convinced that I never want to have a girlfriend ever again.

CHAPTER 1

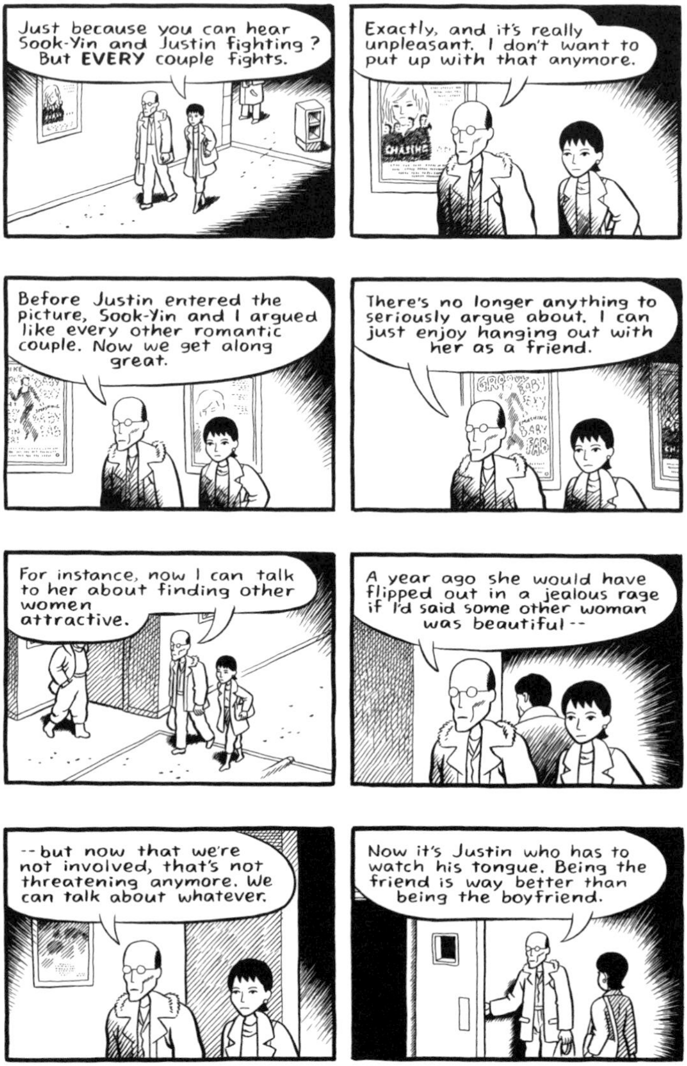

Just because you can hear Sook-Yin and Justin fighting? But EVERY couple fights.
Exactly, and it's really unpleasant. I don't want to put up with that anymore.
Before Justin entered the picture, Sook-Yin and I argued like every other romantic couple. Now we get along great.
There's no longer anything to seriously argue about. I can just enjoy hanging out with her as a friend.
For instance, now I can talk to her about finding other women attractive.
A year ago she would have flipped out in a jealous rage if I'd said some other woman was beautiful--
--but now that we're not involved, that's not threatening anymore. We can talk about whatever.
Now it's Justin who has to watch his tongue. Being the friend is way better than being the boyfriend.

MY LAST GIRLFRIEND

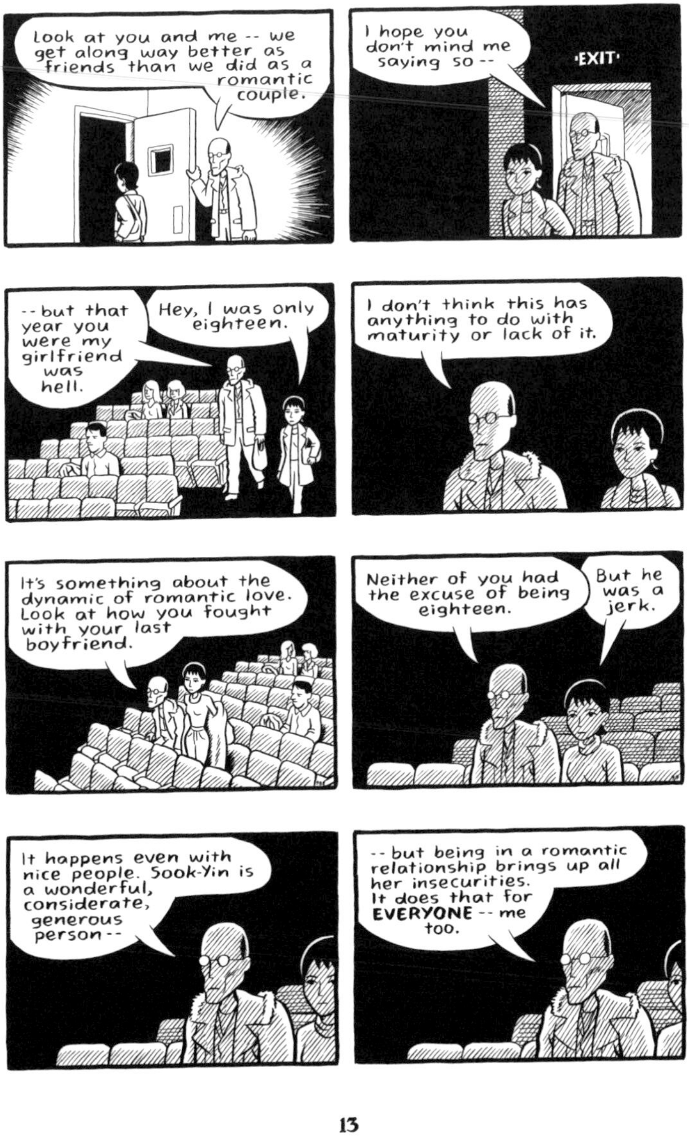

Look at you and me -- we get along way better as friends than we did as a romantic couple.
I hope you don't mind me saying so --
·EXIT·
-- but that year you were my girlfriend was hell.
Hey, I was only eighteen.
I don't think this has anything to do with maturity or lack of it.
It's something about the dynamic of romantic love. Look at how you fought with your last boyfriend.
Neither of you had the excuse of being eighteen.
But he was a jerk.
It happens even with nice people. Sook-Yin is a wonderful, considerate, generous person --
-- but being in a romantic relationship brings up all her insecurities. It does that for EVERYONE -- me too.

CHAPTER 1

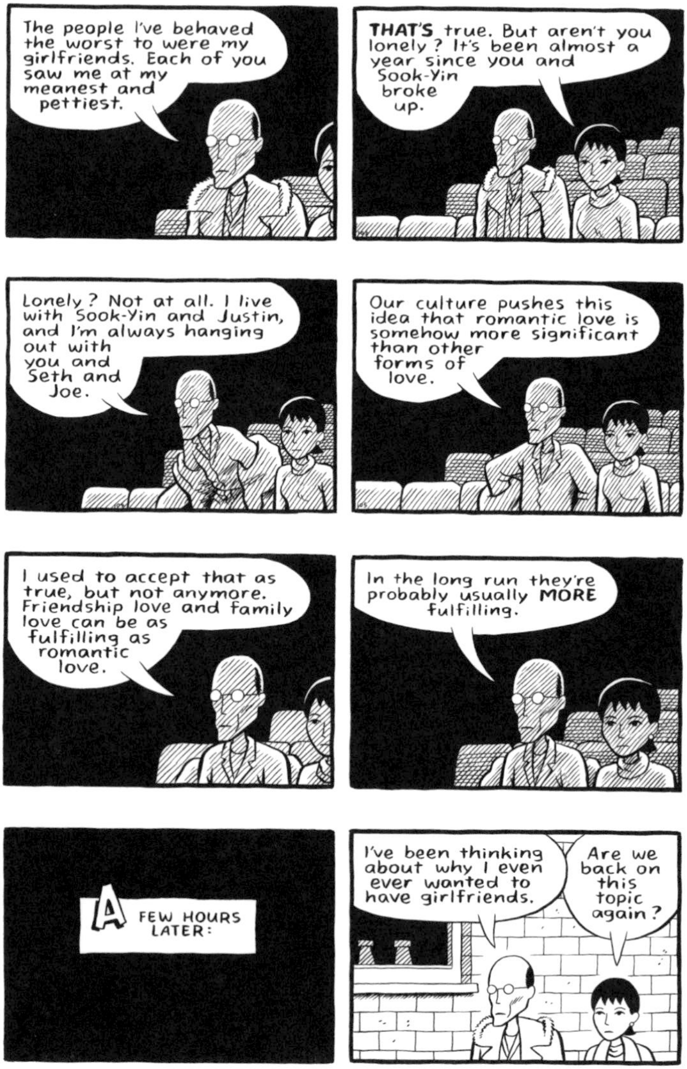
The people I've behaved the worst to were my girlfriends. Each of you saw me at my meanest and pettiest.
THAT'S true. But aren't you lonely? It's been almost a year since you and Sook-Yin broke up.
Lonely? Not at all. I live with Sook-Yin and Justin, and I'm always hanging out with you and Seth and Joe.
Our culture pushes this idea that romantic love is somehow more significant than other forms of love.
I used to accept that as true, but not anymore. Friendship love and family love can be as fulfilling as romantic love.
In the long run they're probably usually MORE fulfilling.
A FEW HOURS LATER:
I've been thinking about why I even ever wanted to have girlfriends.
Are we back on this topic again?

MY LAST GIRLFRIEND

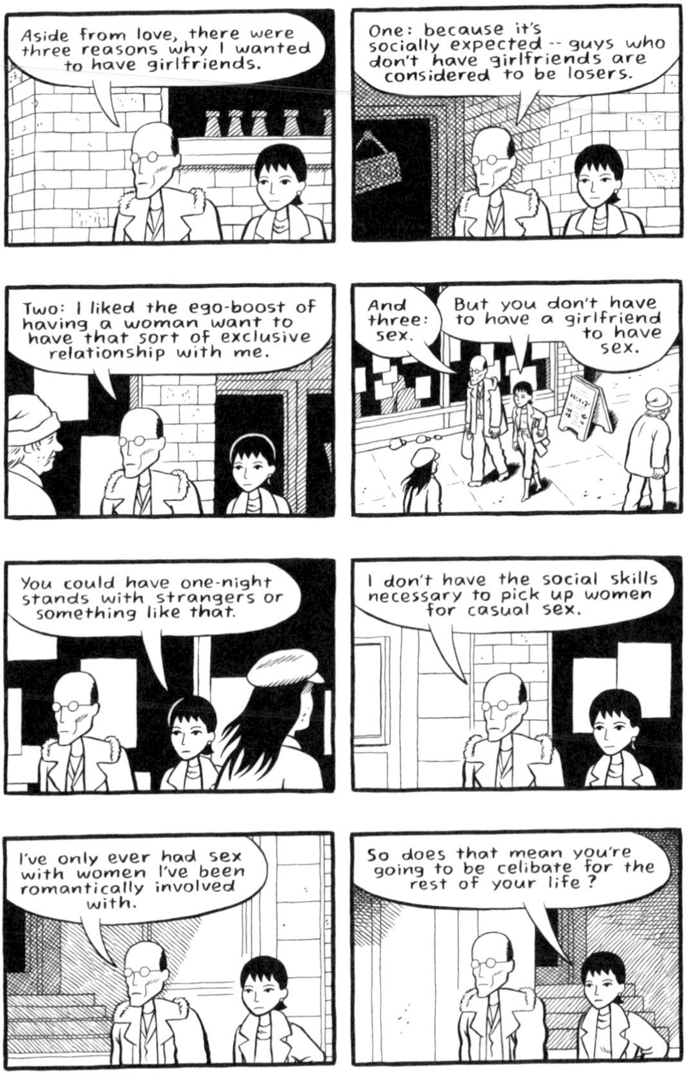

Aside from love, there were three reasons why I wanted to have girlfriends.
One: because it's socially expected -- guys who don't have girlfriends are considered to be losers.
Two: I liked the ego-boost of having a woman want to have that sort of exclusive relationship with me.
And three: sex.
But you don't have to have a girlfriend to have sex.
You could have one-night stands with strangers or something like that.
I don't have the social skills necessary to pick up women for casual sex.
I've only ever had sex with women I've been romantically involved with.
So does that mean you're going to be celibate for the rest of your life?

CHAPTER 1

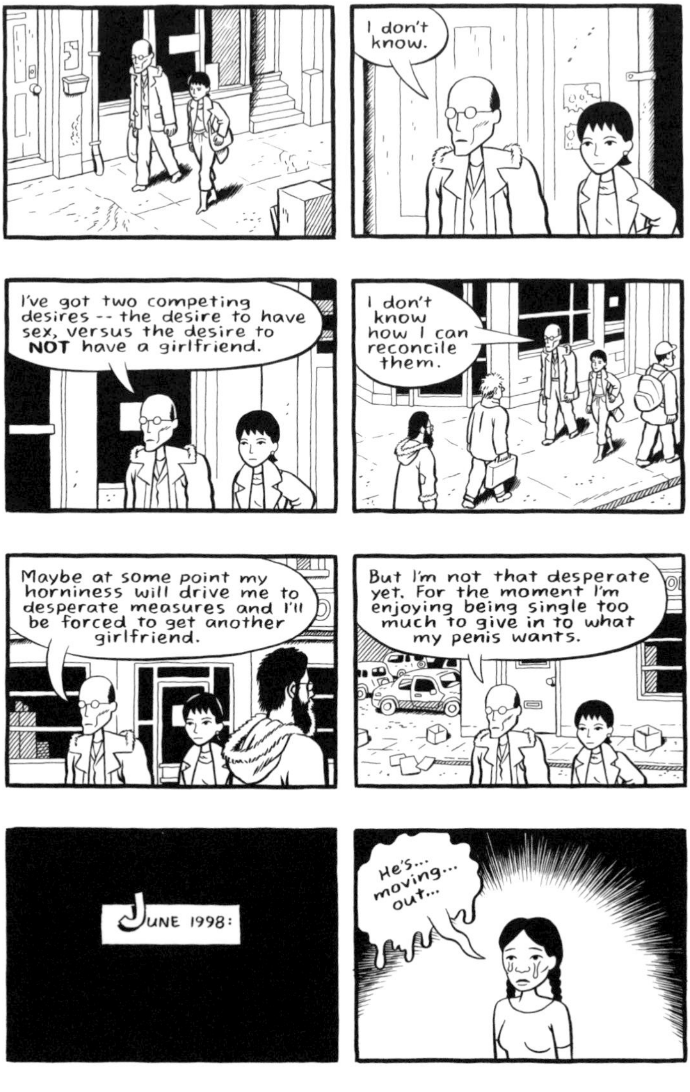
I don't know.
I've got two competing desires -- the desire to have sex, versus the desire to **NOT** have a girlfriend.
I don't know how I can reconcile them.
Maybe at some point my horniness will drive me to desperate measures and I'll be forced to get another girlfriend.
But I'm not that desperate yet. For the moment I'm enjoying being single too much to give in to what my penis wants.
JUNE 1998:
He's... moving... out...

MY LAST GIRLFRIEND

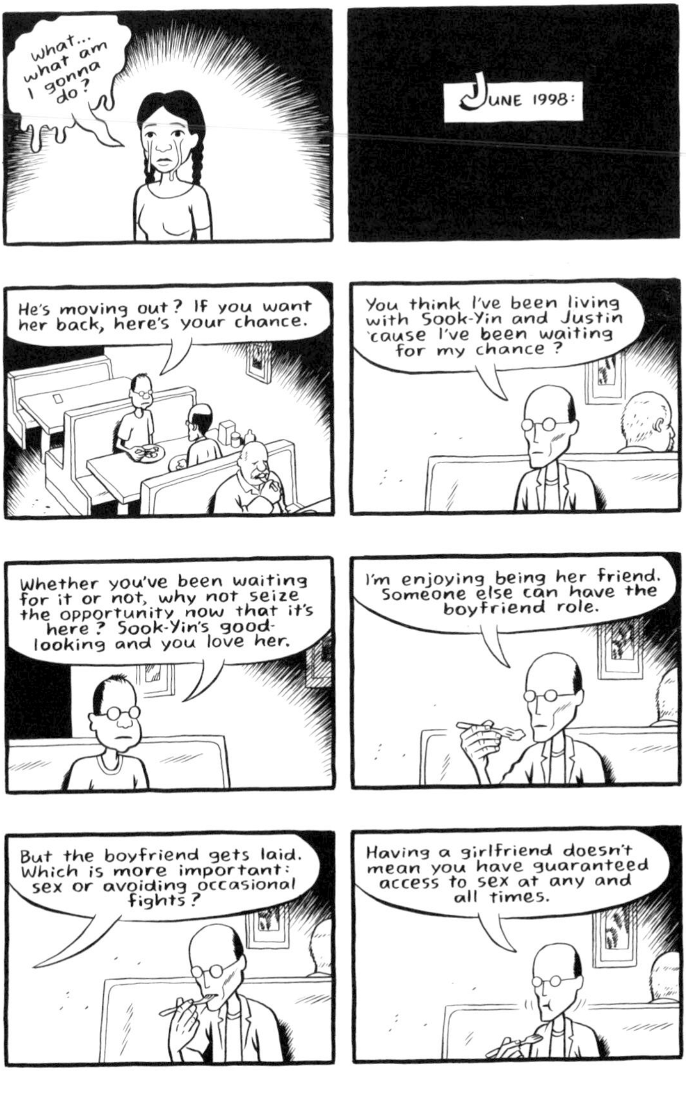
What... what am I gonna do?
JUNE 1998:
He's moving out? If you want her back, here's your chance.
You think I've been living with Sook-Yin and Justin 'cause I've been waiting for my chance?
Whether you've been waiting for it or not, why not seize the opportunity now that it's here? Sook-Yin's good-looking and you love her.
I'm enjoying being her friend. Someone else can have the boyfriend role.
But the boyfriend gets laid. Which is more important: sex or avoiding occasional fights?
Having a girlfriend doesn't mean you have guaranteed access to sex at any and all times.

CHAPTER 1

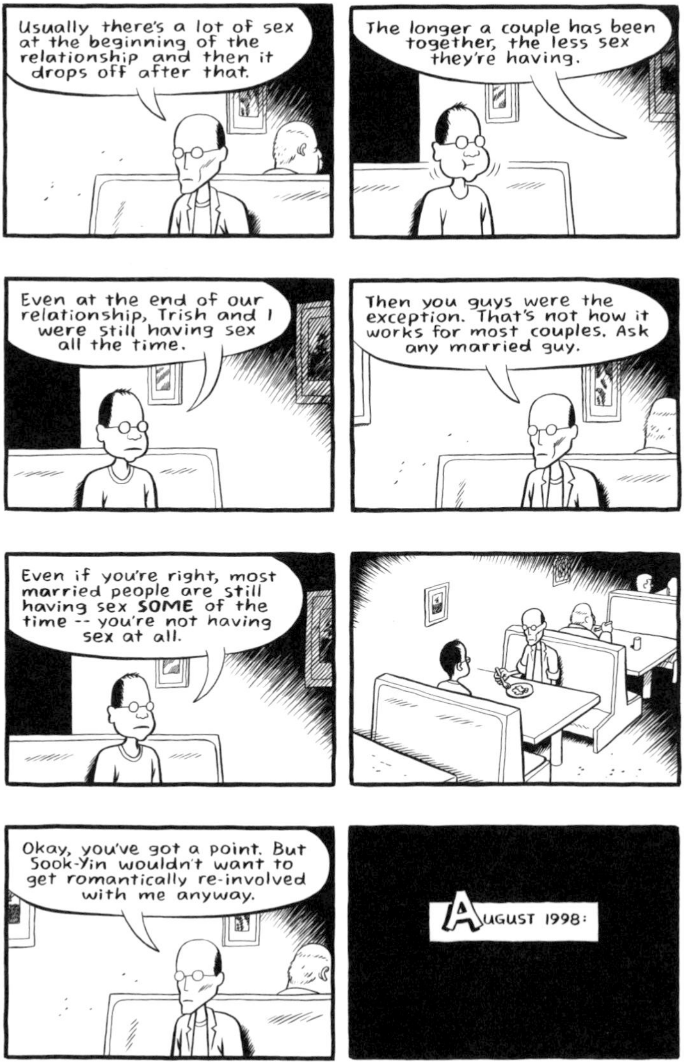
Usually there's a lot of sex at the beginning of the relationship and then it drops off after that.
The longer a couple has been together, the less sex they're having.
Even at the end of our relationship, Trish and I were still having sex all the time.
Then you guys were the exception. That's not how it works for most couples. Ask any married guy.
Even if you're right, most married people are still having sex SOME of the time -- you're not having sex at all.
Okay, you've got a point. But Sook-Yin wouldn't want to get romantically re-involved with me anyway.
AUGUST 1998:

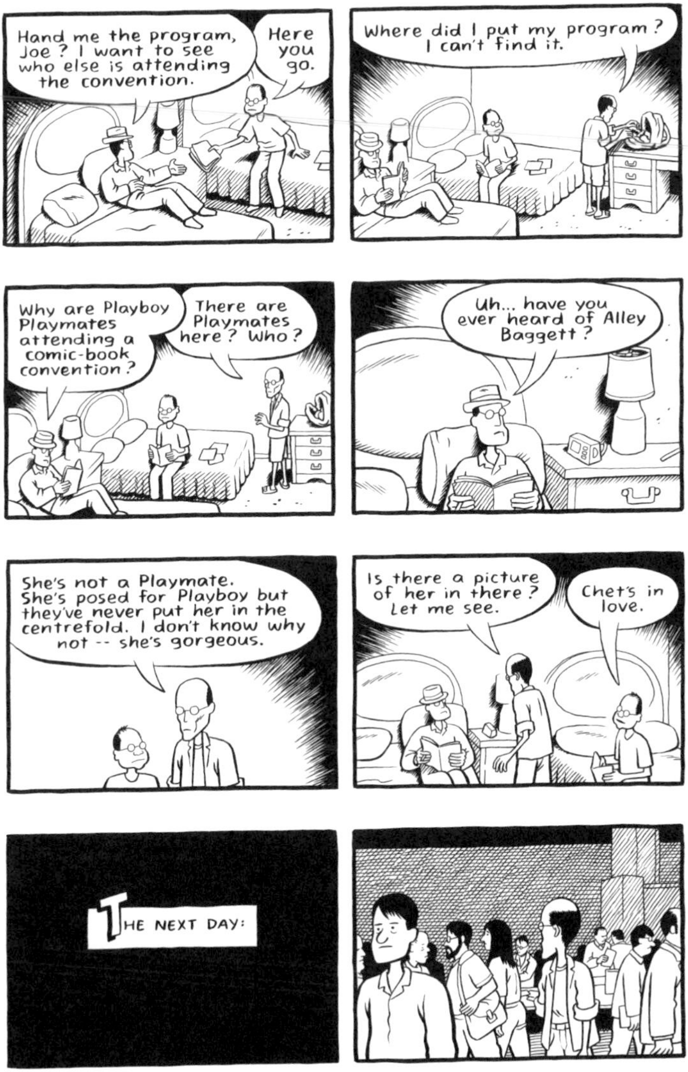
Hand me the program, Joe? I want to see who else is attending the convention.
Here you go.
Where did I put my program? I can't find it.
Why are Playboy Playmates attending a comic-book convention?
There are Playmates here? Who?
Uh... have you ever heard of Alley Baggett?
She's not a Playmate. She's posed for Playboy but they've never put her in the centrefold. I don't know why not -- she's gorgeous.
Is there a picture of her in there? Let me see.
Chet's in love.
THE NEXT DAY:

CHAPTER 1

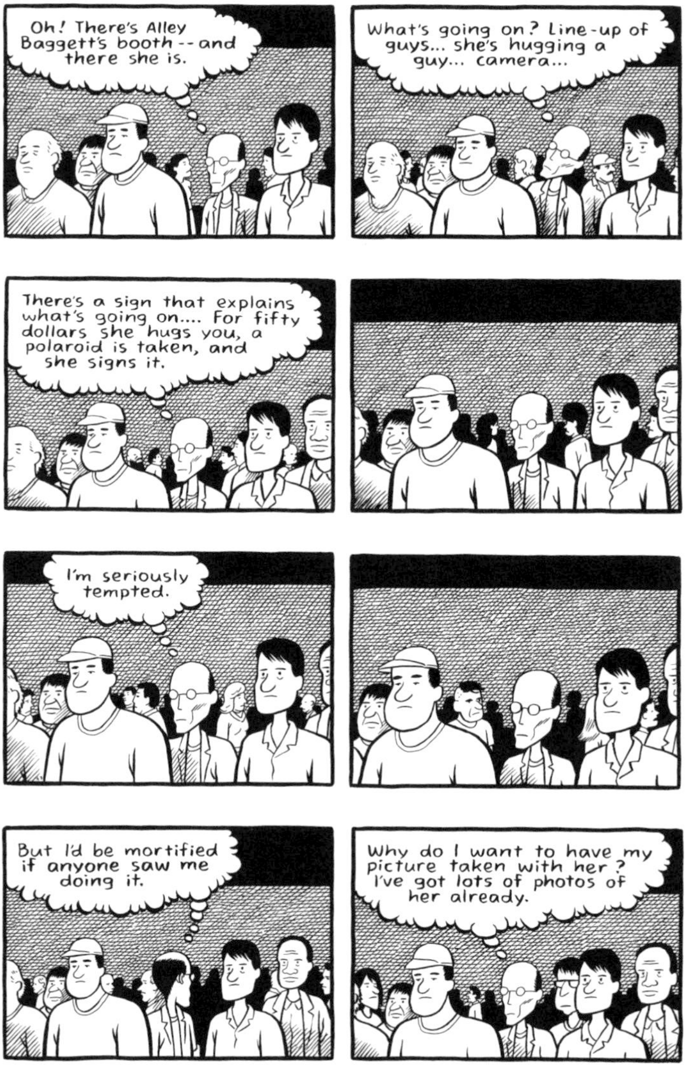
Oh! There's Alley Baggett's booth -- and there she is.
What's going on? Line-up of guys... she's hugging a guy... camera...
There's a sign that explains what's going on.... For fifty dollars she hugs you, a polaroid is taken, and she signs it.
I'm seriously tempted.
But I'd be mortified if anyone saw me doing it.
Why do I want to have my picture taken with her? I've got lots of photos of her already.

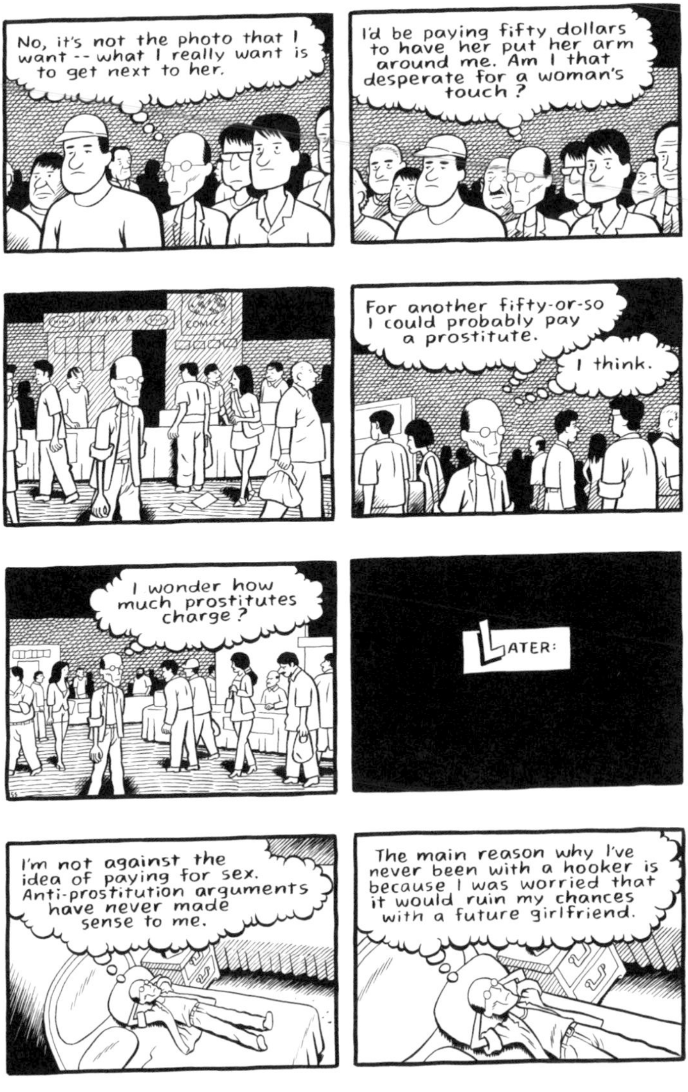
No, it's not the photo that I want -- what I really want is to get next to her.
I'd be paying fifty dollars to have her put her arm around me. Am I that desperate for a woman's touch?
COMICS
For another fifty-or-so I could probably pay a prostitute.
I think.
I wonder how much prostitutes charge?
LATER:
I'm not against the idea of paying for sex. Anti-prostitution arguments have never made sense to me.
The main reason why I've never been with a hooker is because I was worried that it would ruin my chances with a future girlfriend.

CHAPTER 1

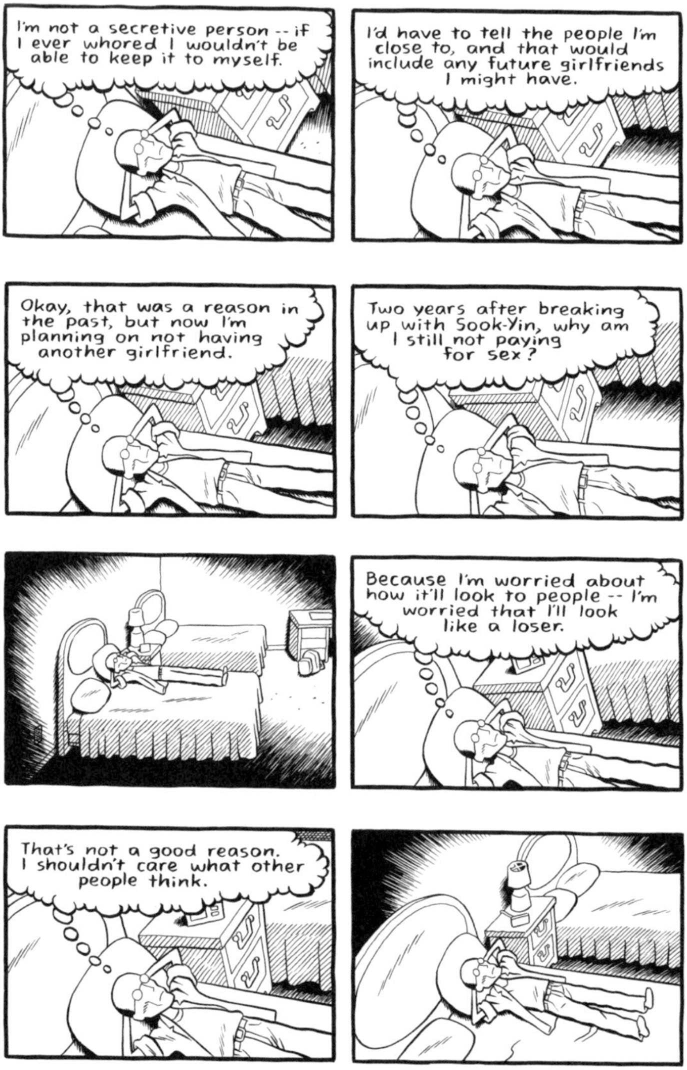
I'm not a secretive person -- if I ever whored I wouldn't be able to keep it to myself.
I'd have to tell the people I'm close to, and that would include any future girlfriends I might have.
Okay, that was a reason in the past, but now I'm planning on not having another girlfriend.
Two years after breaking up with Sook-Yin, why am I still not paying for sex?
Because I'm worried about how it'll look to people -- I'm worried that I'll look like a loser.
That's not a good reason. I shouldn't care what other people think.

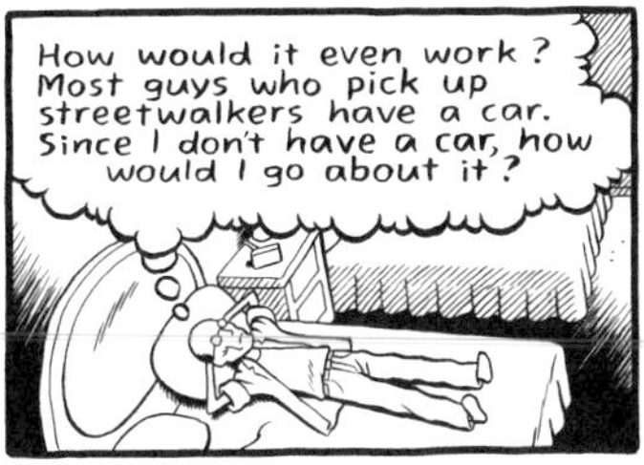
How would it even work? Most guys who pick up streetwalkers have a car. Since I don't have a car, how would I go about it?

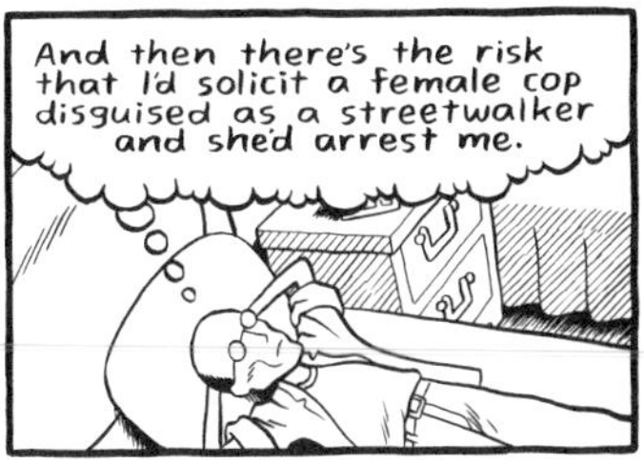
And then there's the risk that I'd solicit a female cop disguised as a streetwalker and she'd arrest me.

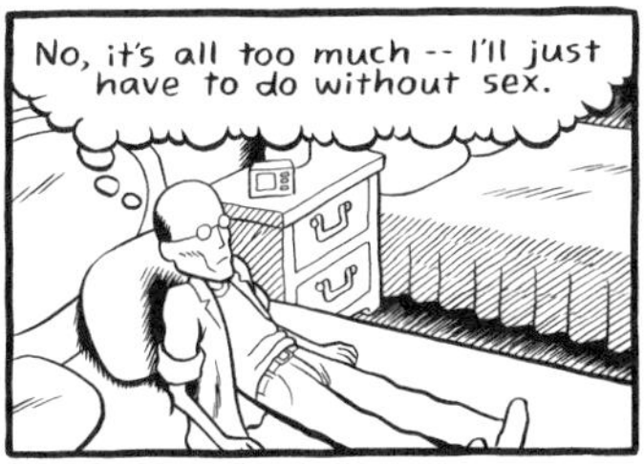
No, it's all too much -- I'll just have to do without sex.

CHAPTER 2
CARLA

MARCH 1999:

Do you mind if I read that Dan Savage book I bought you?

No, go ahead.

LATER:

CHAPTER 2

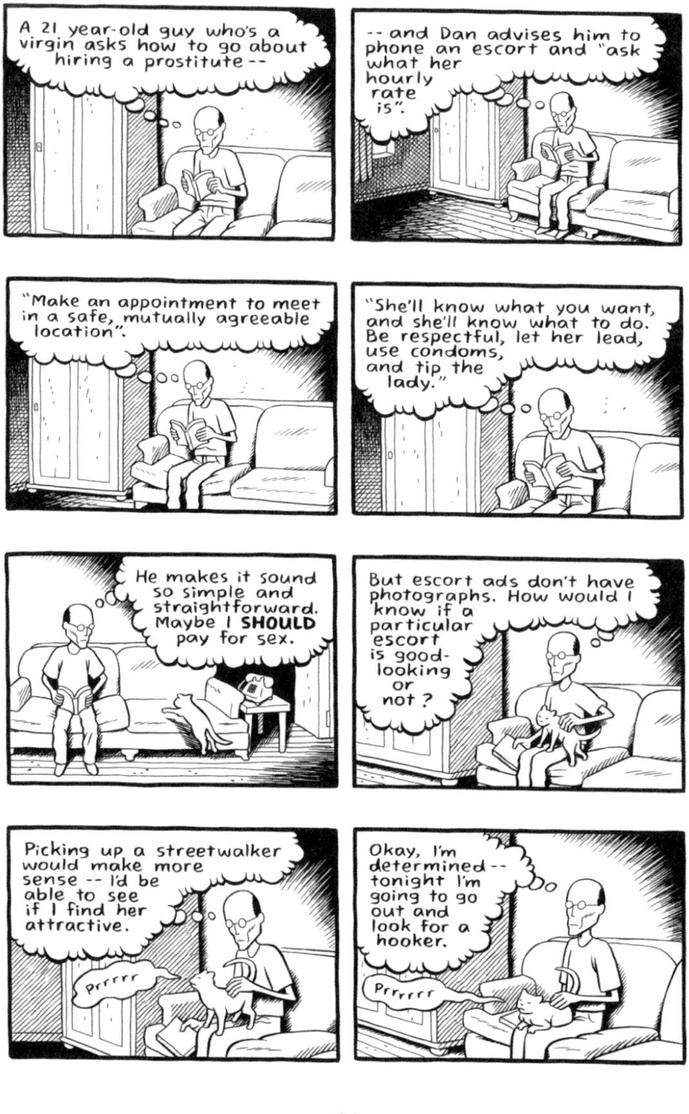
A 21 year-old guy who's a virgin asks how to go about hiring a prostitute --
-- and Dan advises him to phone an escort and "ask what her hourly rate is".
"Make an appointment to meet in a safe, mutually agreeable location".
"She'll know what you want, and she'll know what to do. Be respectful, let her lead, use condoms, and tip the lady."
He makes it sound so simple and straightforward. Maybe I SHOULD pay for sex.
But escort ads don't have photographs. How would I know if a particular escort is good-looking or not?
Picking up a streetwalker would make more sense -- I'd be able to see if I find her attractive.
Prrrrr
Okay, I'm determined -- tonight I'm going to go out and look for a hooker.
Prrrrrr

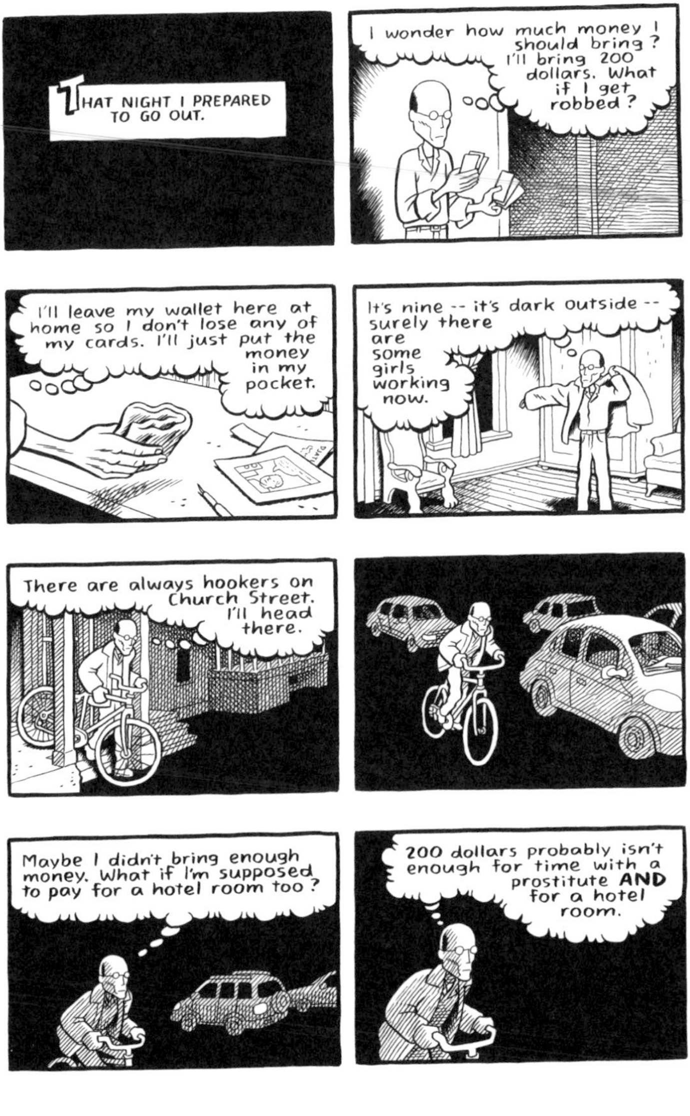
THAT NIGHT I PREPARED TO GO OUT.
I wonder how much money I should bring? I'll bring 200 dollars. What if I get robbed?
I'll leave my wallet here at home so I don't lose any of my cards. I'll just put the money in my pocket.
It's nine -- it's dark outside -- surely there are some girls working now.
There are always hookers on Church Street. I'll head there.
Maybe I didn't bring enough money. What if I'm supposed to pay for a hotel room too?
200 dollars probably isn't enough for time with a prostitute AND for a hotel room.

CHAPTER 2

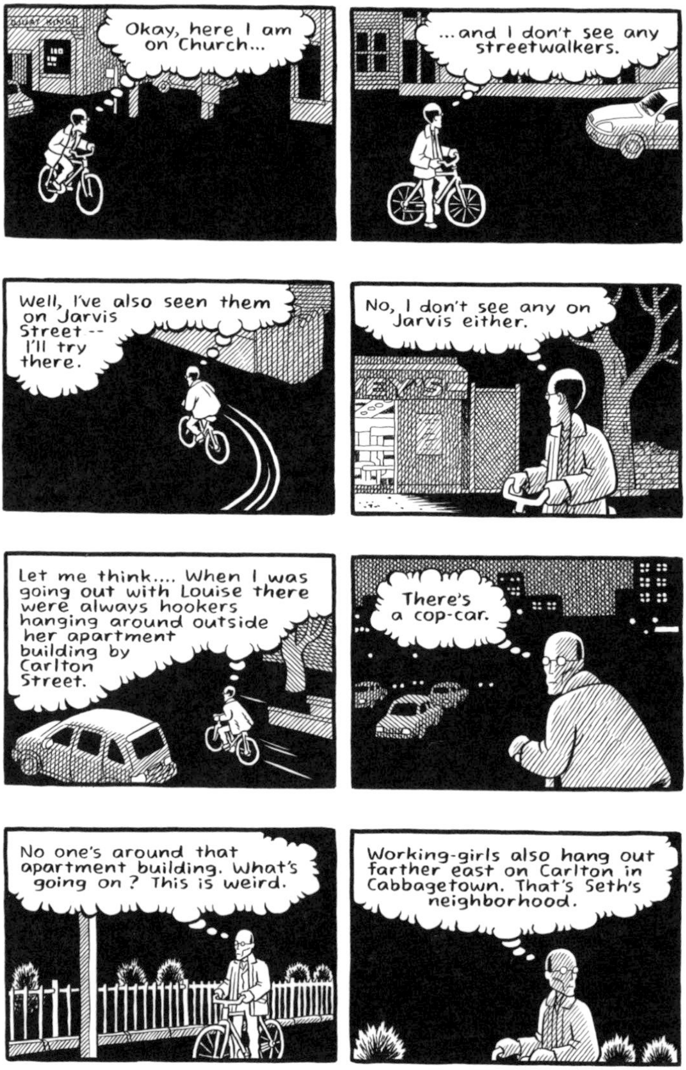
Okay, here I am on Church...
...and I don't see any streetwalkers.
Well, I've also seen them on Jarvis Street -- I'll try there.
No, I don't see any on Jarvis either.
Let me think.... When I was going out with Louise there were always hookers hanging around outside her apartment building by Carlton Street.
There's a cop-car.
No one's around that apartment building. What's going on? This is weird.
Working-girls also hang out farther east on Carlton in Cabbagetown. That's Seth's neighborhood.

It'd be embarrassing if he walked by while I was negotiating something, but I'm running out of options.

There's another cop-car.

Nope, no streetwalkers here in Cabbagetown.

Maybe police pressure has driven them into other neighborhoods. Maybe there was a recent police crackdown. Or maybe I'm just too early.

Oh well, I'm giving up and going home.

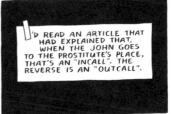

THE NEXT DAY -- MARCH 26th 1999:

Let's take a closer look at the escort ads.

I'D READ AN ARTICLE THAT HAD EXPLAINED THAT, WHEN THE JOHN GOES TO THE PROSTITUTE'S PLACE, THAT'S AN "INCALL". THE REVERSE IS AN "OUTCALL".

CHAPTER 2

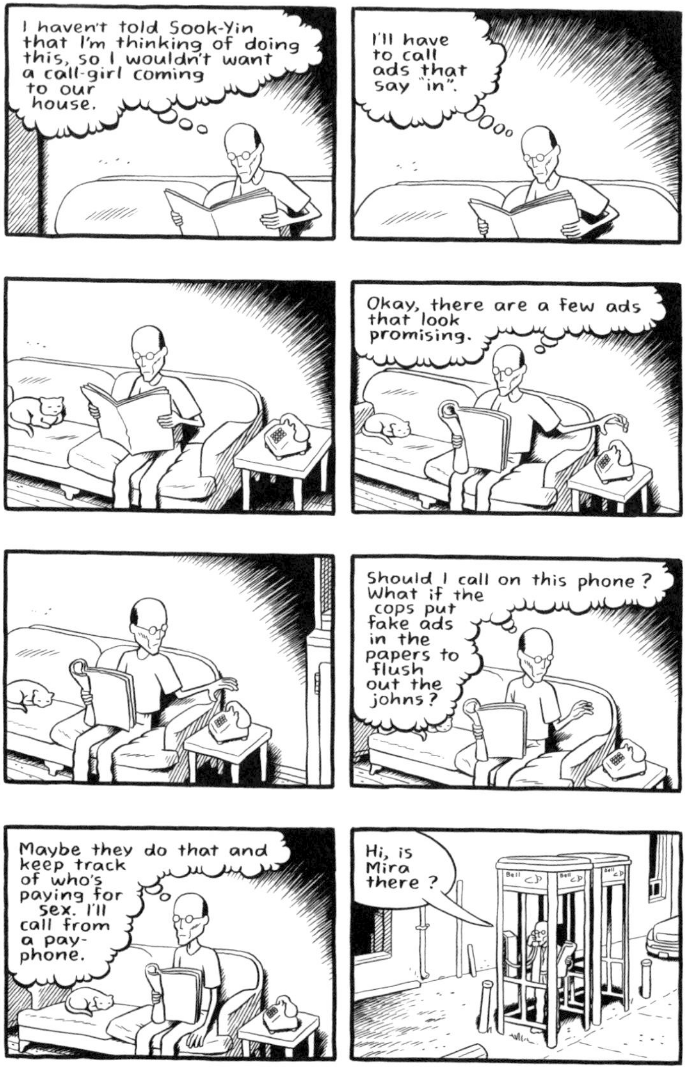
I haven't told Sook-Yin that I'm thinking of doing this, so I wouldn't want a call-girl coming to our house.
I'll have to call ads that say "in".
Okay, there are a few ads that look promising.
Should I call on this phone? What if the cops put fake ads in the papers to flush out the johns?
Maybe they do that and keep track of who's paying for sex. I'll call from a pay-phone.
Hi, is Mira there?
Bell
Bell
Bell

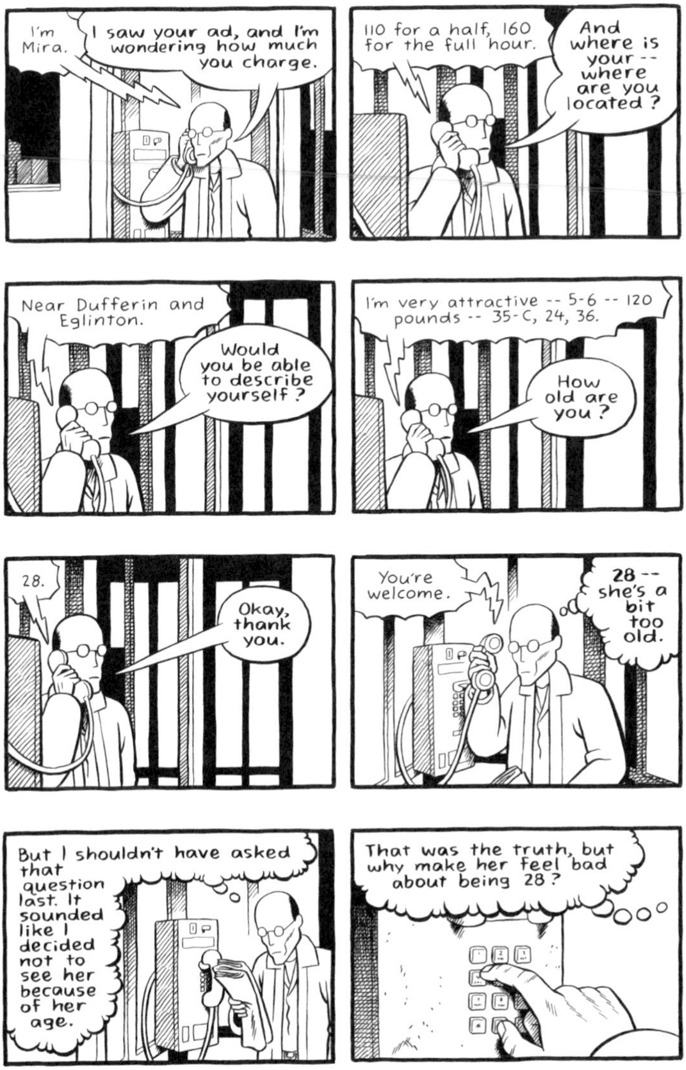
I'm Mira.
I saw your ad, and I'm wondering how much you charge.
110 for a half, 160 for the full hour.
And where is your -- where are you located?
Near Dufferin and Eglinton.
Would you be able to describe yourself?
I'm very attractive -- 5-6 -- 120 pounds -- 35-C, 24, 36.
How old are you?
28.
Okay, thank you.
You're welcome.
28 -- she's a bit too old.
But I shouldn't have asked that question last. It sounded like I decided not to see her because of her age.
That was the truth, but why make her feel bad about being 28?

CHAPTER 2

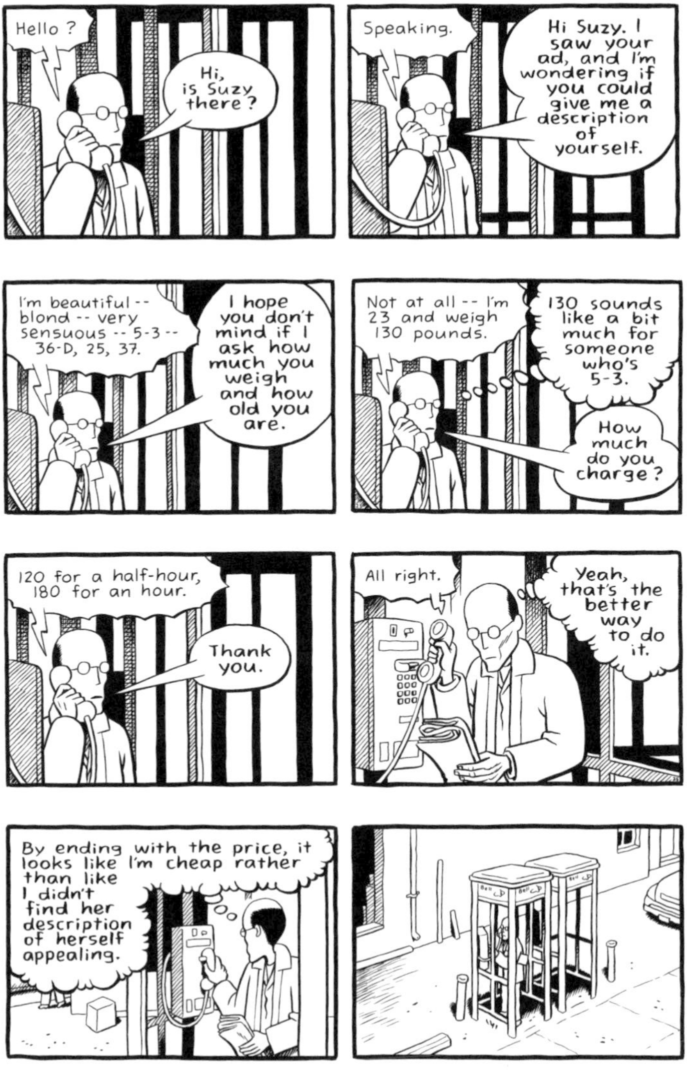

Hello ?
Hi, is Suzy there ?
Speaking.
Hi Suzy. I saw your ad, and I'm wondering if you could give me a description of yourself.
I'm beautiful -- blond -- very sensuous -- 5-3 -- 36-D, 25, 37.
I hope you don't mind if I ask how much you weigh and how old you are.
Not at all -- I'm 23 and weigh 130 pounds.
130 sounds like a bit much for someone who's 5-3.
How much do you charge ?
120 for a half-hour, 180 for an hour.
Thank you.
All right.
Yeah, that's the better way to do it.
By ending with the price, it looks like I'm cheap rather than like I didn't find her description of herself appealing.

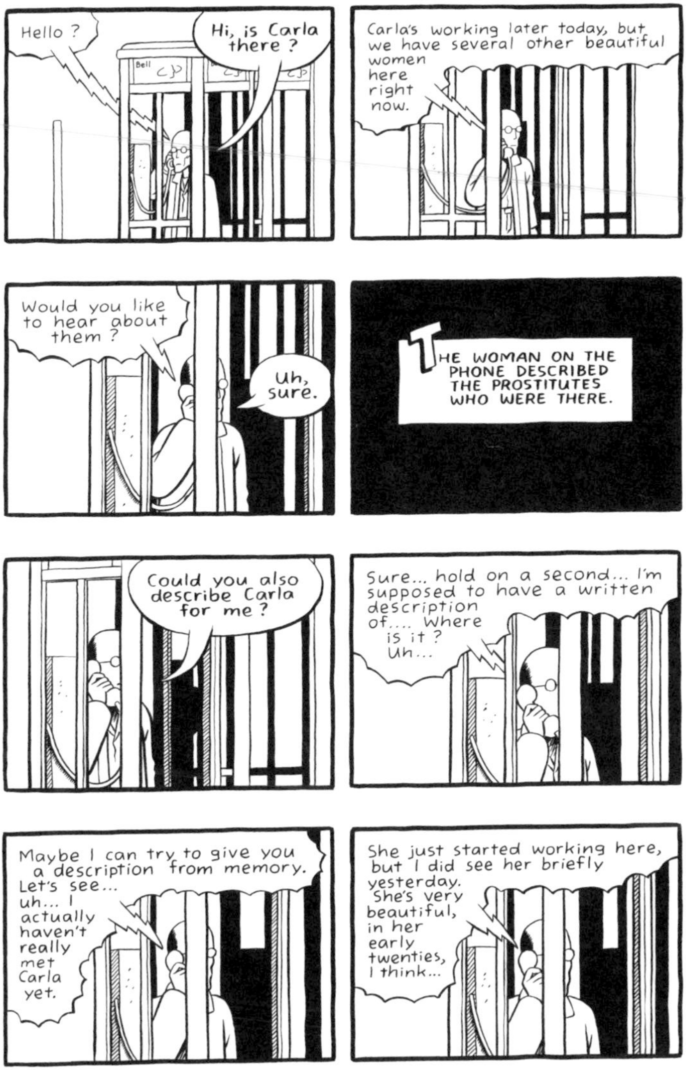
Hello ?
Hi, is Carla there ?
Bell
Carla's working later today, but we have several other beautiful women here right now.
Would you like to hear about them ?
Uh, sure.
THE WOMAN ON THE PHONE DESCRIBED THE PROSTITUTES WHO WERE THERE.
Could you also describe Carla for me ?
Sure... hold on a second... I'm supposed to have a written description of.... Where is it ? Uh...
Maybe I can try to give you a description from memory. Let's see... uh... I actually haven't really met Carla yet.
She just started working here, but I did see her briefly yesterday. She's very beautiful, in her early twenties, I think...

CHAPTER 2

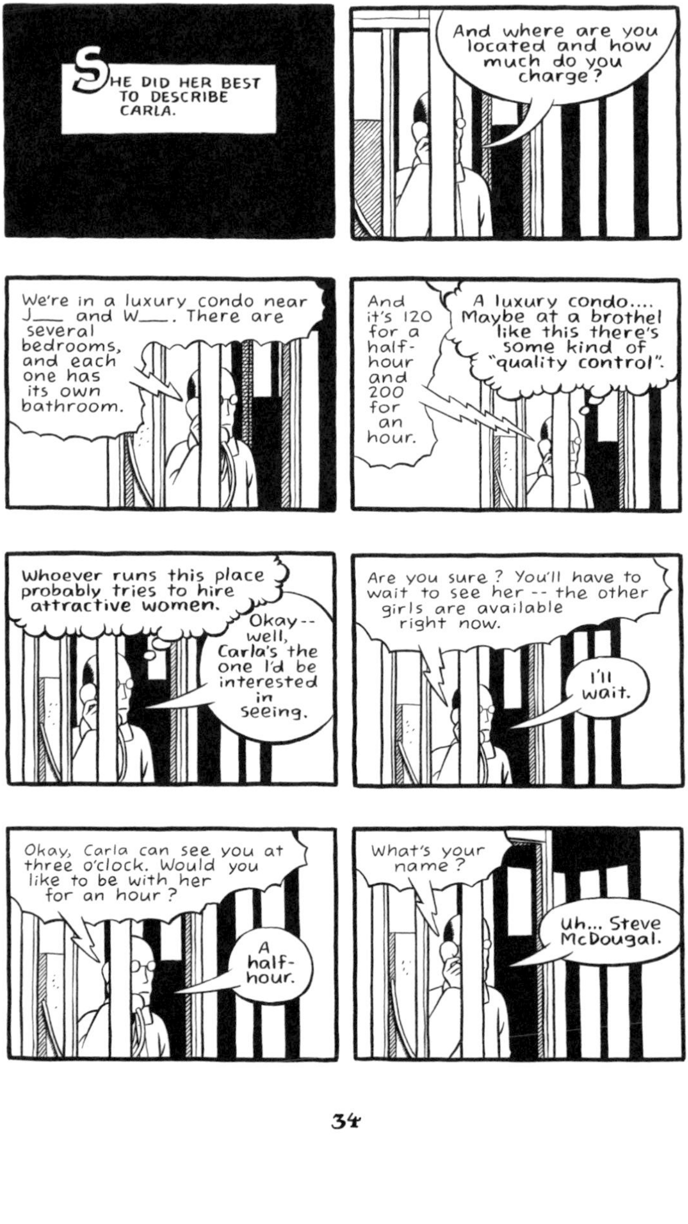

SHE DID HER BEST TO DESCRIBE CARLA.
And where are you located and how much do you charge?
We're in a luxury condo near J___ and W___. There are several bedrooms, and each one has its own bathroom.
And it's 120 for a half-hour and 200 for an hour.
A luxury condo.... Maybe at a brothel like this there's some kind of "quality control".
Whoever runs this place probably tries to hire attractive women.
Okay-- well, Carla's the one I'd be interested in seeing.
Are you sure? You'll have to wait to see her -- the other girls are available right now.
I'll wait.
Okay, Carla can see you at three o'clock. Would you like to be with her for an hour?
A half-hour.
What's your name?
Uh... Steve McDougal.

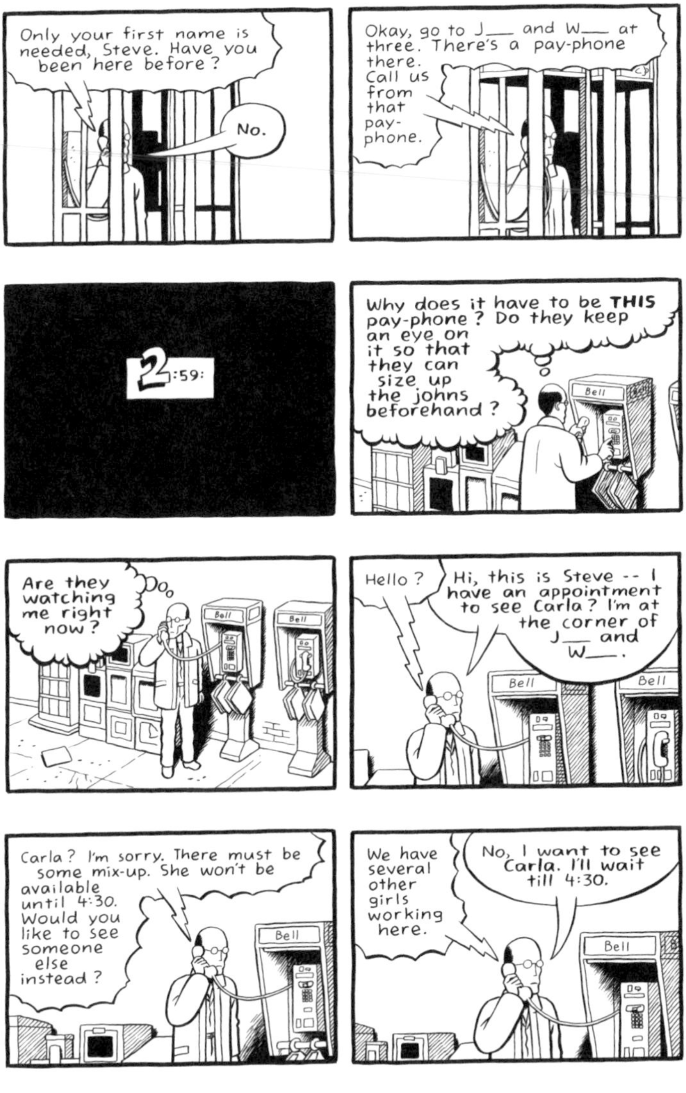
Only your first name is needed, Steve. Have you been here before?
No.
Okay, go to J___ and W___ at three. There's a pay-phone there. Call us from that pay-phone.
2:59:
Why does it have to be THIS pay-phone? Do they keep an eye on it so that they can size up the johns beforehand?
Bell
Are they watching me right now?
Bell
Bell
Hello?
Hi, this is Steve -- I have an appointment to see Carla? I'm at the corner of J___ and W___.
Bell
Bell
Carla? I'm sorry. There must be some mix-up. She won't be available until 4:30. Would you like to see someone else instead?
Bell
We have several other girls working here.
No, I want to see Carla. I'll wait till 4:30.
Bell

CHAPTER 2

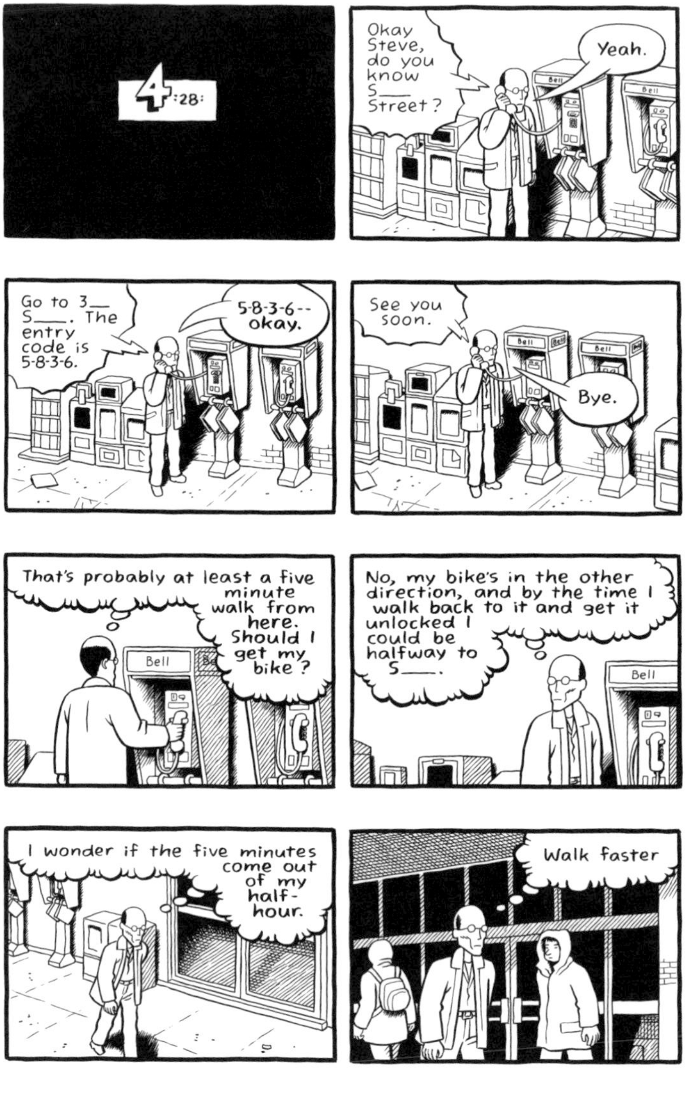
4:28:
Okay Steve, do you know S___ Street?
Yeah.
Go to 3__ S___. The entry code is 5-8-3-6.
5-8-3-6-- okay.
See you soon.
Bye.
That's probably at least a five minute walk from here. Should I get my bike?
No, my bike's in the other direction, and by the time I walk back to it and get it unlocked I could be halfway to S___.
I wonder if the five minutes come out of my half-hour.
Walk faster

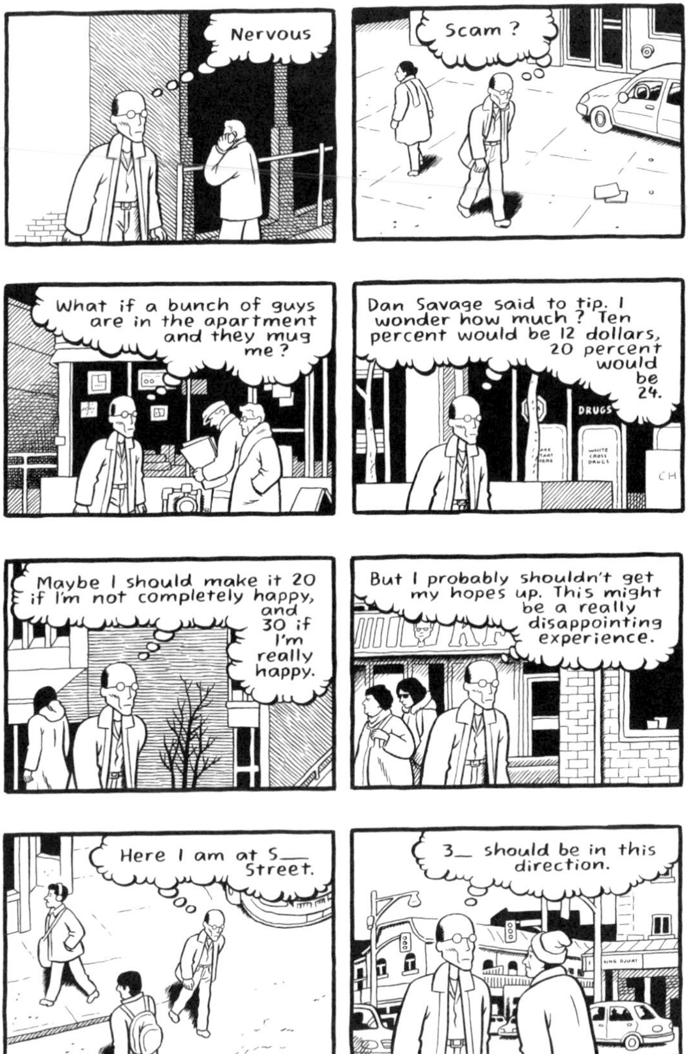
Nervous
Scam?
What if a bunch of guys are in the apartment and they mug me?
Dan Savage said to tip. I wonder how much? Ten percent would be 12 dollars, 20 percent would be 24.
DRUGS
Maybe I should make it 20 if I'm not completely happy, and 30 if I'm really happy.
But I probably shouldn't get my hopes up. This might be a really disappointing experience.
Here I am at S___ Street.
3_ should be in this direction.

CHAPTER 2

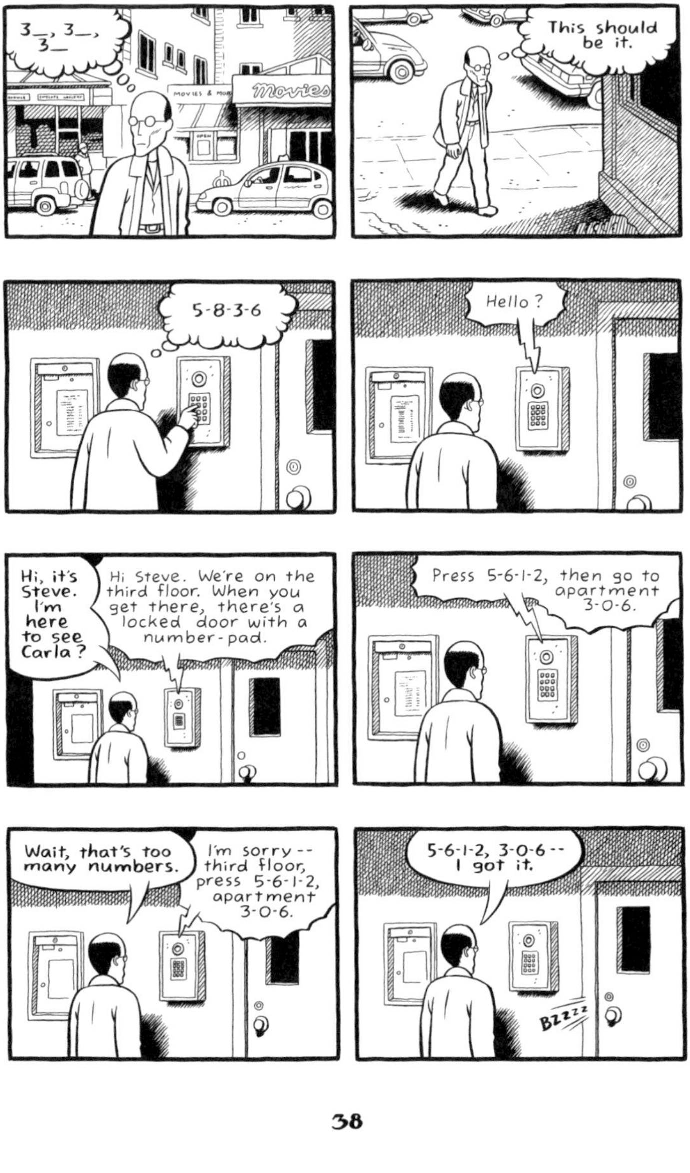
3_, 3_, 3_
MOVIES & MORE
Movies
OPEN
This should be it.
5-8-3-6
Hello?
Hi, it's Steve. I'm here to see Carla?
Hi Steve. We're on the third floor. When you get there, there's a locked door with a number-pad.
Press 5-6-1-2, then go to apartment 3-0-6.
Wait, that's too many numbers.
I'm sorry -- third floor, press 5-6-1-2, apartment 3-0-6.
5-6-1-2, 3-0-6 -- I got it.
BZZZZ

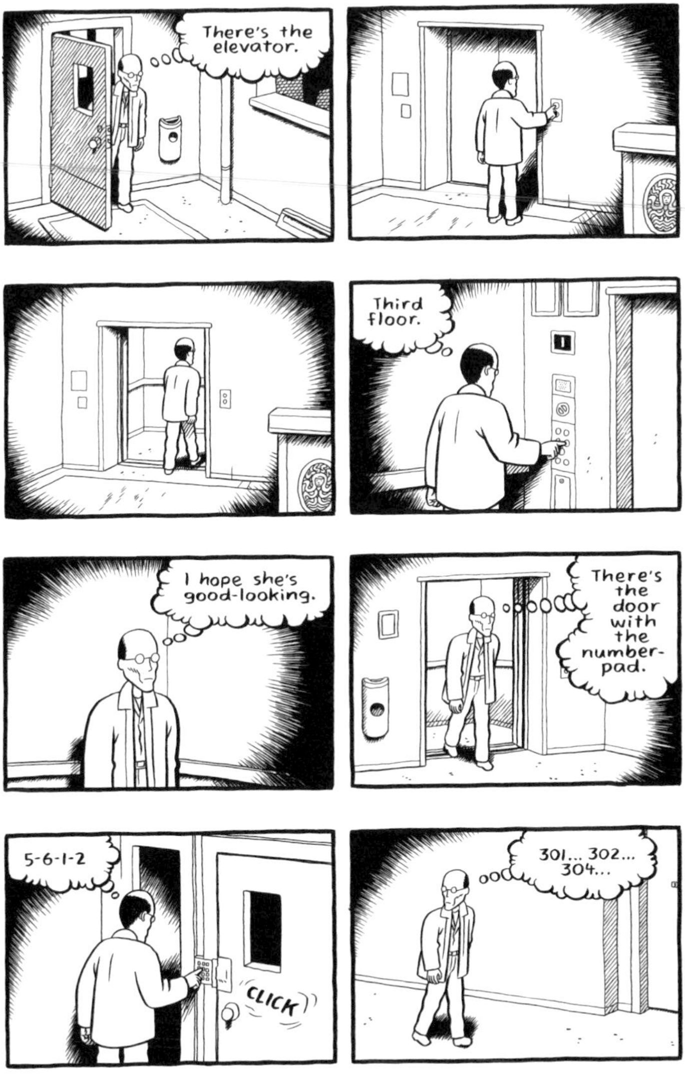
There's the elevator.
Third floor.
I hope she's good-looking.
There's the door with the number-pad.
5-6-1-2
CLICK
301... 302... 304...

CHAPTER 2

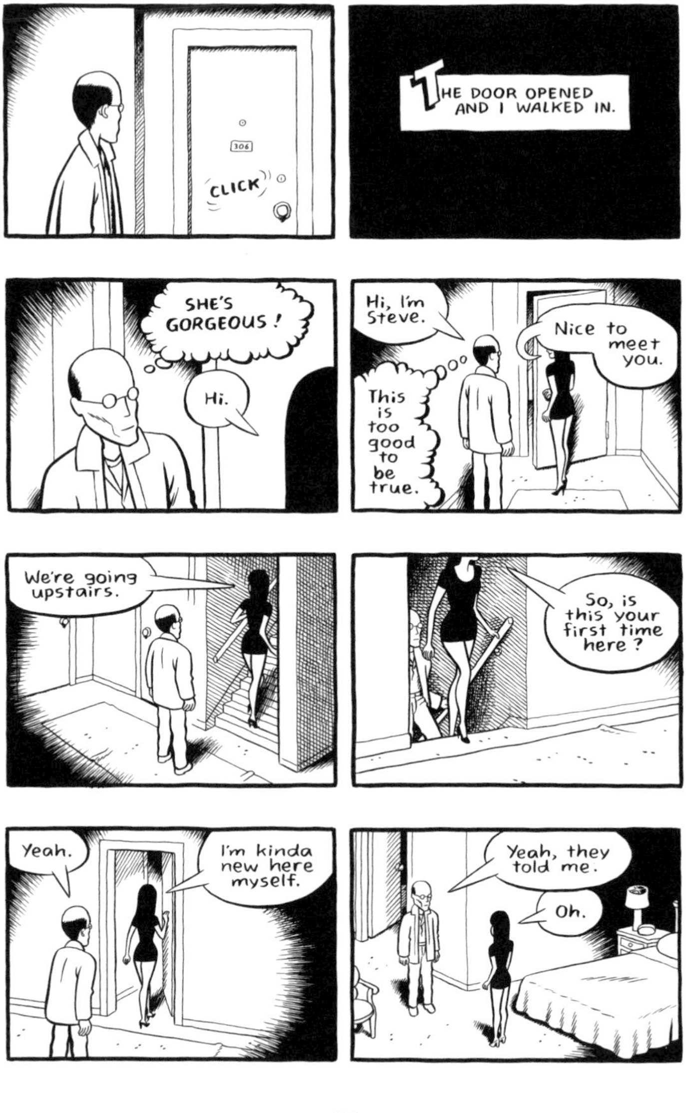

306
CLICK
THE DOOR OPENED AND I WALKED IN.
SHE'S GORGEOUS!
Hi.
Hi, I'm Steve.
Nice to meet you.
This is too good to be true.
We're going upstairs.
So, is this your first time here?
Yeah.
I'm kinda new here myself.
Yeah, they told me.
Oh.

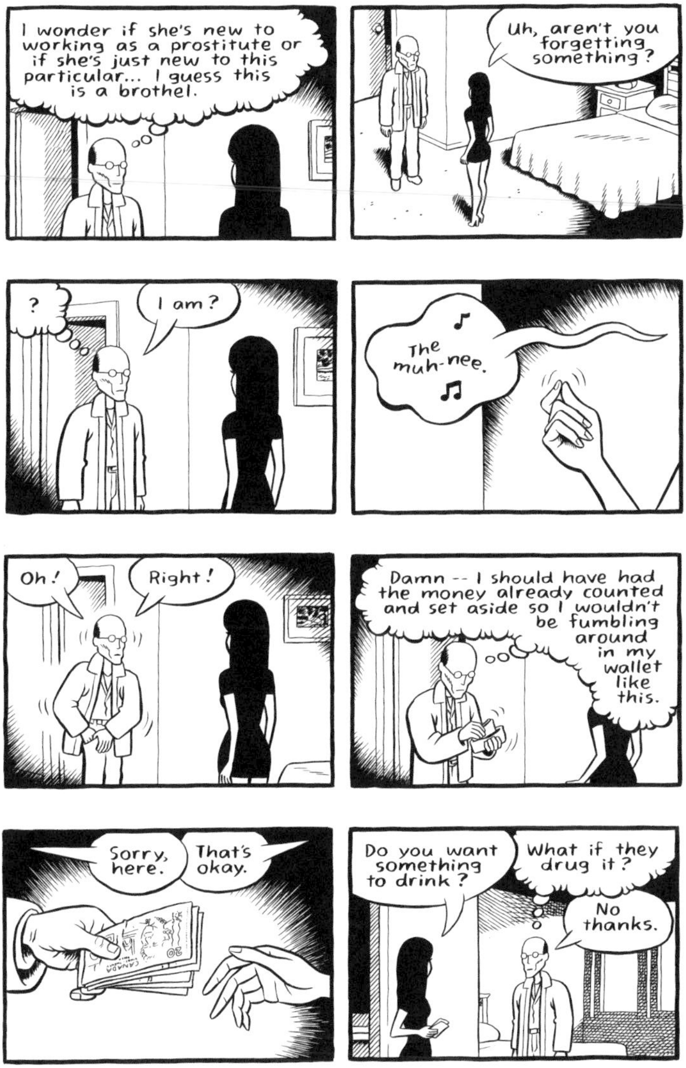
I wonder if she's new to working as a prostitute or if she's just new to this particular... I guess this is a brothel.
Uh, aren't you forgetting something?
?
I am?
The muh-nee.
Oh!
Right!
Damn -- I should have had the money already counted and set aside so I wouldn't be fumbling around in my wallet like this.
Sorry, here.
That's okay.
Do you want something to drink?
What if they drug it?
No thanks.

CHAPTER 2

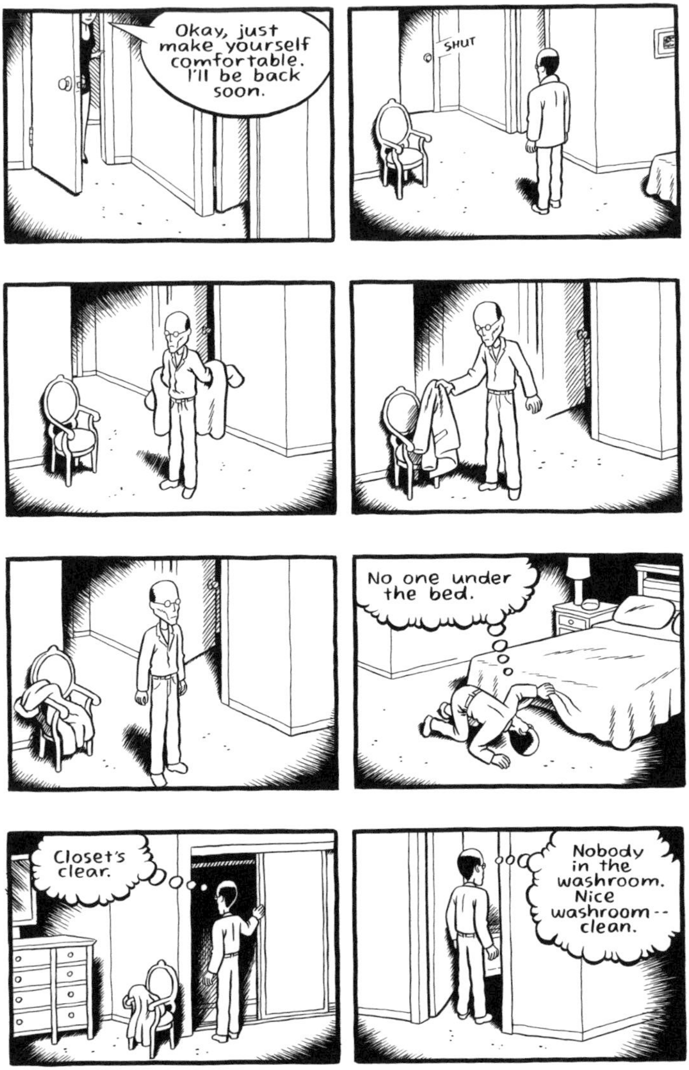
Okay, just make yourself comfortable. I'll be back soon.
SHUT
No one under the bed.
Closet's clear.
Nobody in the washroom. Nice washroom -- clean.

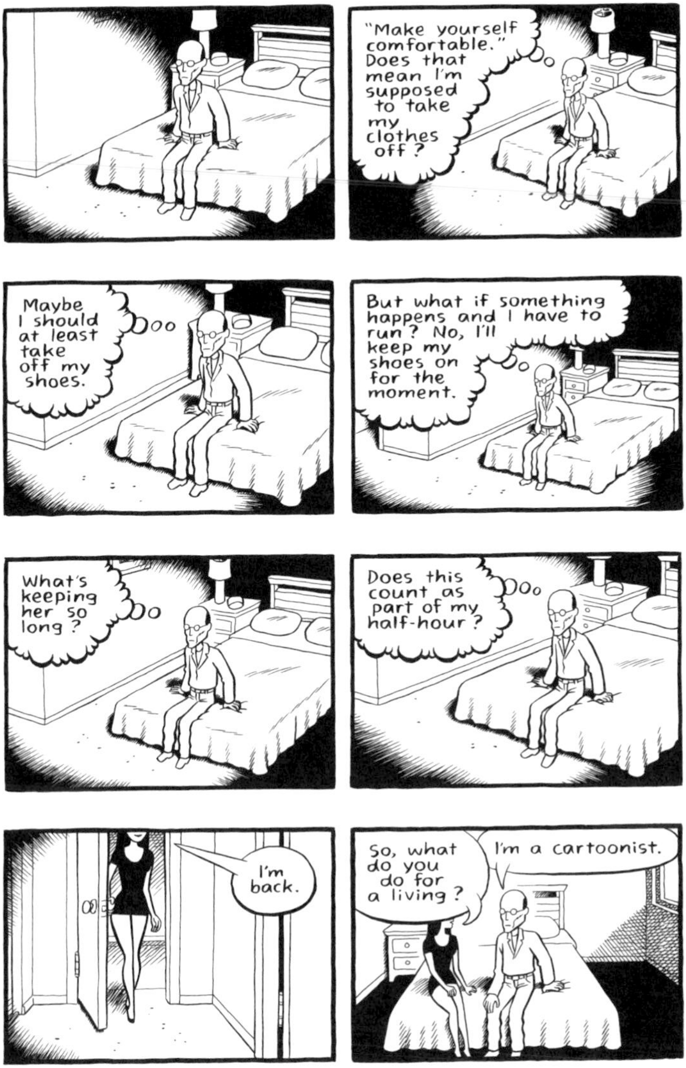
"Make yourself comfortable." Does that mean I'm supposed to take my clothes off?
Maybe I should at least take off my shoes.
But what if something happens and I have to run? No, I'll keep my shoes on for the moment.
What's keeping her so long?
Does this count as part of my half-hour?
I'm back.
So, what do you do for a living?
I'm a cartoonist.

CHAPTER 2

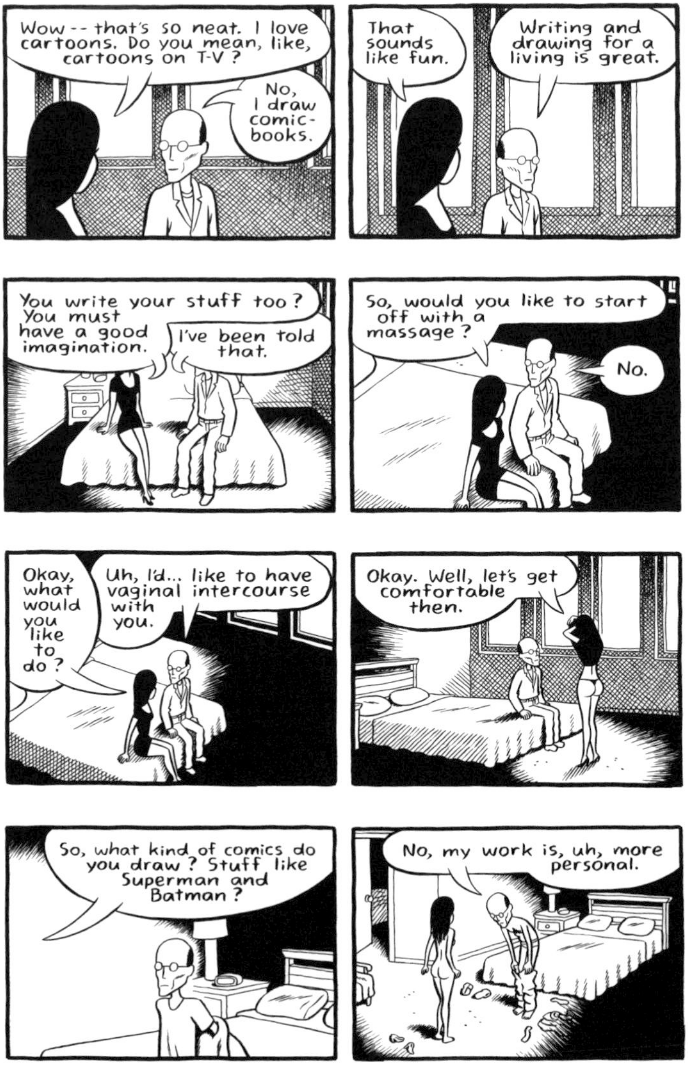
Wow -- that's so neat. I love cartoons. Do you mean, like, cartoons on T-V?
No, I draw comic-books.
That sounds like fun.
Writing and drawing for a living is great.
You write your stuff too? You must have a good imagination.
I've been told that.
So, would you like to start off with a massage?
No.
Okay, what would you like to do?
Uh, I'd... like to have vaginal intercourse with you.
Okay. Well, let's get comfortable then.
So, what kind of comics do you draw? Stuff like Superman and Batman?
No, my work is, uh, more personal.

Why don't you lie back?
It's really happening.
She's not a cop, she's not a rip-off -- she's the real thing.
Should I take my glasses off? It's going to be weird leaving them on, but I want to see what's happening.
What would you like? Me on the bottom?
Sure.
Hold on a second.

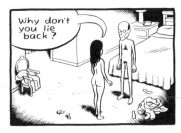

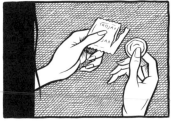

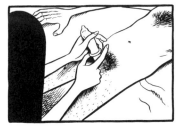

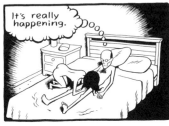

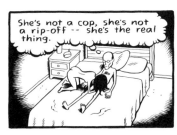

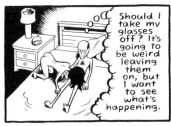

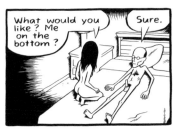

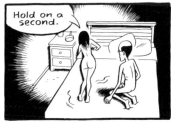

CHAPTER 2

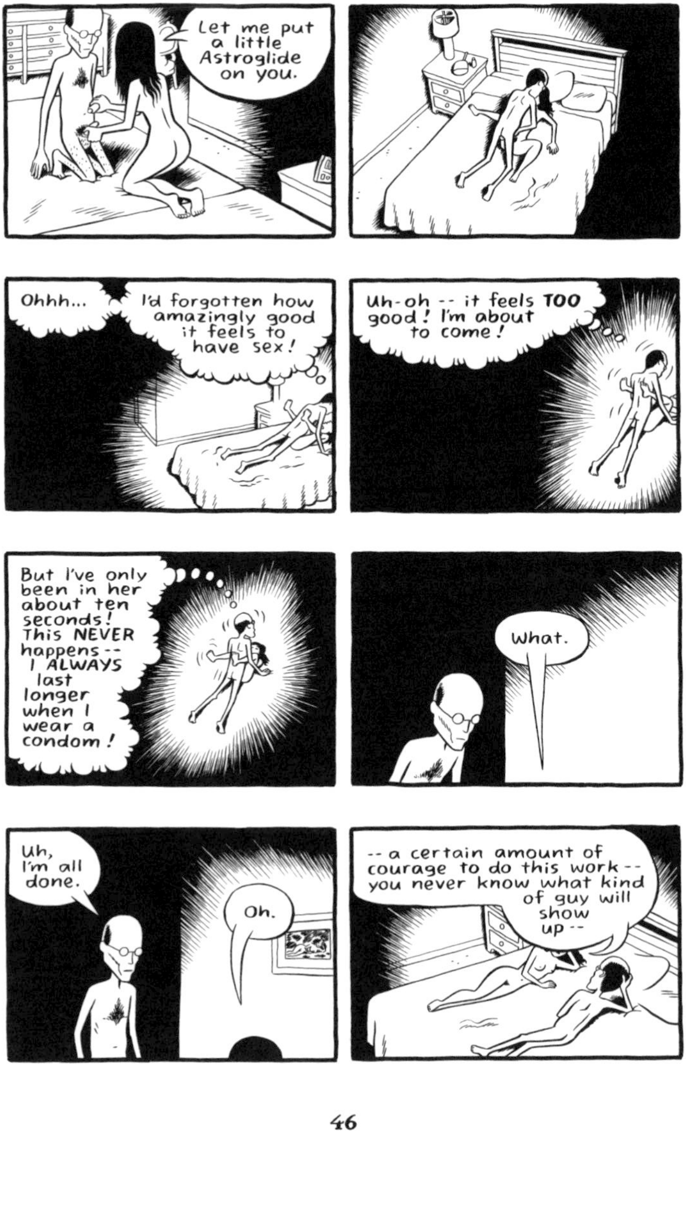

Let me put a little Astroglide on you.
Ohhh...
I'd forgotten how amazingly good it feels to have sex!
Uh-oh -- it feels TOO good! I'm about to come!
But I've only been in her about ten seconds! This NEVER happens -- I ALWAYS last longer when I wear a condom!
What.
Uh, I'm all done.
Oh.
-- a certain amount of courage to do this work -- you never know what kind of guy will show up --

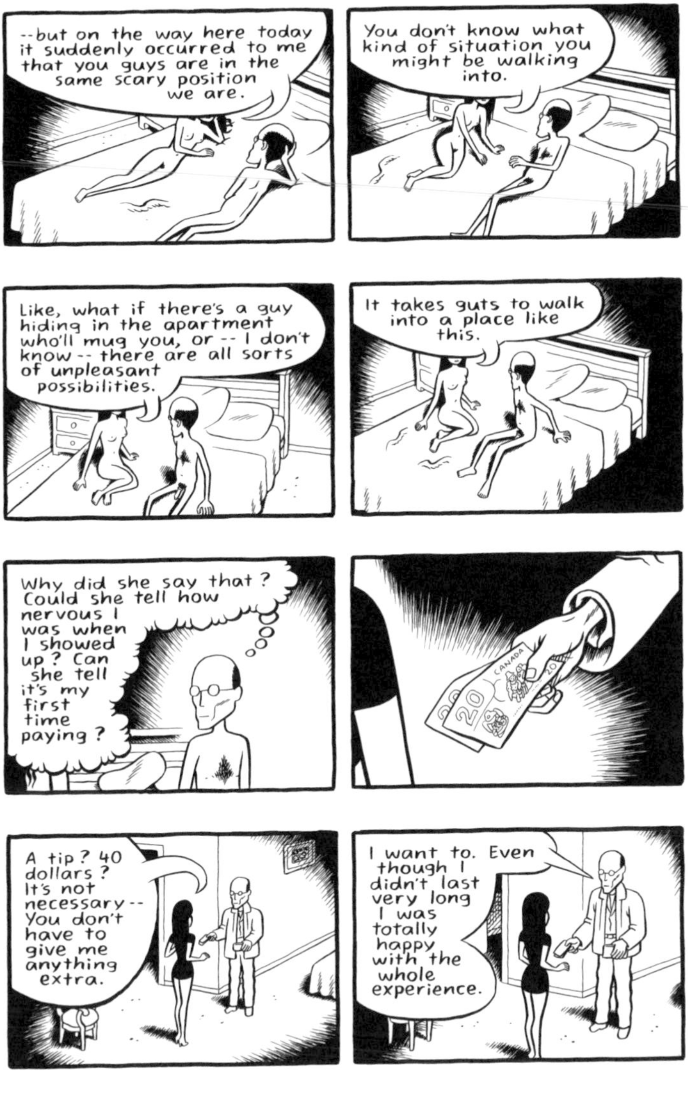
--but on the way here today it suddenly occurred to me that you guys are in the same scary position we are.
You don't know what kind of situation you might be walking into.
Like, what if there's a guy hiding in the apartment who'll mug you, or -- I don't know -- there are all sorts of unpleasant possibilities.
It takes guts to walk into a place like this.
Why did she say that? Could she tell how nervous I was when I showed up? Can she tell it's my first time paying?
CANADA
20
A tip? 40 dollars? It's not necessary -- You don't have to give me anything extra.
I want to. Even though I didn't last very long I was totally happy with the whole experience.

CHAPTER 2

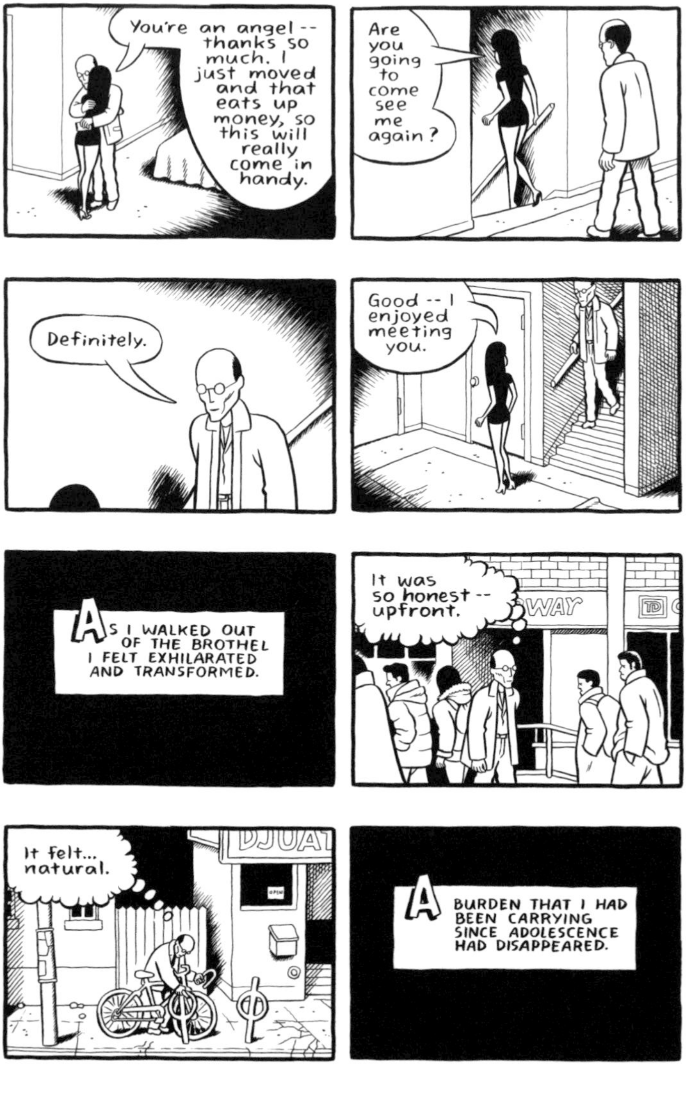

You're an angel -- thanks so much. I just moved and that eats up money, so this will really come in handy.
Are you going to come see me again?
Definitely.
Good -- I enjoyed meeting you.
AS I WALKED OUT OF THE BROTHEL I FELT EXHILARATED AND TRANSFORMED.
It was so honest -- upfront.
It felt... natural.
A BURDEN THAT I HAD BEEN CARRYING SINCE ADOLESCENCE HAD DISAPPEARED.

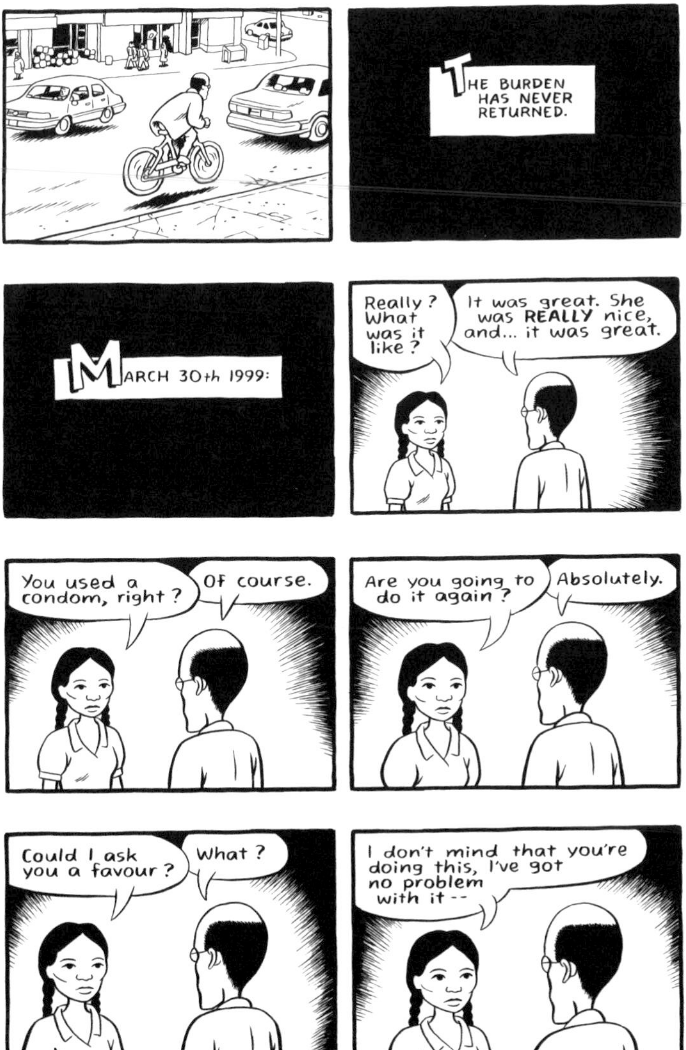
THE BURDEN HAS NEVER RETURNED.
MARCH 30th 1999:
Really? What was it like?
It was great. She was REALLY nice, and... it was great.
You used a condom, right?
Of course.
Are you going to do it again?
Absolutely.
Could I ask you a favour?
What?
I don't mind that you're doing this, I've got no problem with it --

CHAPTER 2

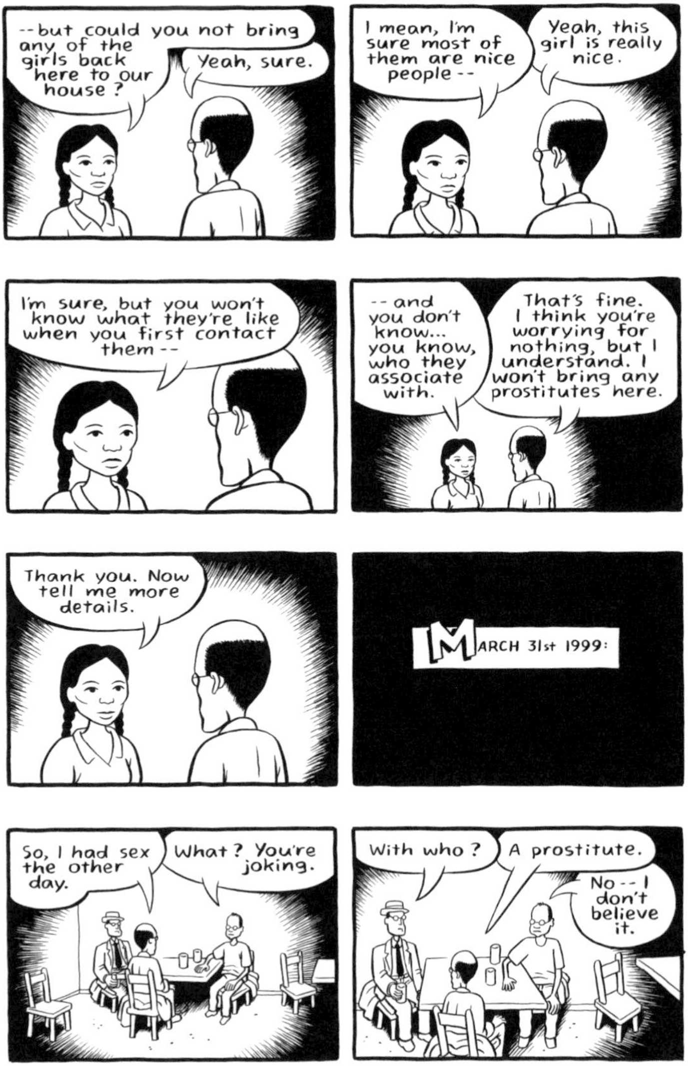
--but could you not bring any of the girls back here to our house?
Yeah, sure.
I mean, I'm sure most of them are nice people--
Yeah, this girl is really nice.
I'm sure, but you won't know what they're like when you first contact them--
--and you don't know... you know, who they associate with.
That's fine. I think you're worrying for nothing, but I understand. I won't bring any prostitutes here.
Thank you. Now tell me more details.
MARCH 31st 1999:
So, I had sex the other day.
What? You're joking.
With who?
A prostitute.
No--I don't believe it.

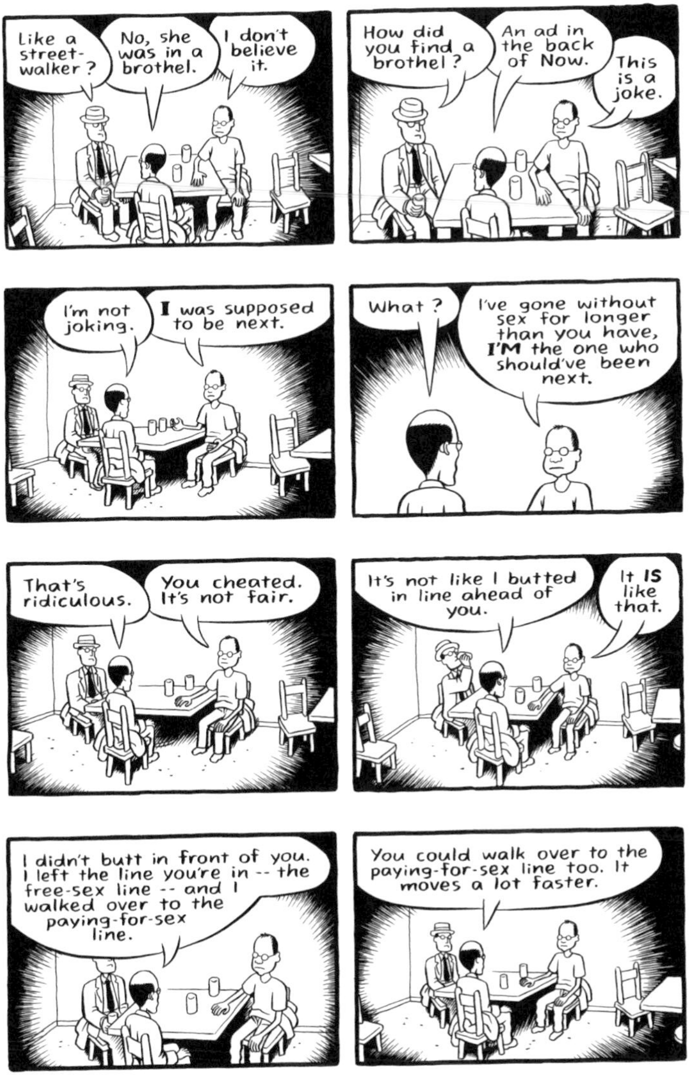
Like a street-walker?
No, she was in a brothel.
I don't believe it.
How did you find a brothel?
An ad in the back of Now.
This is a joke.
I'm not joking.
I was supposed to be next.
What?
I've gone without sex for longer than you have, I'M the one who should've been next.
That's ridiculous.
You cheated. It's not fair.
It's not like I butted in line ahead of you.
It IS like that.
I didn't butt in front of you. I left the line you're in -- the free-sex line -- and I walked over to the paying-for-sex line.
You could walk over to the paying-for-sex line too. It moves a lot faster.

CHAPTER 2

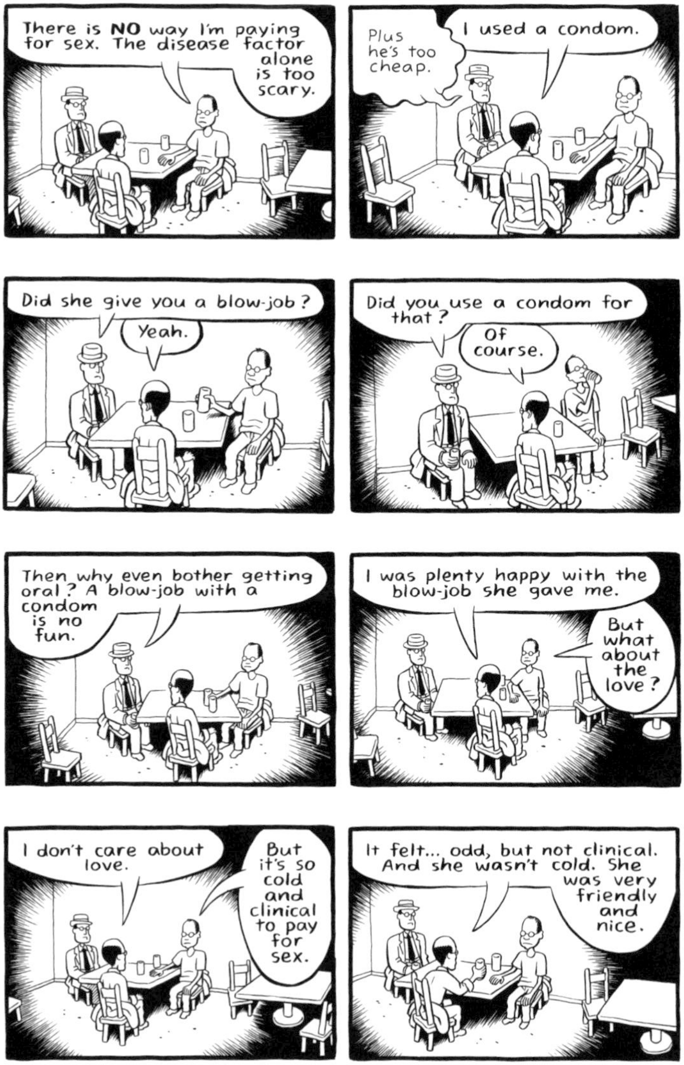
There is NO way I'm paying for sex. The disease factor alone is too scary.
Plus he's too cheap.
I used a condom.
Did she give you a blow-job?
Yeah.
Did you use a condom for that?
Of course.
Then why even bother getting oral? A blow-job with a condom is no fun.
I was plenty happy with the blow-job she gave me.
But what about the love?
I don't care about love.
But it's so cold and clinical to pay for sex.
It felt... odd, but not clinical. And she wasn't cold. She was very friendly and nice.

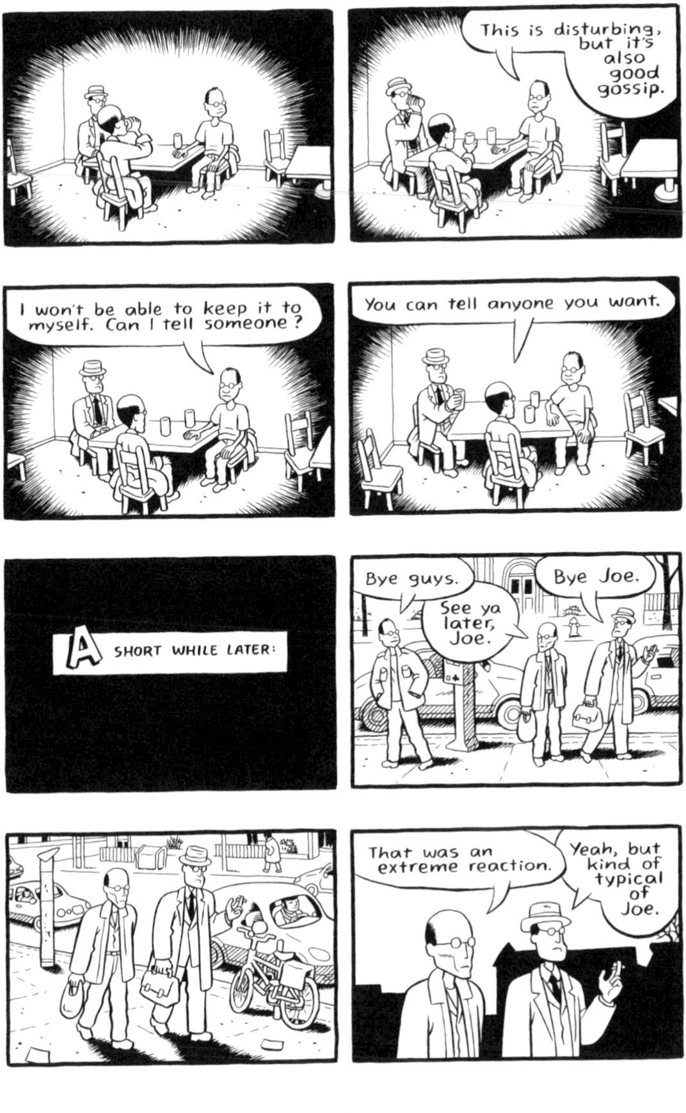
This is disturbing, but it's also good gossip.
I won't be able to keep it to myself. Can I tell someone?
You can tell anyone you want.
A SHORT WHILE LATER:
Bye guys.
See ya later, Joe.
Bye Joe.
That was an extreme reaction.
Yeah, but kind of typical of Joe.

He was upset but not for any reason connected to a moral principal -- he's bothered because you're getting laid and he's not.

Right. Do **YOU** have an opinion on the morality of prostitution?

I think it should be legal, but that's not the same thing as saying it's right.

I'm not sure that I can address it as an issue of simple right and wrong. To be honest it just seems sad to me.

It's sad that you're resorting to this, and it's sad that women are in circumstances that force them to have sex for money.

Don't feel sad for me. I feel great.

And you don't see it as sad for the girl?

One would have to know how she views sex to know whether or not it's sad for her.

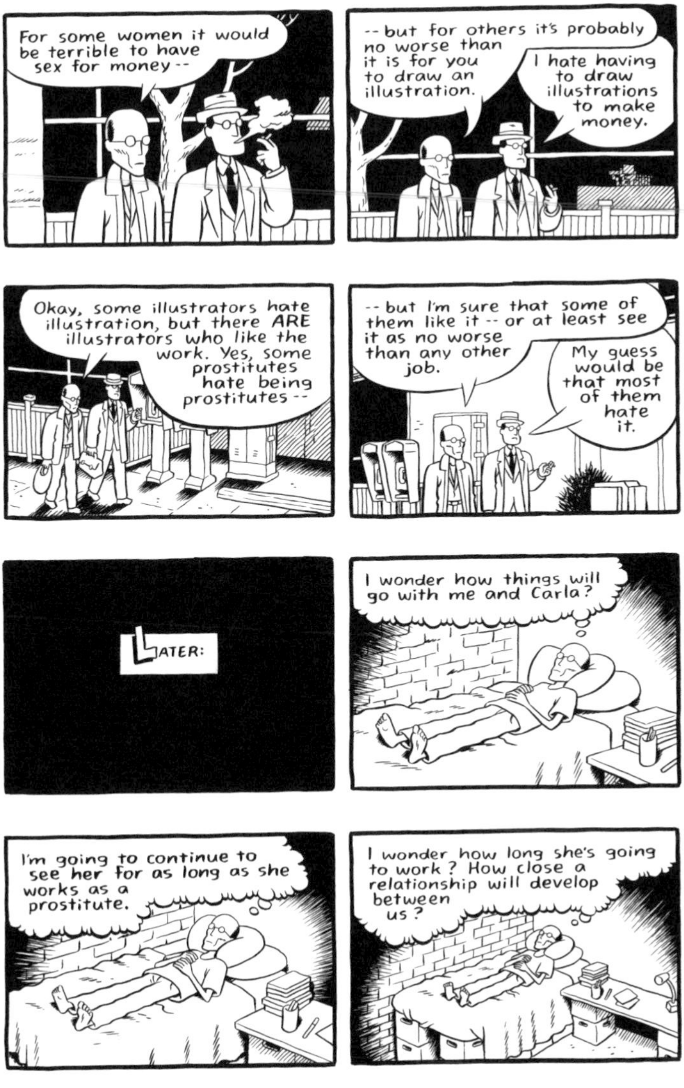
For some women it would be terrible to have sex for money --
-- but for others it's probably no worse than it is for you to draw an illustration.
I hate having to draw illustrations to make money.
Okay, some illustrators hate illustration, but there ARE illustrators who like the work. Yes, some prostitutes hate being prostitutes --
-- but I'm sure that some of them like it -- or at least see it as no worse than any other job.
My guess would be that most of them hate it.
LATER:
I wonder how things will go with me and Carla?
I'm going to continue to see her for as long as she works as a prostitute.
I wonder how long she's going to work? How close a relationship will develop between us?

CHAPTER 2

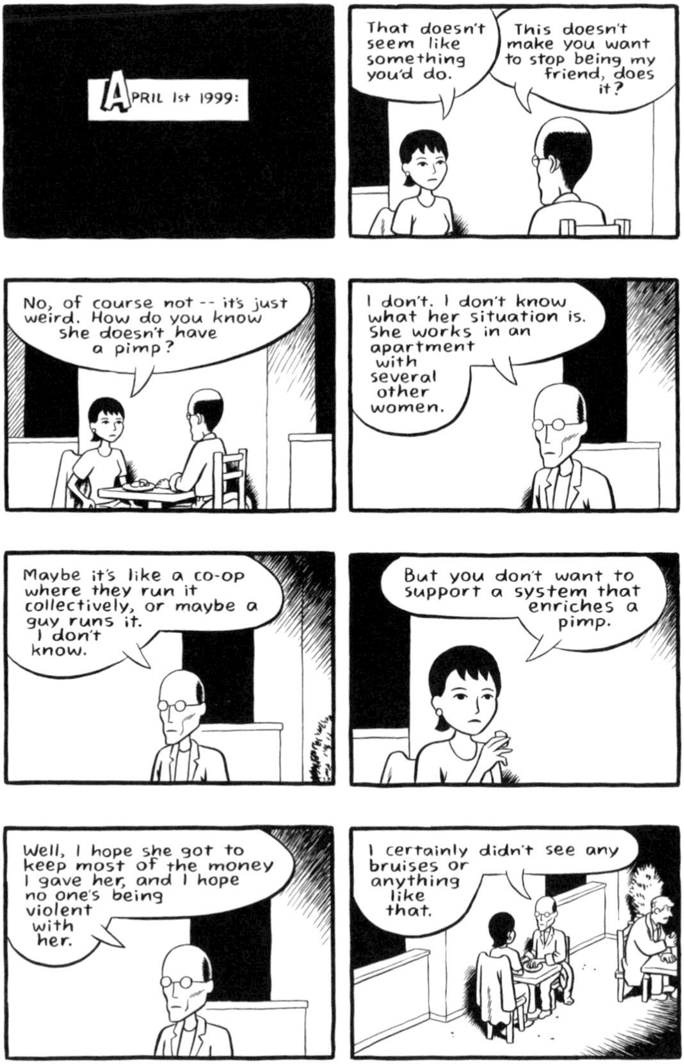
APRIL 1st 1999:
That doesn't seem like something you'd do.
This doesn't make you want to stop being my friend, does it?
No, of course not -- it's just weird. How do you know she doesn't have a pimp?
I don't. I don't know what her situation is. She works in an apartment with several other women.
Maybe it's like a co-op where they run it collectively, or maybe a guy runs it. I don't know.
But you don't want to support a system that enriches a pimp.
Well, I hope she got to keep most of the money I gave her, and I hope no one's being violent with her.
I certainly didn't see any bruises or anything like that.

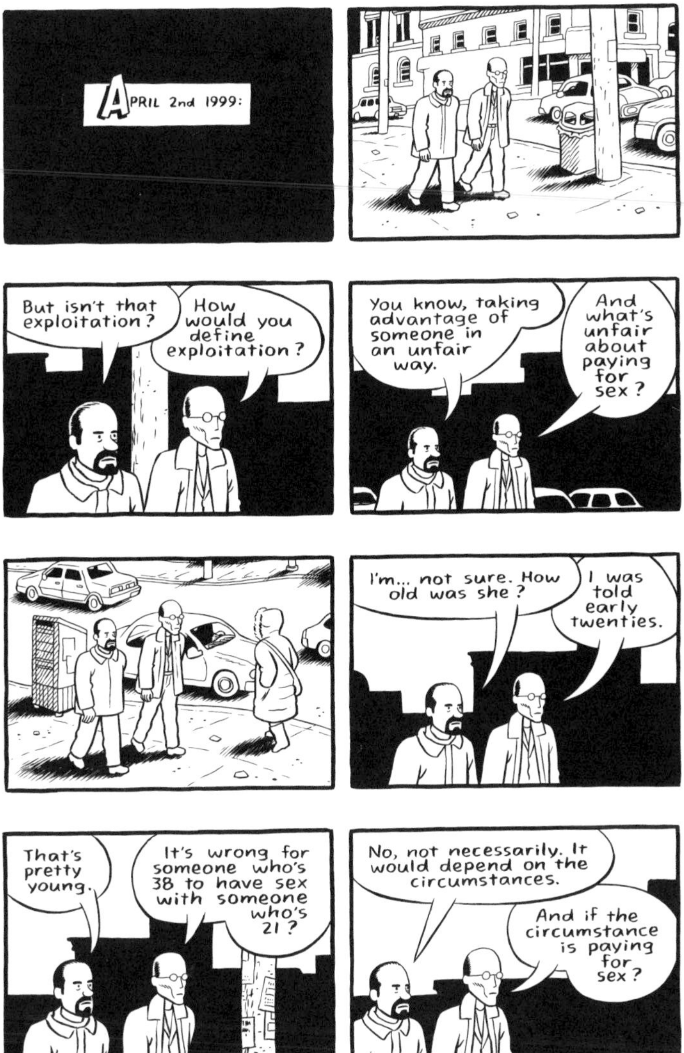
APRIL 2nd 1999:
But isn't that exploitation?
How would you define exploitation?
You know, taking advantage of someone in an unfair way.
And what's unfair about paying for sex?
I'm... not sure. How old was she?
I was told early twenties.
That's pretty young.
It's wrong for someone who's 38 to have sex with someone who's 21?
No, not necessarily. It would depend on the circumstances.
And if the circumstance is paying for sex?

CHAPTER 2

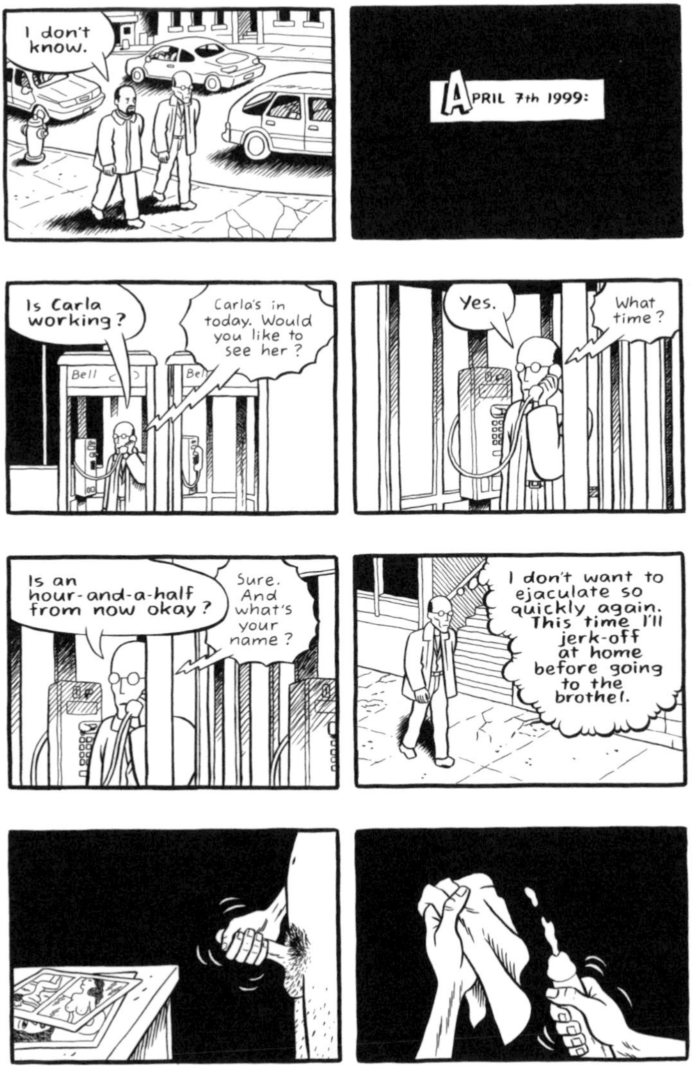
I don't know.
APRIL 7th 1999:
Is Carla working?
Carla's in today. Would you like to see her?
Bell
Yes.
What time?
Is an hour-and-a-half from now okay?
Sure. And what's your name?
I don't want to ejaculate so quickly again. This time I'll jerk-off at home before going to the brothel.

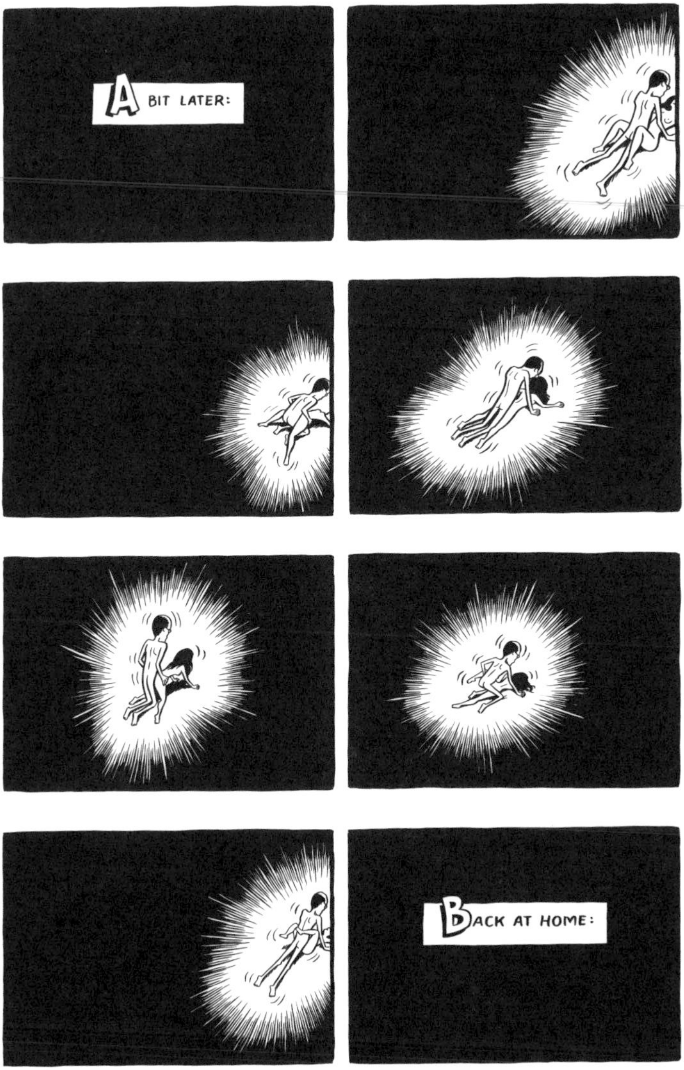
A BIT LATER:
BACK AT HOME:

CHAPTER 2

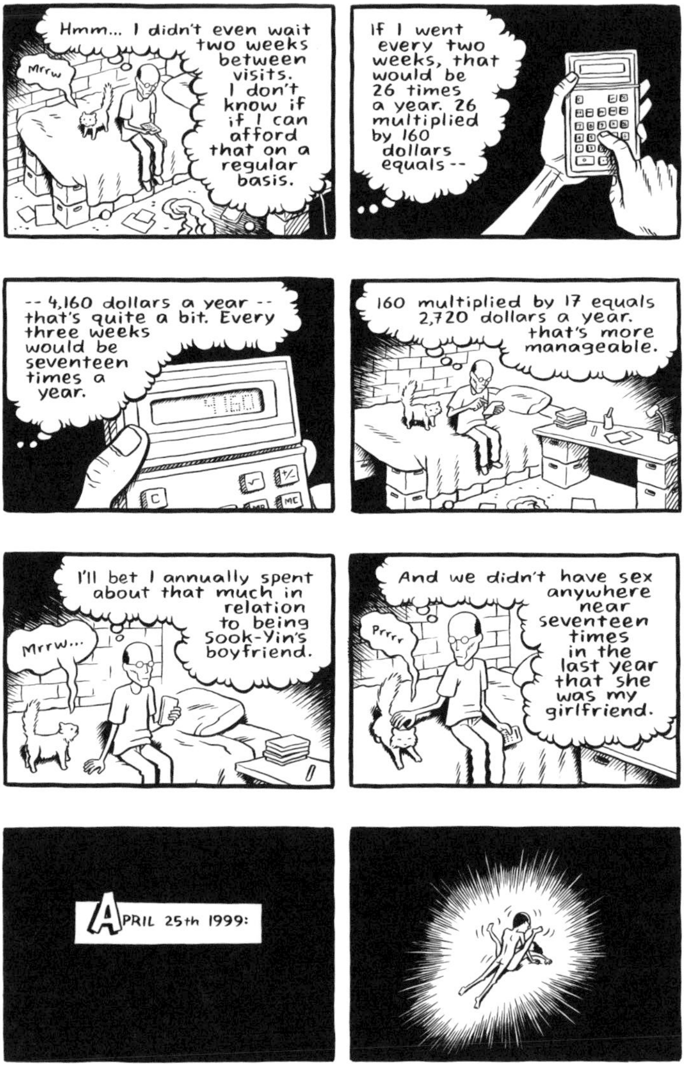
Hmm... I didn't even wait two weeks between visits. I don't know if if I can afford that on a regular basis.
Mrrw
If I went every two weeks, that would be 26 times a year. 26 multiplied by 160 dollars equals --
-- 4,160 dollars a year -- that's quite a bit. Every three weeks would be seventeen times a year.
4160
160 multiplied by 17 equals 2,720 dollars a year. that's more manageable.
I'll bet I annually spent about that much in relation to being Sook-Yin's boyfriend.
Mrrw...
And we didn't have sex anywhere near seventeen times in the last year that she was my girlfriend.
Prrrr
APRIL 25th 1999:

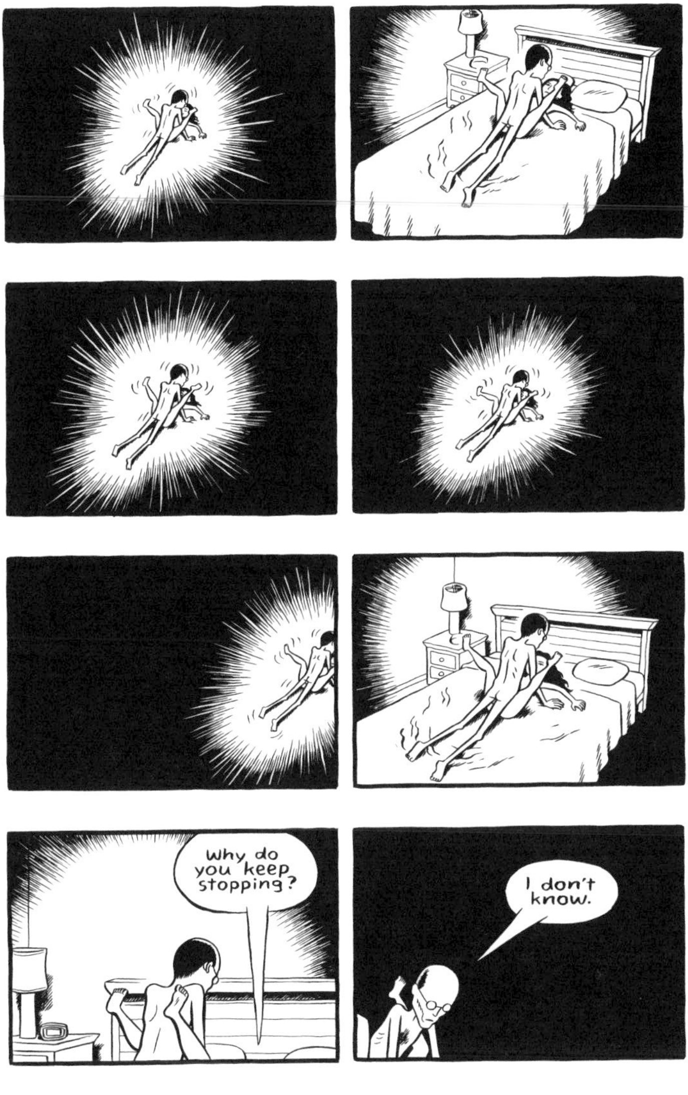
Why do you keep stopping?
I don't know.

CHAPTER 2

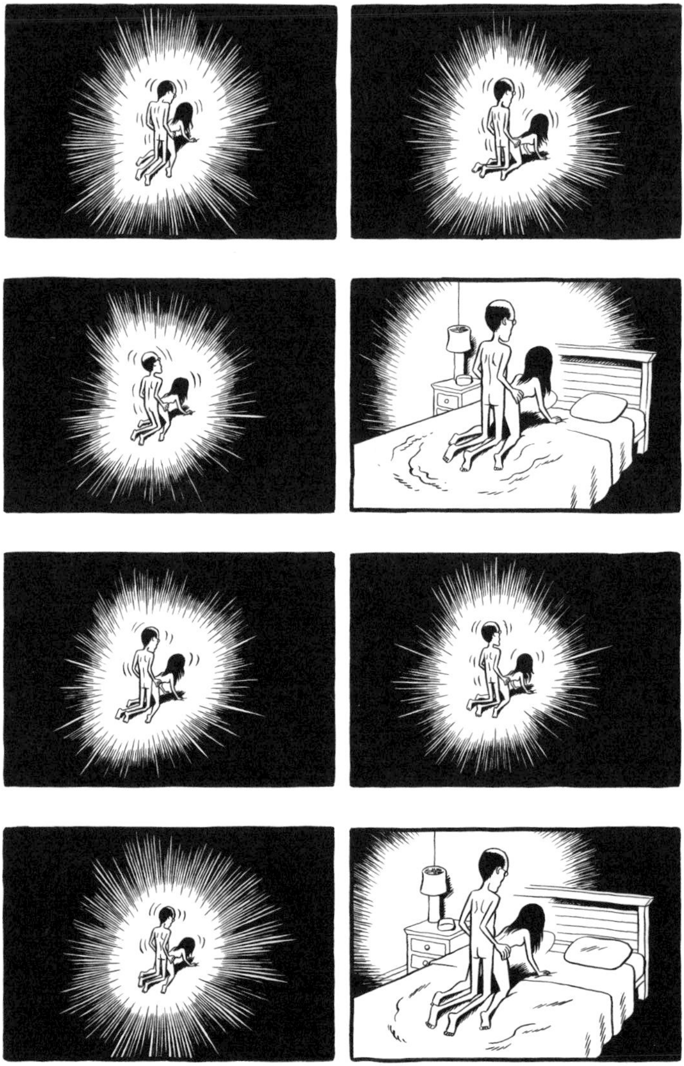

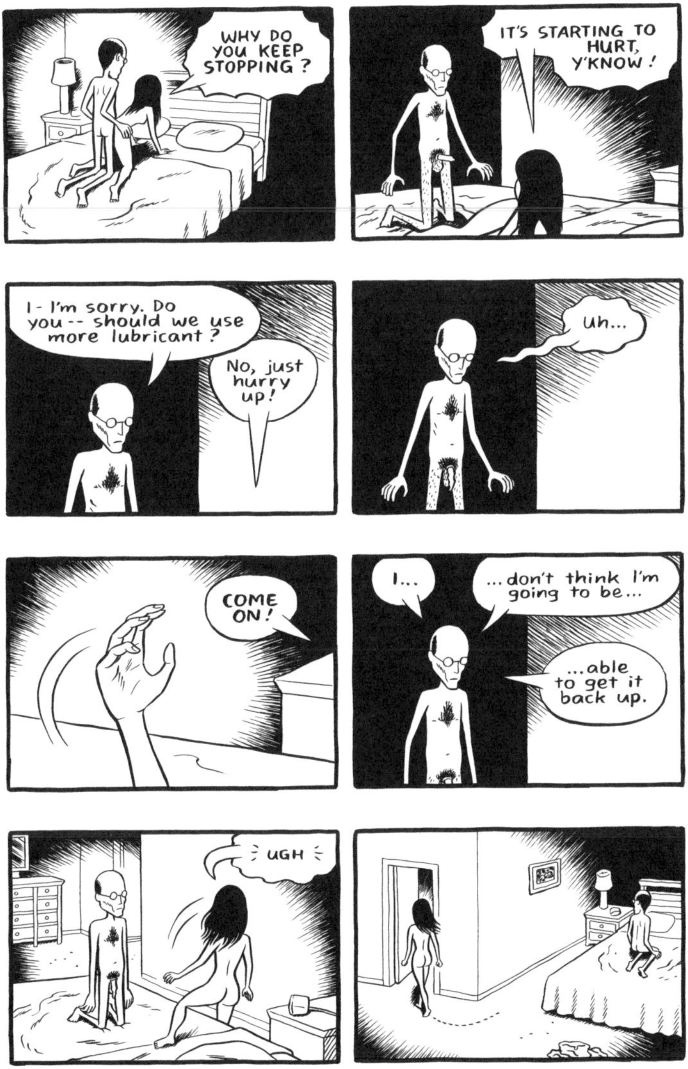
WHY DO YOU KEEP STOPPING ?
IT'S STARTING TO HURT, Y'KNOW !
I- I'm sorry. Do you -- should we use more lubricant ?
No, just hurry up !
Uh...
COME ON !
I...
...don't think I'm going to be...
...able to get it back up.
UGH

CHAPTER 2

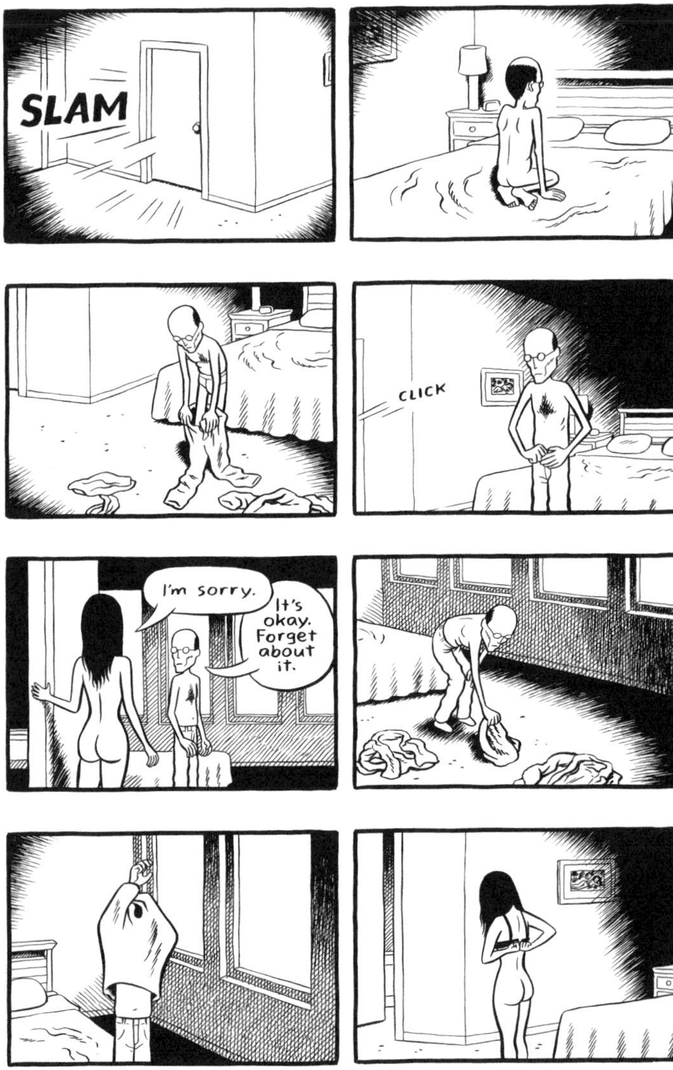
SLAM
CLICK
I'm sorry.
It's okay. Forget about it.

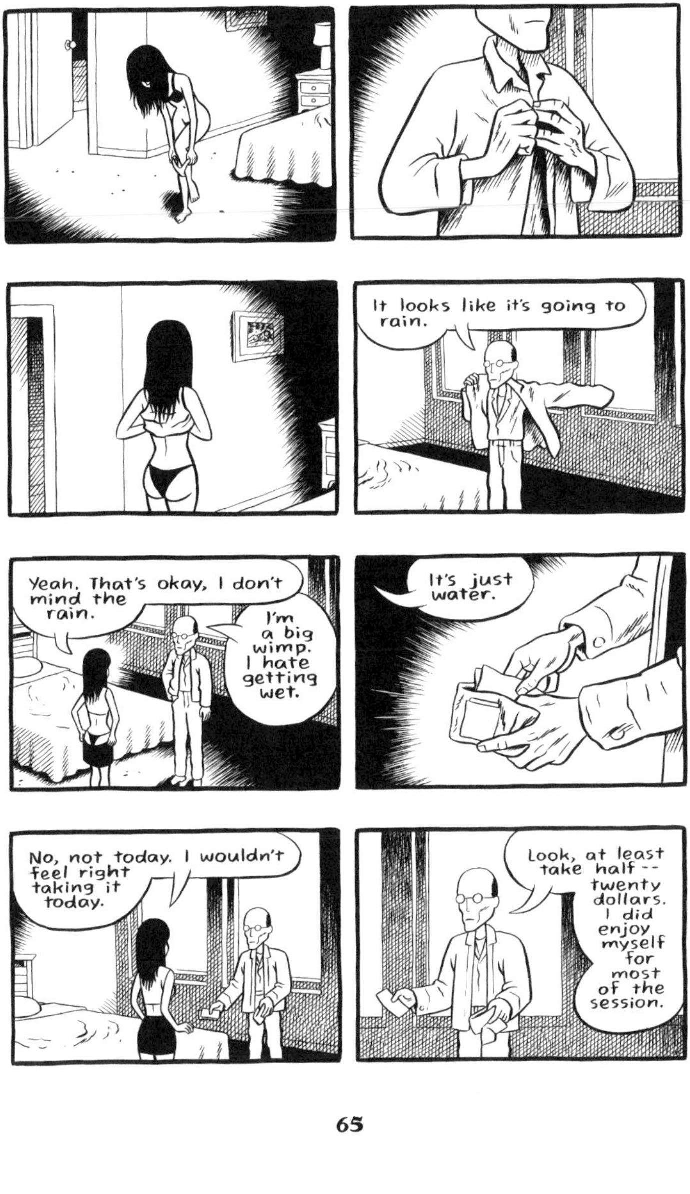
It looks like it's going to rain.
Yeah. That's okay, I don't mind the rain.
I'm a big wimp. I hate getting wet.
It's just water.
No, not today. I wouldn't feel right taking it today.
Look, at least take half -- twenty dollars. I did enjoy myself for most of the session.

CHAPTER 2

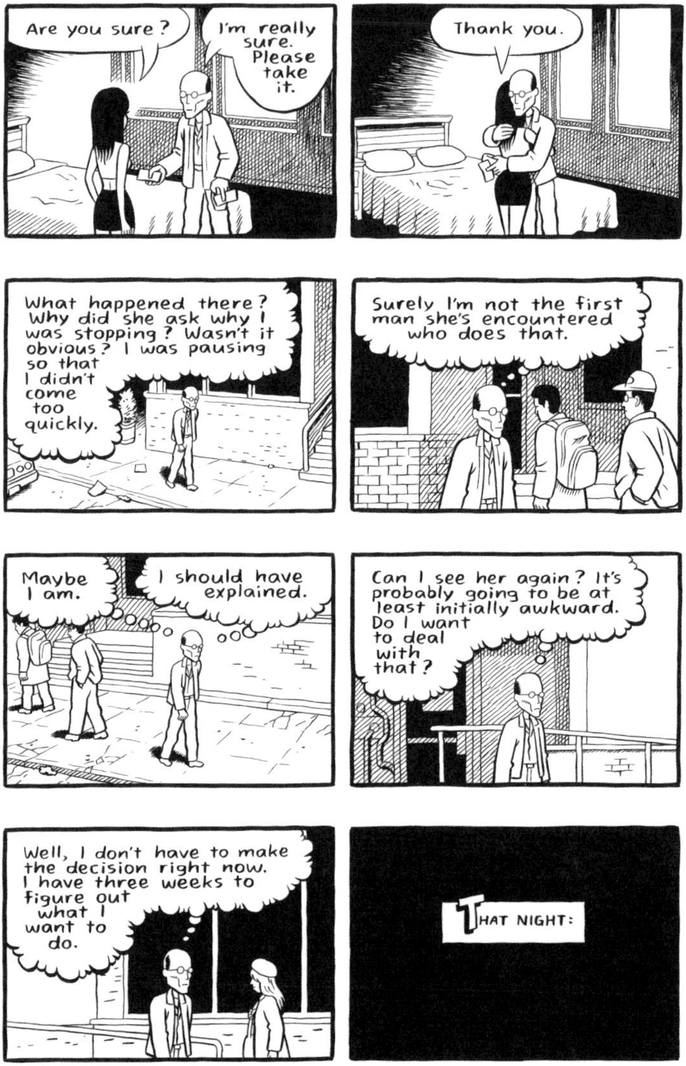

Are you sure?
I'm really sure. Please take it.
Thank you.
What happened there? Why did she ask why I was stopping? Wasn't it obvious? I was pausing so that I didn't come too quickly.
Surely I'm not the first man she's encountered who does that.
Maybe I am.
I should have explained.
Can I see her again? It's probably going to be at least initially awkward. Do I want to deal with that?
Well, I don't have to make the decision right now. I have three weeks to figure out what I want to do.
THAT NIGHT:

The second time I saw her, we went through a lot of positions and the sex lasted maybe twenty minutes.
Obviously I was trying to do the same today. I guess, for her, a half-hour session doesn't mean twenty minutes of fucking.
In the future I'll try to limit myself to ten minutes of sex in a thirty minute appointment.

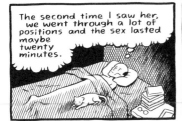

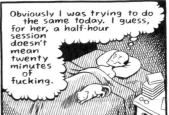

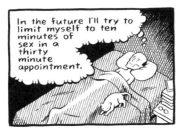

CHAPTER 3
—
ANGELINA

May 13th 1999:

Here's an ad for a girl named Tina -- "19, thin, busty, very pretty".

I'm calling about Tina. How much does she charge?

80 dollars for a half-hour.

Wow! That's a lot less than 120.

And where are you located?

CHAPTER 3

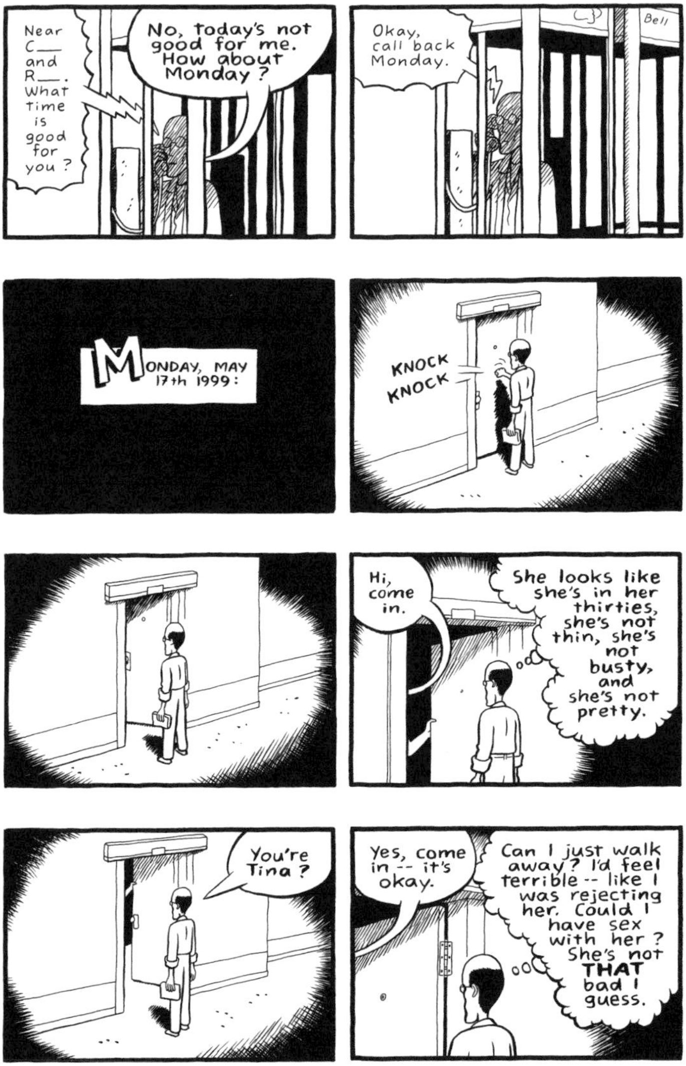
Near C___ and R___. What time is good for you?
No, today's not good for me. How about Monday?
Okay, call back Monday.
Bell
MONDAY, MAY 17th 1999:
KNOCK KNOCK
Hi, come in.
She looks like she's in her thirties, she's not thin, she's not busty, and she's not pretty.
You're Tina?
Yes, come in -- it's okay.
Can I just walk away? I'd feel terrible -- like I was rejecting her. Could I have sex with her? She's not THAT bad I guess.

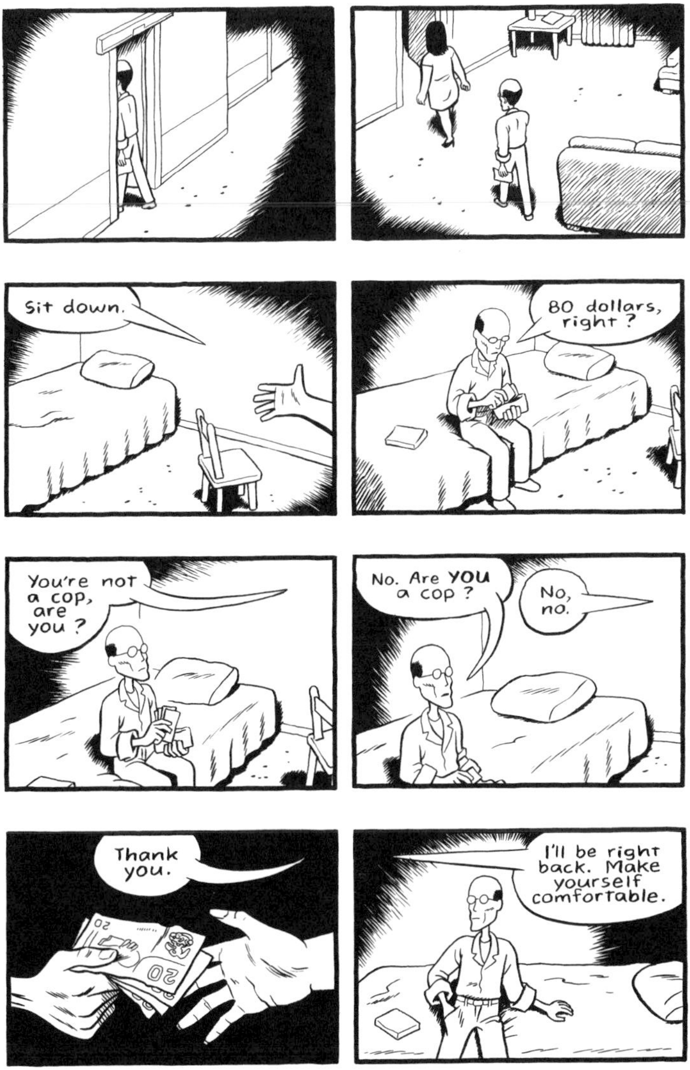
Sit down.
80 dollars, right ?
You're not a cop, are you ?
No. Are YOU a cop ?
No, no.
Thank you.
I'll be right back. Make yourself comfortable.

CHAPTER 3

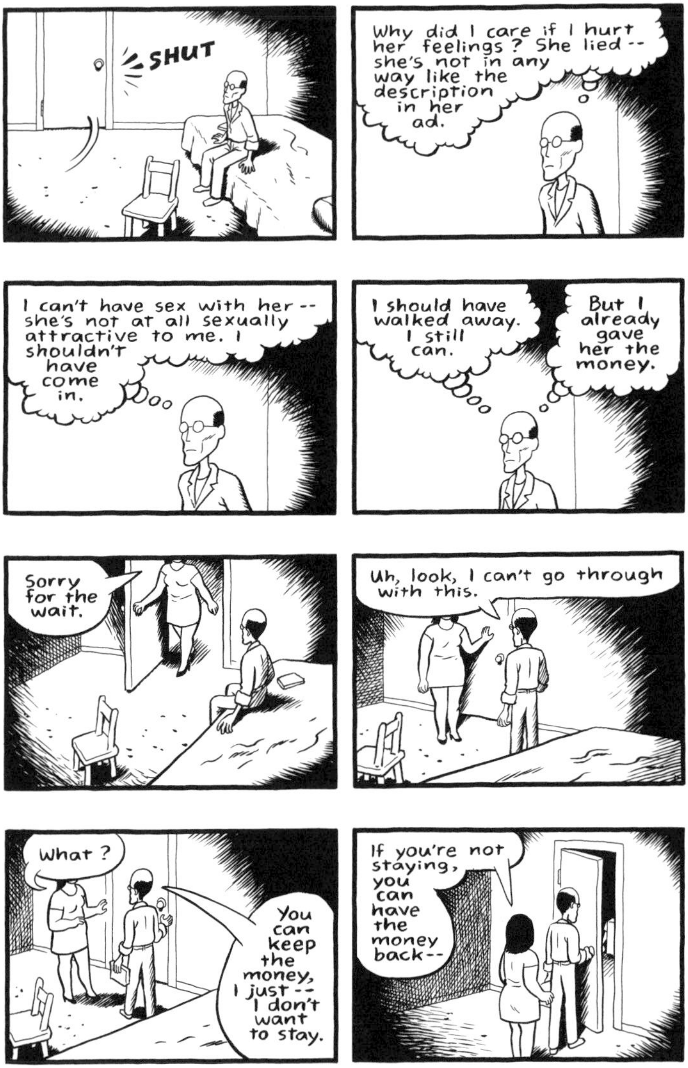
SHUT
Why did I care if I hurt her feelings? She lied -- she's not in any way like the description in her ad.
I can't have sex with her -- she's not at all sexually attractive to me. I shouldn't have come in.
I should have walked away. I still can.
But I already gave her the money.
Sorry for the wait.
Uh, look, I can't go through with this.
What?
You can keep the money, I just -- I don't want to stay.
If you're not staying, you can have the money back--

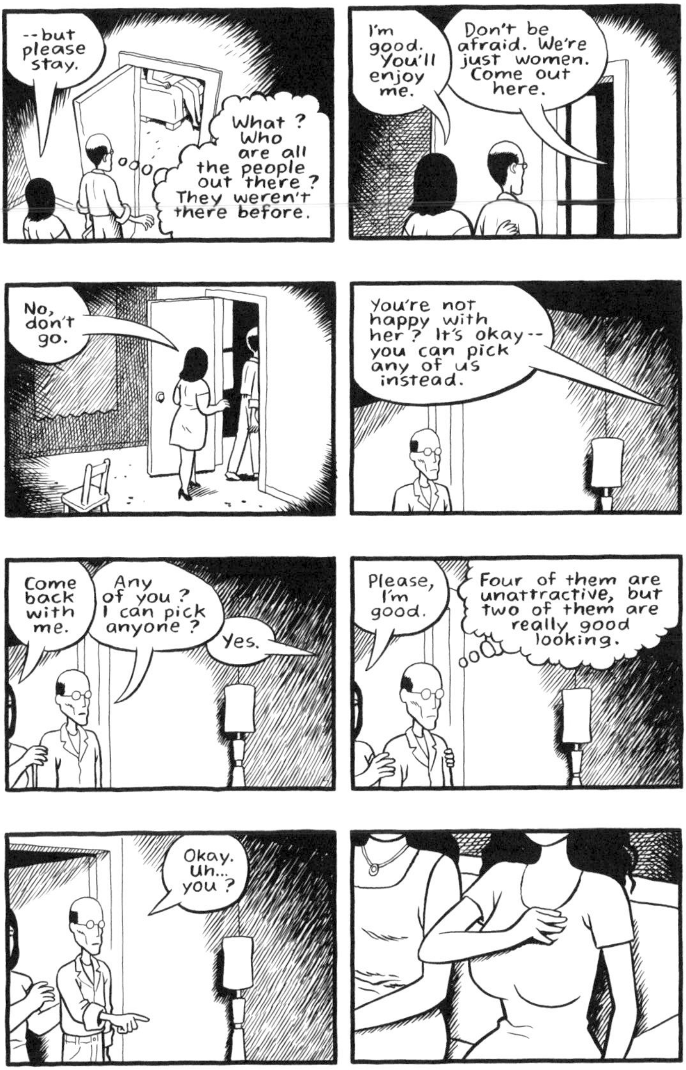
--but please stay.
What? Who are all the people out there? They weren't there before.
I'm good. You'll enjoy me.
Don't be afraid. We're just women. Come out here.
No, don't go.
You're not happy with her? It's okay-- you can pick any of us instead.
Come back with me.
Any of you? I can pick anyone?
Yes.
Please, I'm good.
Four of them are unattractive, but two of them are really good looking.
Okay. Uh... you?

CHAPTER 3

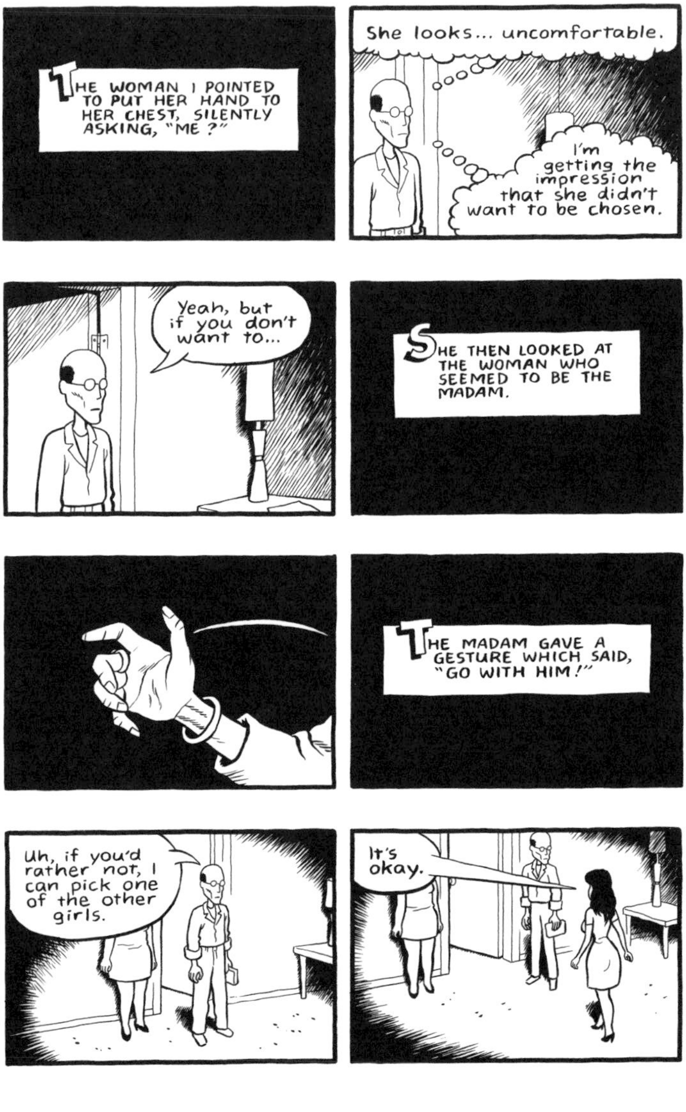
THE WOMAN I POINTED TO PUT HER HAND TO HER CHEST, SILENTLY ASKING, "ME?"
She looks... uncomfortable.
I'm getting the impression that she didn't want to be chosen.
Yeah, but if you don't want to...
SHE THEN LOOKED AT THE WOMAN WHO SEEMED TO BE THE MADAM.
THE MADAM GAVE A GESTURE WHICH SAID, "GO WITH HIM!"
Uh, if you'd rather not, I can pick one of the other girls.
It's okay.

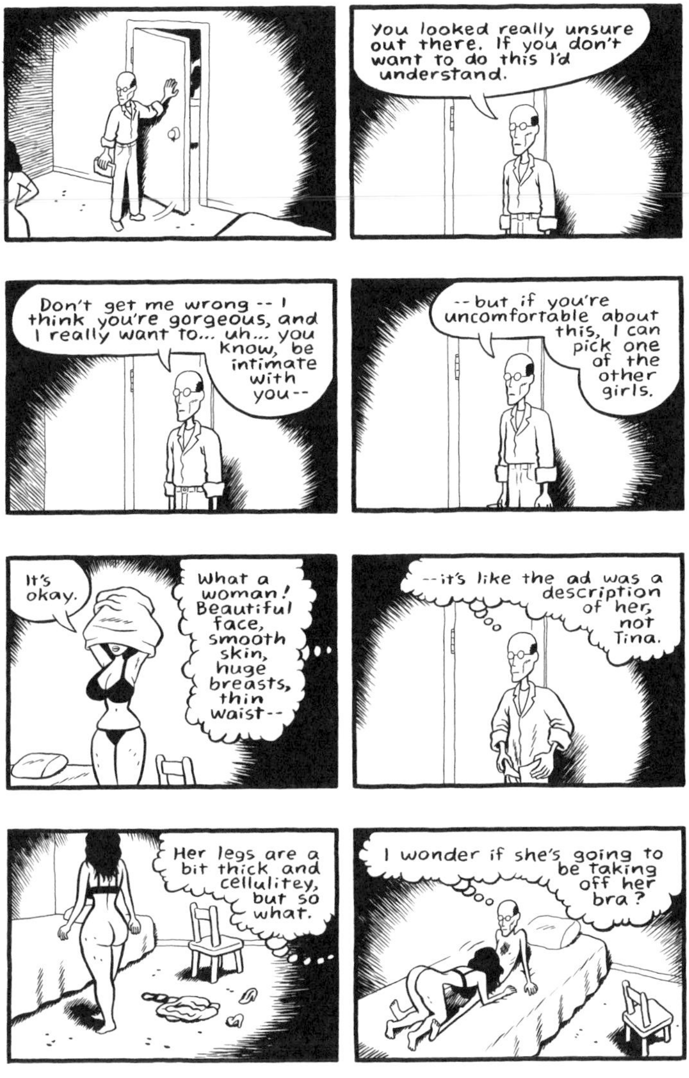
You looked really unsure out there. If you don't want to do this I'd understand.
Don't get me wrong -- I think you're gorgeous, and I really want to... uh... you know, be intimate with you--
--but if you're uncomfortable about this, I can pick one of the other girls.
It's okay.
What a woman! Beautiful face, smooth skin, huge breasts, thin waist--
--it's like the ad was a description of her, not Tina.
Her legs are a bit thick and cellulitey, but so what.
I wonder if she's going to be taking off her bra?

CHAPTER 3

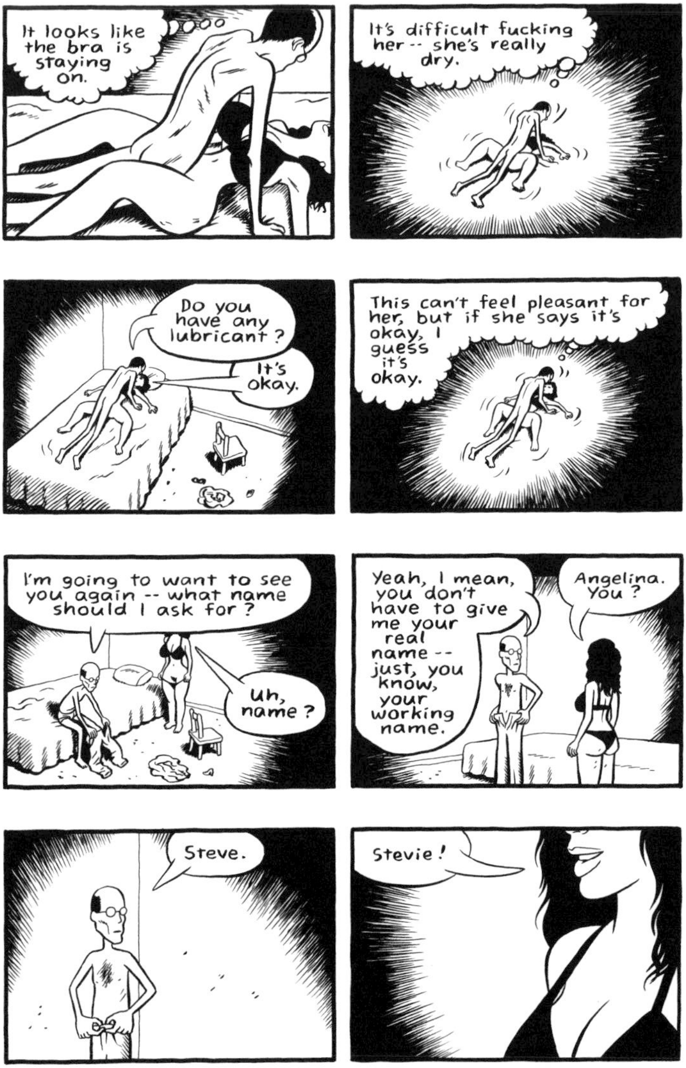
It looks like the bra is staying on.
It's difficult fucking her -- she's really dry.
Do you have any lubricant?
It's okay.
This can't feel pleasant for her, but if she says it's okay, I guess it's okay.
I'm going to want to see you again -- what name should I ask for?
Uh, name?
Yeah, I mean, you don't have to give me your real name -- just, you know, your working name.
Angelina. You?
Steve.
Stevie!

CHAPTER
4
—
ANNE

MAY 31st 1999:

I want to see Angelina again, but I'm also curious to see the petite 18 year-old described in this ad.

LATER THAT DAY:

KNOCK KNOCK

CHAPTER 4

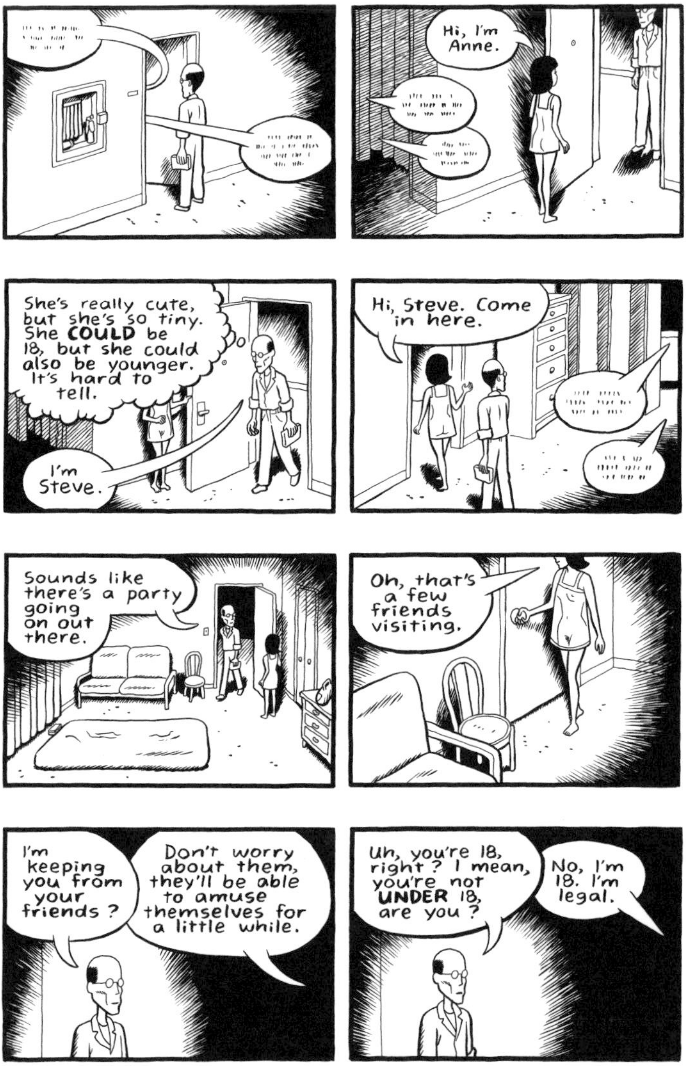
Hi, I'm Anne.
She's really cute, but she's so tiny. She COULD be 18, but she could also be younger. It's hard to tell.
I'm Steve.
Hi, Steve. Come in here.
Sounds like there's a party going on out there.
Oh, that's a few friends visiting.
I'm keeping you from your friends?
Don't worry about them, they'll be able to amuse themselves for a little while.
Uh, you're 18, right? I mean, you're not UNDER 18, are you?
No, I'm 18. I'm legal.

Her body's kinda the opposite of Angelina's, but it's just as amazing.
JUNE 1999:
I was telling my step-mother about your whoring and she was disgusted. She said, "He's obviously got no self-respect."
I don't know, I think I've got a pretty high opinion of myself. I think I've got a lot of respect for myself.
Yeah, you are pretty arrogant.

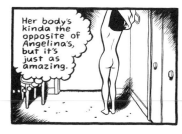

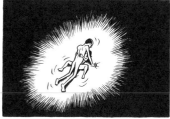

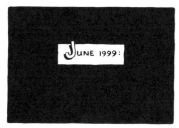

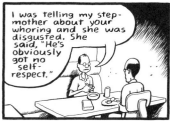

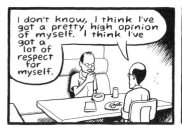

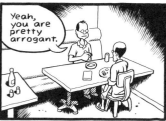

CHAPTER
5
—
BACK TO
ANGELINA

JULY 5th 1999:

Hi, I'd like an appointment to see Angelina.

ABOUT TWO HOURS LATER:

KNOCK KNOCK

CHAPTER 5

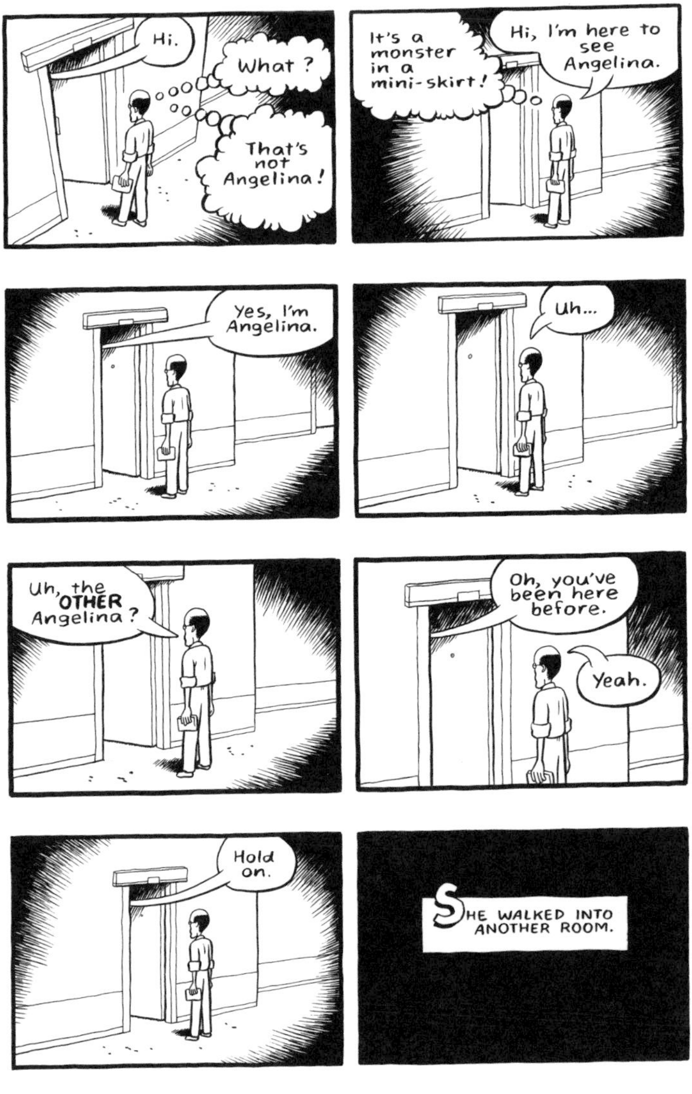
Hi.
What ?
That's not Angelina!
It's a monster in a mini-skirt!
Hi, I'm here to see Angelina.
Yes, I'm Angelina.
Uh...
Uh, the OTHER Angelina?
Oh, you've been here before.
Yeah.
Hold on.
SHE WALKED INTO ANOTHER ROOM.

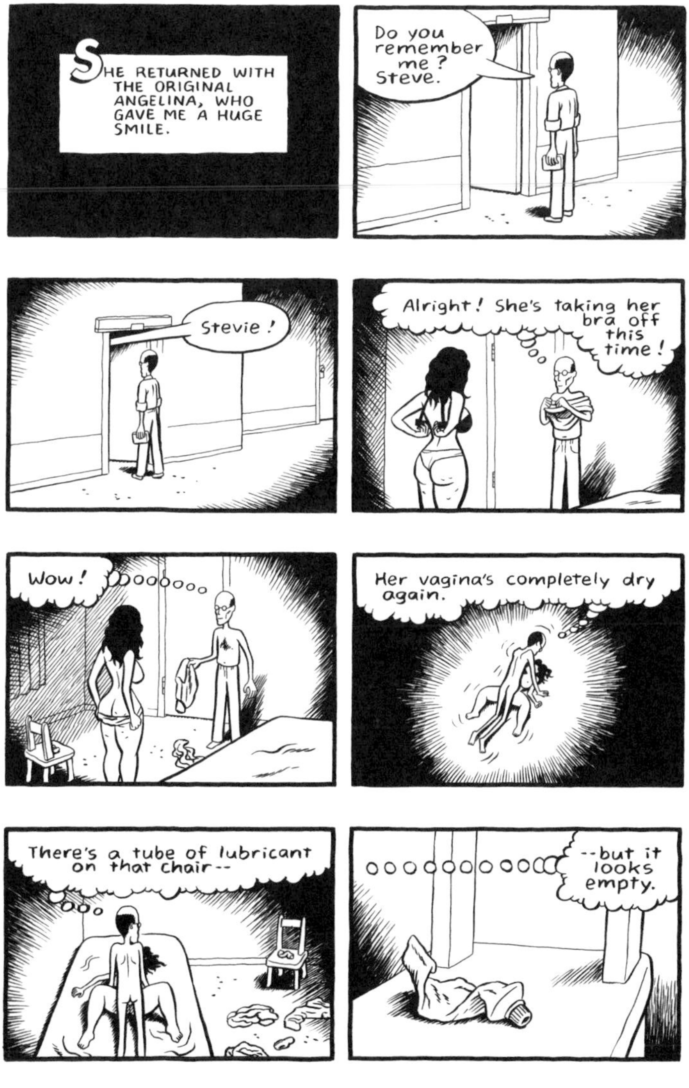
SHE RETURNED WITH THE ORIGINAL ANGELINA, WHO GAVE ME A HUGE SMILE.
Do you remember me? Steve.
Stevie!
Alright! She's taking her bra off this time!
Wow!
Her vagina's completely dry again.
There's a tube of lubricant on that chair--
--but it looks empty.

CHAPTER 5

How long have you lived in Toronto ?
I... no English.
You can't speak English ?
No speak English.
How did I not notice that ? I guess I followed her lead in not speaking much.

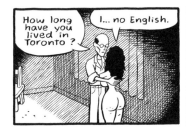

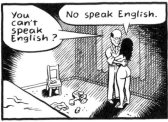

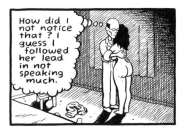

CHAPTER 6

BACK TO ANNE

JUNE 14th 1999:
You draw comic-books? That's awesome.
The next time you come to see me, you should bring me one. I used to like Archie comics.
My stuff's quite different from Archie, but I'll bring you something.

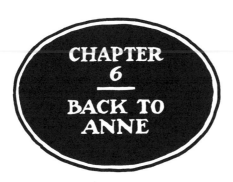

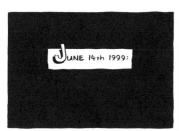

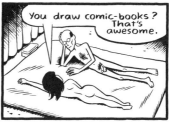

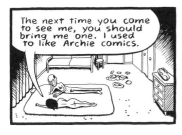

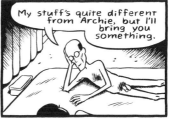

CHAPTER 6

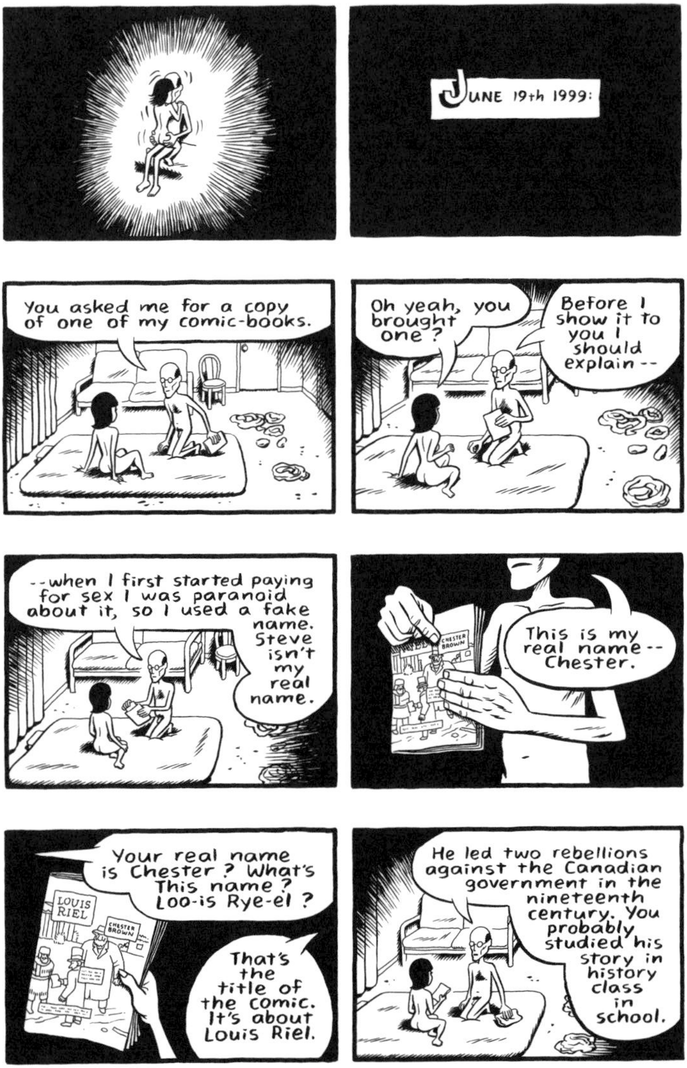
JUNE 19th 1999:
You asked me for a copy of one of my comic-books.
Oh yeah, you brought one?
Before I show it to you I should explain --
--when I first started paying for sex I was paranoid about it, so I used a fake name. Steve isn't my real name.
This is my real name -- Chester.
CHESTER BROWN
Your real name is Chester? What's This name? Loo-is Rye-el?
LOUIS RIEL
CHESTER BROWN
That's the title of the comic. It's about Louis Riel.
He led two rebellions against the Canadian government in the nineteenth century. You probably studied his story in history class in school.

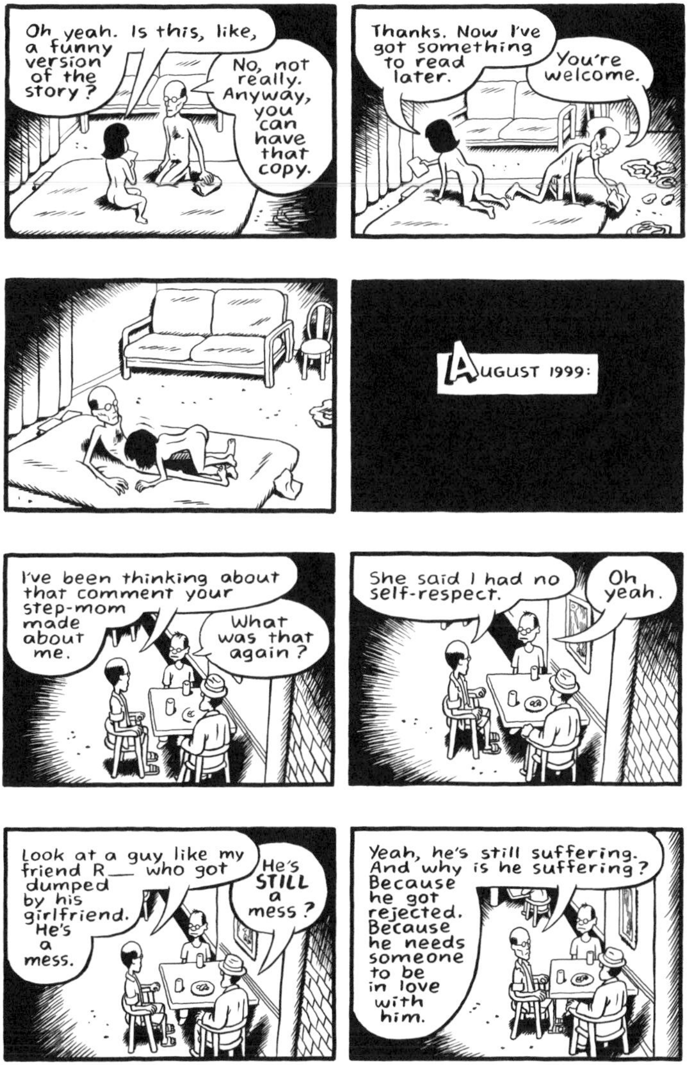
Oh yeah. Is this, like, a funny version of the story?
No, not really. Anyway, you can have that copy.
Thanks. Now I've got something to read later.
You're welcome.
AUGUST 1999:
I've been thinking about that comment your step-mom made about me.
What was that again?
She said I had no self-respect.
Oh yeah.
Look at a guy like my friend R__ who got dumped by his girlfriend. He's a mess.
He's STILL a mess?
Yeah, he's still suffering. And why is he suffering? Because he got rejected. Because he needs someone to be in love with him.

CHAPTER 6

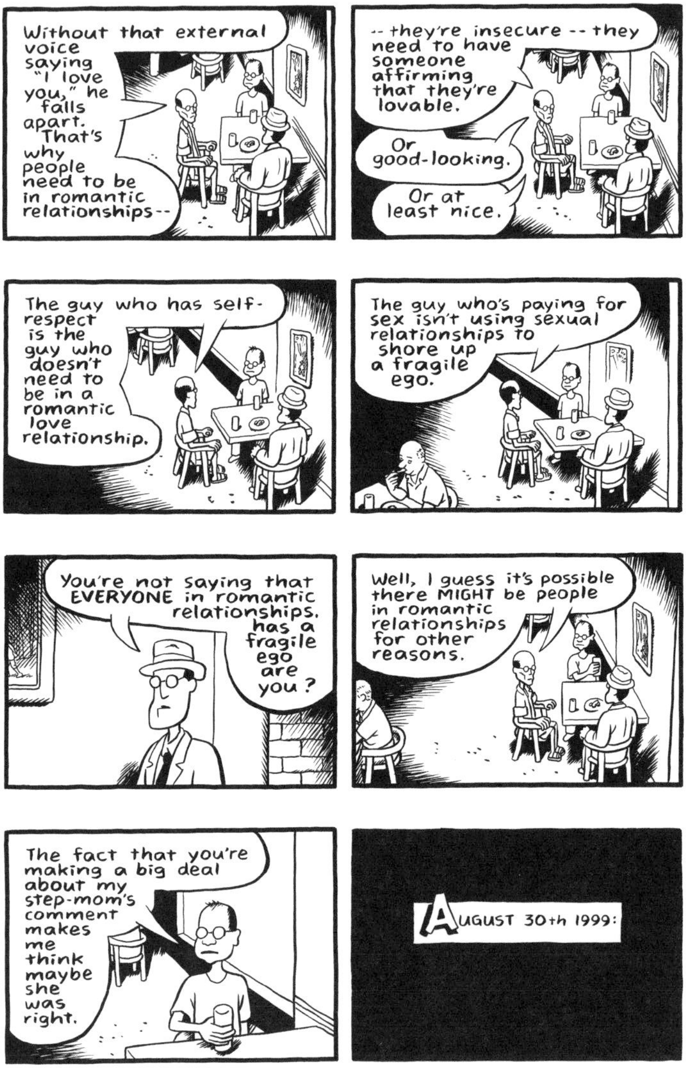

Without that external voice saying "I love you," he falls apart. That's why people need to be in romantic relationships--
-- they're insecure -- they need to have someone affirming that they're lovable.
Or good-looking.
Or at least nice.
The guy who has self-respect is the guy who doesn't need to be in a romantic love relationship.
The guy who's paying for sex isn't using sexual relationships to shore up a fragile ego.
You're not saying that EVERYONE in romantic relationships has a fragile ego are you?
Well, I guess it's possible there MIGHT be people in romantic relationships for other reasons.
The fact that you're making a big deal about my step-mom's comment makes me think maybe she was right.
AUGUST 30th 1999:

There's another girl who works here -- if you want to see her sometime, it's okay with me.
What's she look like?
Big breasts, thin, pretty. Her name's Amanda.
I'll think about it.

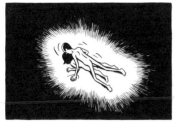

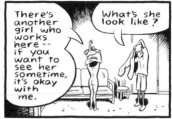

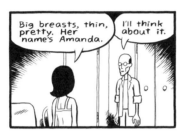

CHAPTER
7
—
AMANDA

SEPTEMBER 21st 1999:

Anne has nothing but good things to say about you.

Her face is reasonably attractive, but those boobs look too fake for my liking.

Can I look at your penis?

?

Okay.

91

CHAPTER 7

She's obviously really careful-- this is a very thorough inspection.
Would you like a blow-job?
Very much.
OH GOD! OH GOD! FASTER!
HARDER! FASTER! OH GOD! LIKE THAT! FASTER!
She wants me to go faster 'cause she wants me to come quickly.

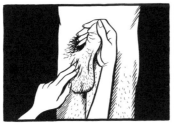

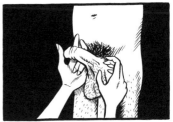

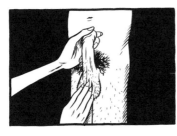

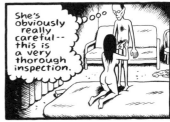

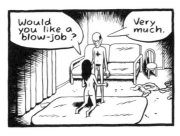

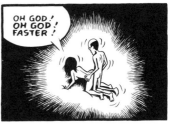

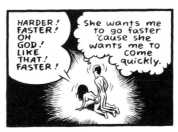

CHAPTER 8

BACK TO ANNE

OCTOBER 12th 1999:

So how did things go with Amanda?

Fine. She was nice, but those fake breasts were disturbing.

Disturbing?

They didn't look right, and they didn't feel right.

Your breasts feel the way breasts should. You're never going to get breast-implants are you?

CHAPTER 8

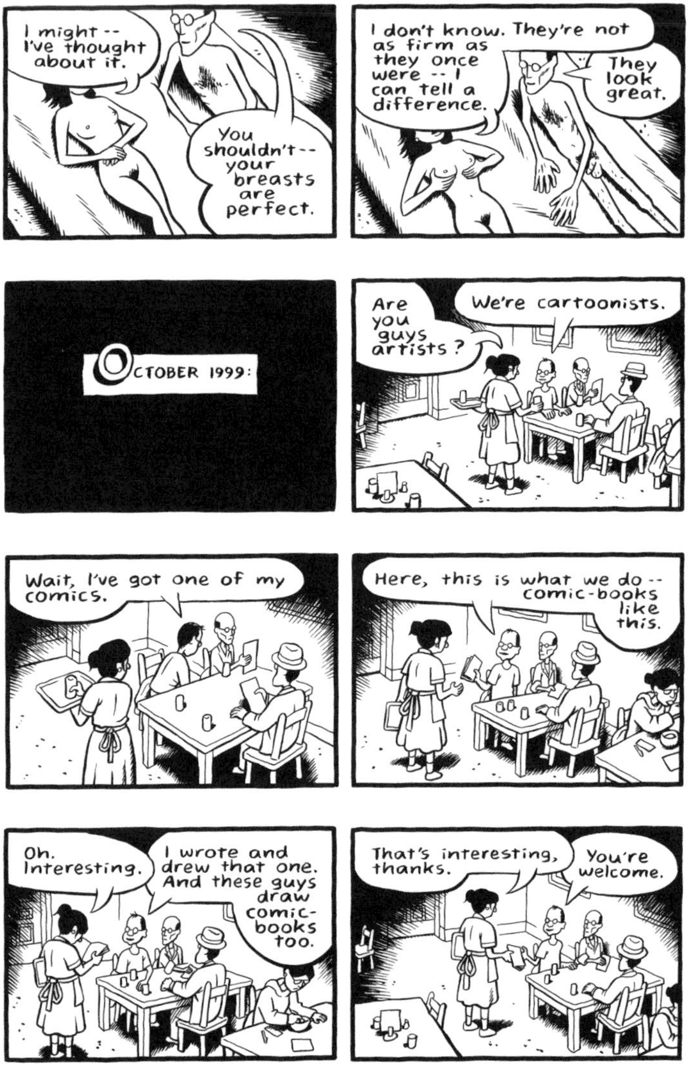
I might -- I've thought about it.
You shouldn't -- your breasts are perfect.
I don't know. They're not as firm as they once were -- I can tell a difference.
They look great.
OCTOBER 1999:
Are you guys artists?
We're cartoonists.
Wait, I've got one of my comics.
Here, this is what we do -- comic-books like this.
Oh. Interesting.
I wrote and drew that one. And these guys draw comic-books too.
That's interesting, thanks.
You're welcome.

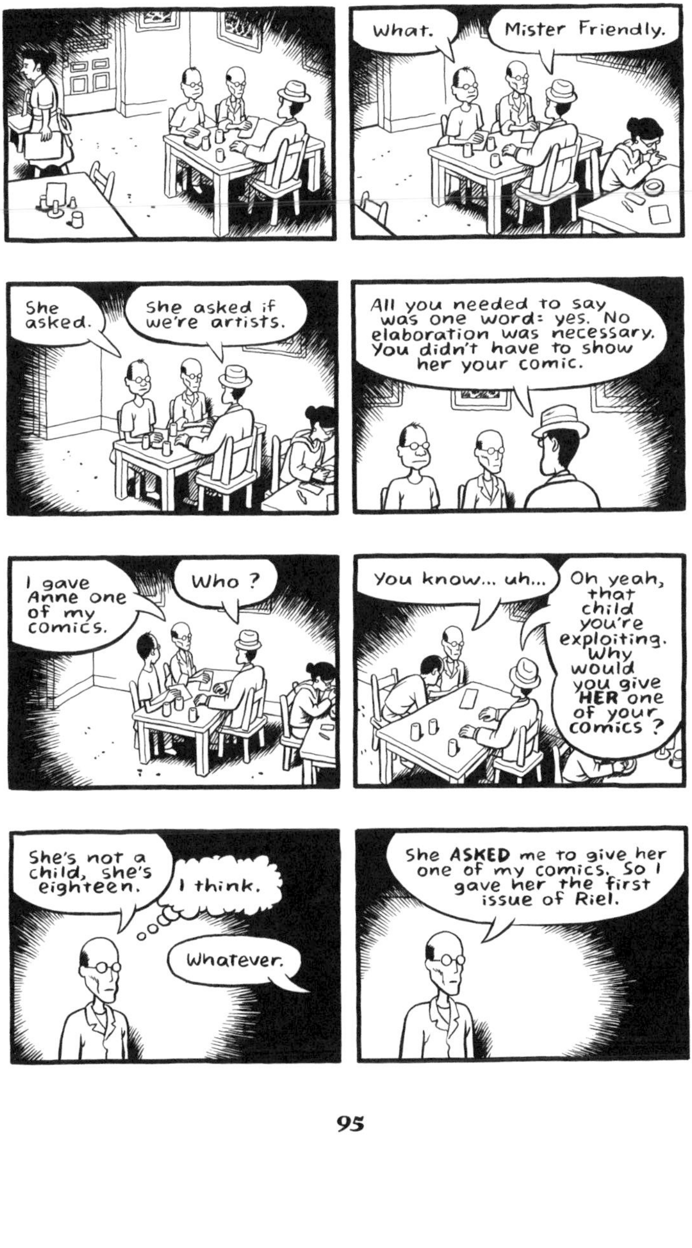
What.
Mister Friendly.
She asked.
She asked if we're artists.
All you needed to say was one word: yes. No elaboration was necessary. You didn't have to show her your comic.
I gave Anne one of my comics.
Who?
You know... uh...
Oh yeah, that child you're exploiting. Why would you give HER one of your comics?
She's not a child, she's eighteen.
I think.
Whatever.
She ASKED me to give her one of my comics. So I gave her the first issue of Riel.

CHAPTER 8

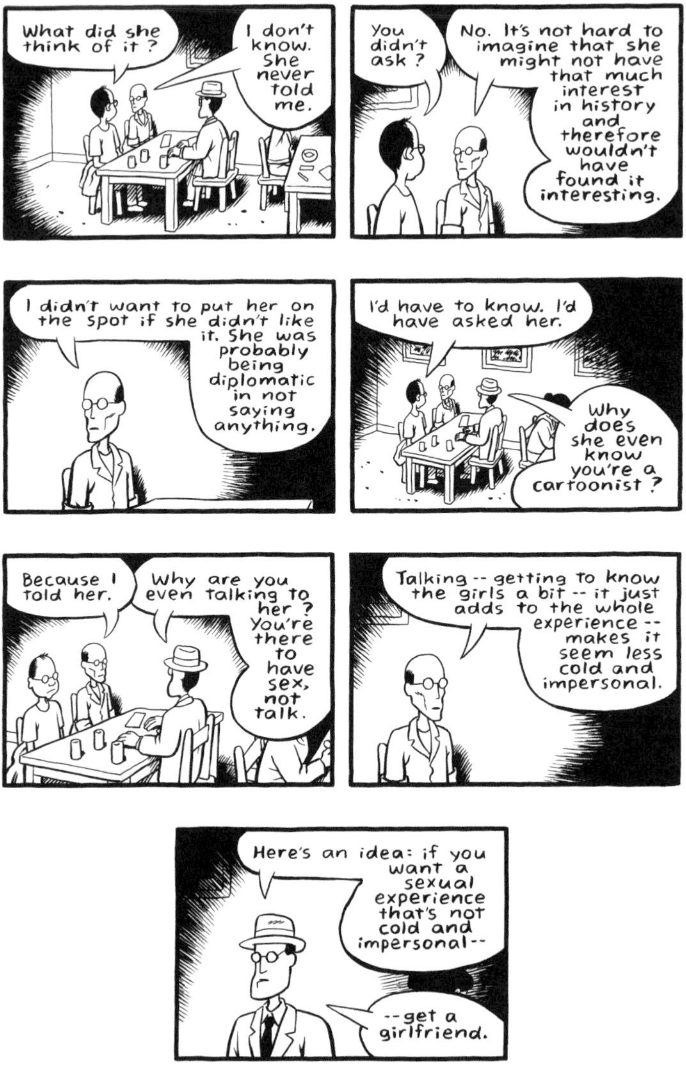
What did she think of it?
I don't know. She never told me.
You didn't ask?
No. It's not hard to imagine that she might not have that much interest in history and therefore wouldn't have found it interesting.
I didn't want to put her on the spot if she didn't like it. She was probably being diplomatic in not saying anything.
I'd have to know. I'd have asked her.
Why does she even know you're a cartoonist?
Because I told her.
Why are you even talking to her? You're there to have sex, not talk.
Talking -- getting to know the girls a bit -- it just adds to the whole experience -- makes it seem less cold and impersonal.
Here's an idea: if you want a sexual experience that's not cold and impersonal--
--get a girlfriend.

CHAPTER 9

SUSAN

NOVEMBER 1st 1999:
Let's see if Angelina is in today.
This number is out of service.
Damn!
Well, let's look at the ads.

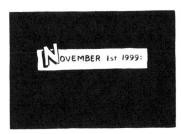

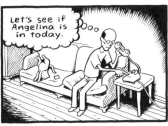

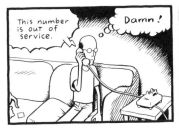

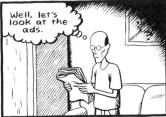

CHAPTER 9

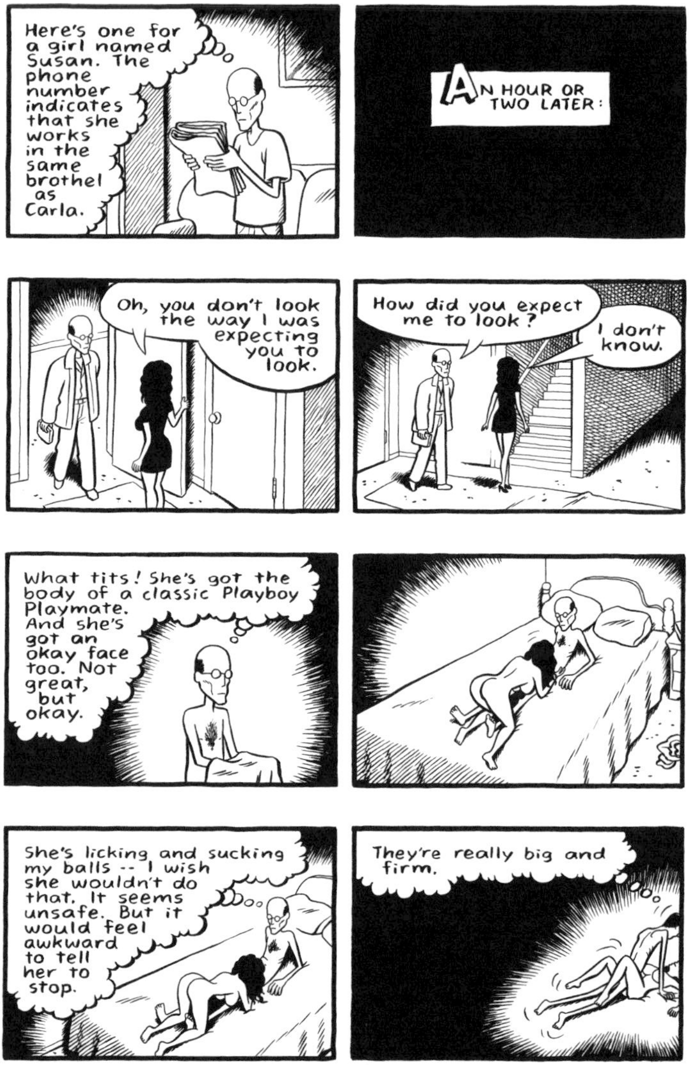
Here's one for a girl named Susan. The phone number indicates that she works in the same brothel as Carla.
AN HOUR OR TWO LATER:
Oh, you don't look the way I was expecting you to look.
How did you expect me to look?
I don't know.
What tits! She's got the body of a classic Playboy Playmate. And she's got an okay face too. Not great, but okay.
She's licking and sucking my balls -- I wish she wouldn't do that. It seems unsafe. But it would feel awkward to tell her to stop.
They're really big and firm.

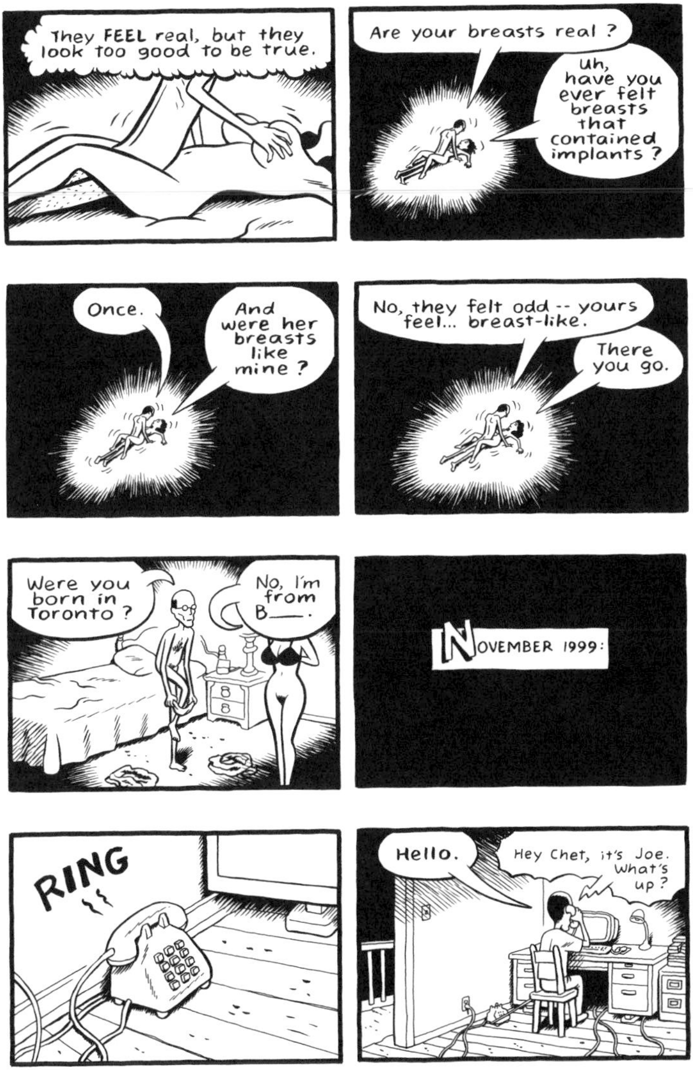
They FEEL real, but they look too good to be true.
Are your breasts real ?
Uh, have you ever felt breasts that contained implants ?
Once.
And were her breasts like mine ?
No, they felt odd -- yours feel... breast-like.
There you go.
Were you born in Toronto ?
No, I'm from B___.
NOVEMBER 1999:
RING
Hello.
Hey Chet, it's Joe. What's up ?

CHAPTER 9

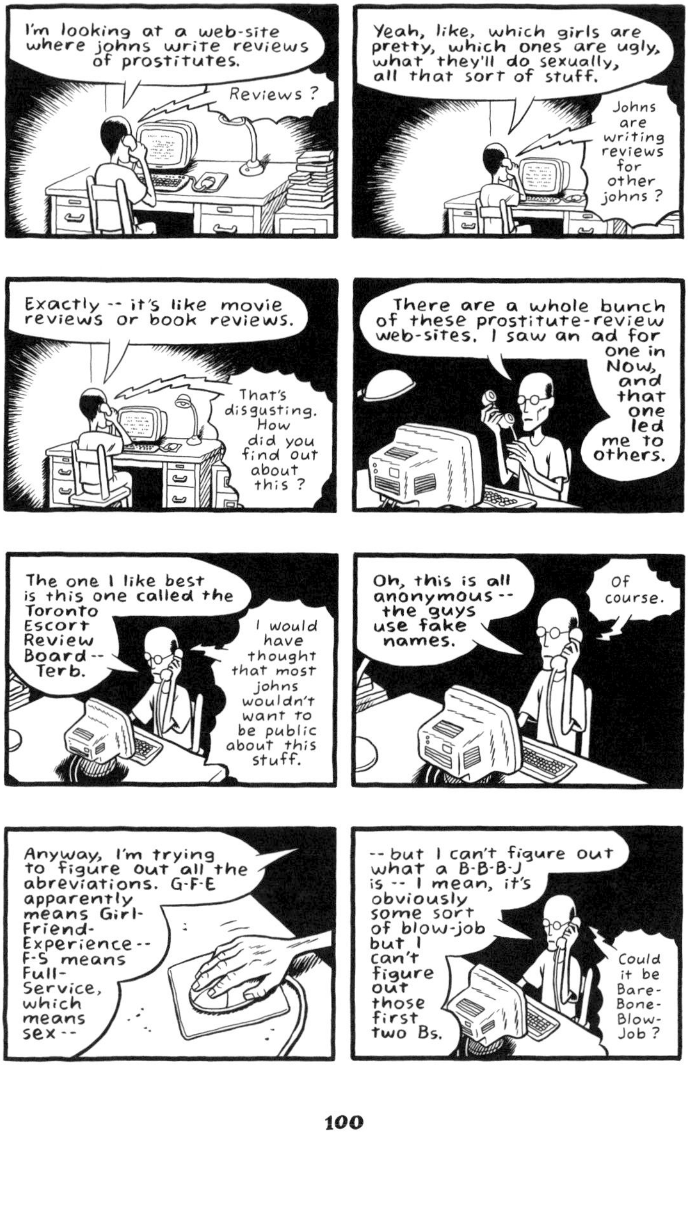
I'm looking at a web-site where johns write reviews of prostitutes.
Reviews ?
Yeah, like, which girls are pretty, which ones are ugly, what they'll do sexually, all that sort of stuff.
Johns are writing reviews for other johns ?
Exactly -- it's like movie reviews or book reviews.
That's disgusting. How did you find out about this ?
There are a whole bunch of these prostitute-review web-sites. I saw an ad for one in Now, and that one led me to others.
The one I like best is this one called the Toronto Escort Review Board -- Terb.
I would have thought that most johns wouldn't want to be public about this stuff.
Oh, this is all anonymous -- the guys use fake names.
Of course.
Anyway, I'm trying to figure out all the abreviations. G-F-E apparently means Girl-Friend-Experience -- F-S means Full-Service, which means sex --
-- but I can't figure out what a B-B-B-J is -- I mean, it's obviously some sort of blow-job but I can't figure out those first two Bs.
Could it be Bare-Bone-Blow-Job ?

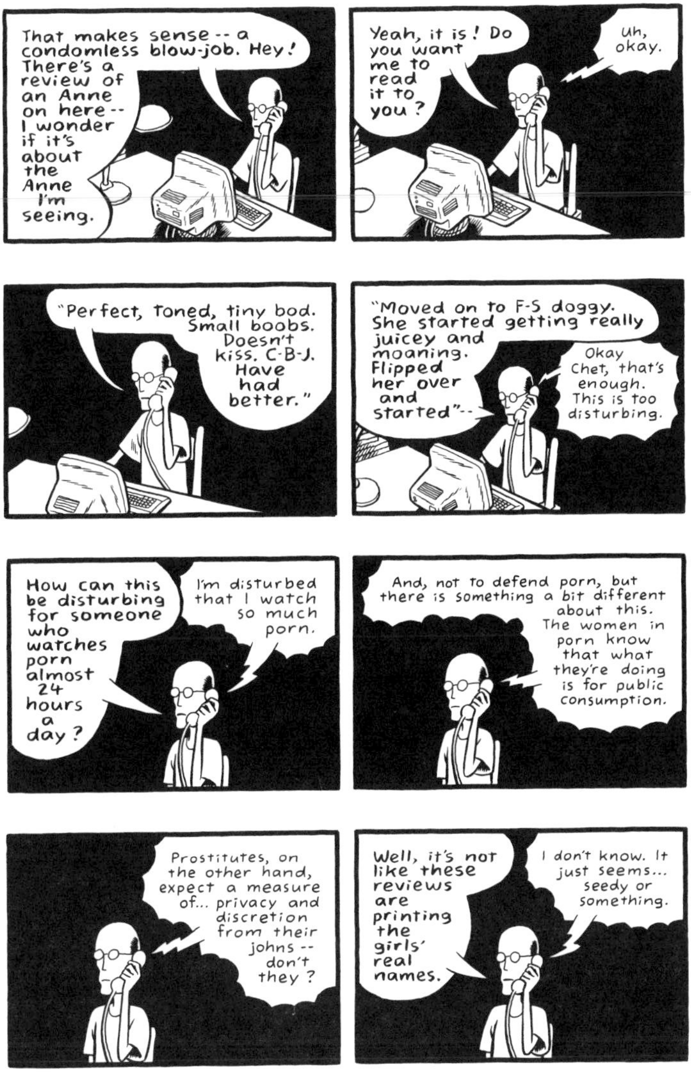
That makes sense -- a condomless blow-job. Hey! There's a review of an Anne on here -- I wonder if it's about the Anne I'm seeing.
Yeah, it is! Do you want me to read it to you?
Uh, okay.
"Perfect, toned, tiny bod. Small boobs. Doesn't kiss. C-B-J. Have had better."
"Moved on to F-S doggy. She started getting really juicey and moaning. Flipped her over and started"--
Okay Chet, that's enough. This is too disturbing.
How can this be disturbing for someone who watches porn almost 24 hours a day?
I'm disturbed that I watch so much porn.
And, not to defend porn, but there is something a bit different about this. The women in porn know that what they're doing is for public consumption.
Prostitutes, on the other hand, expect a measure of... privacy and discretion from their johns -- don't they?
Well, it's not like these reviews are printing the girls' real names.
I don't know. It just seems... seedy or something.

CHAPTER
10
BACK TO ANNE

N OVEMBER 22nd 1999:

A friend of mine was doing it, and she convinced me to try it.

She was, like, "Just try it a few days -- if you don't like it, you can quit."

I worked at the place she worked for maybe a half-year before I started working here with Amanda.

103

CHAPTER 10

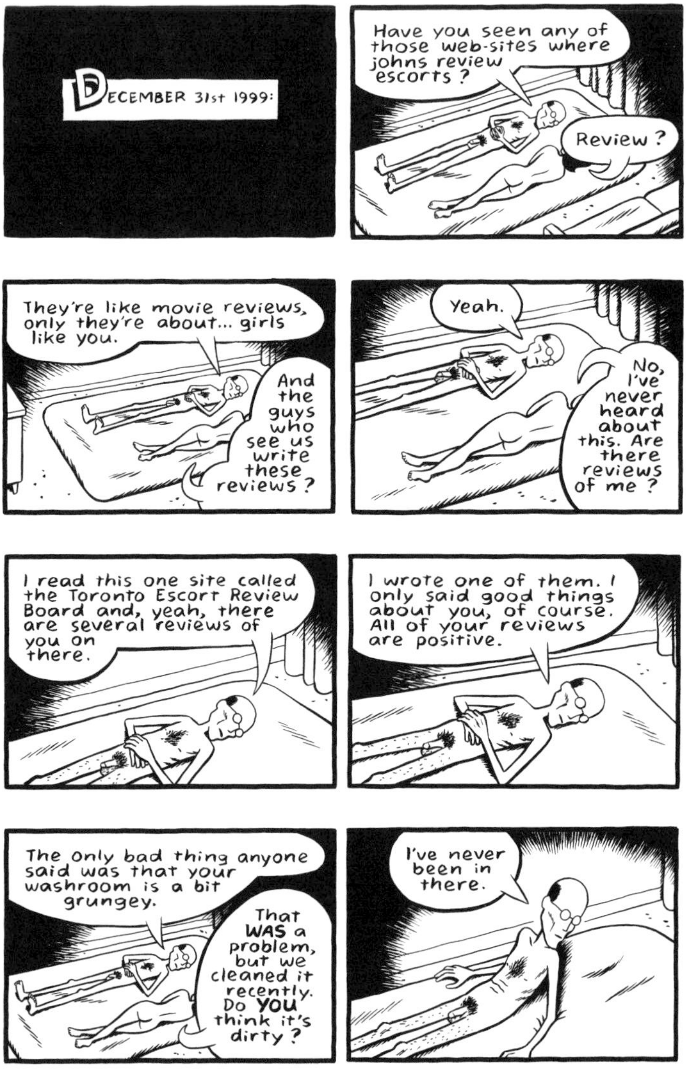
DECEMBER 31st 1999:
Have you seen any of those web-sites where johns review escorts?
Review?
They're like movie reviews, only they're about... girls like you.
And the guys who see us write these reviews?
Yeah.
No, I've never heard about this. Are there reviews of me?
I read this one site called the Toronto Escort Review Board and, yeah, there are several reviews of you on there.
I wrote one of them. I only said good things about you, of course. All of your reviews are positive.
The only bad thing anyone said was that your washroom is a bit grungey.
That WAS a problem, but we cleaned it recently. Do YOU think it's dirty?
I've never been in there.

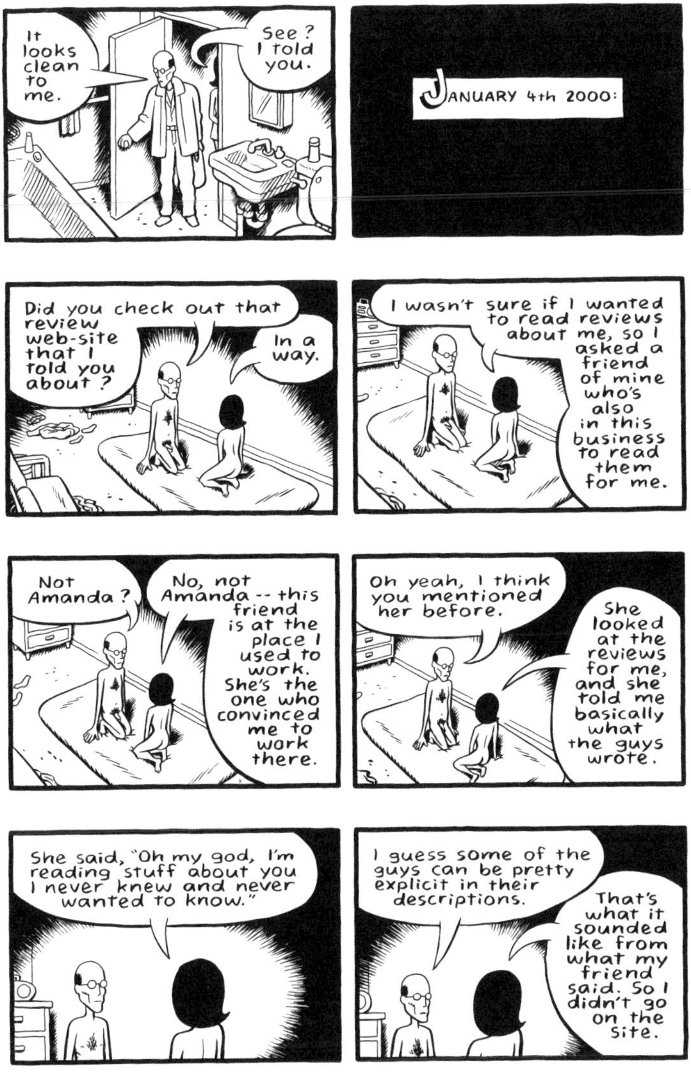
It looks clean to me.
See? I told you.
JANUARY 4th 2000:
Did you check out that review web-site that I told you about?
In a way.
I wasn't sure if I wanted to read reviews about me, so I asked a friend of mine who's also in this business to read them for me.
Not Amanda?
No, not Amanda -- this friend is at the place I used to work. She's the one who convinced me to work there.
Oh yeah, I think you mentioned her before.
She looked at the reviews for me, and she told me basically what the guys wrote.
She said, "Oh my god, I'm reading stuff about you I never knew and never wanted to know."
I guess some of the guys can be pretty explicit in their descriptions.
That's what it sounded like from what my friend said. So I didn't go on the site.

CHAPTER 10

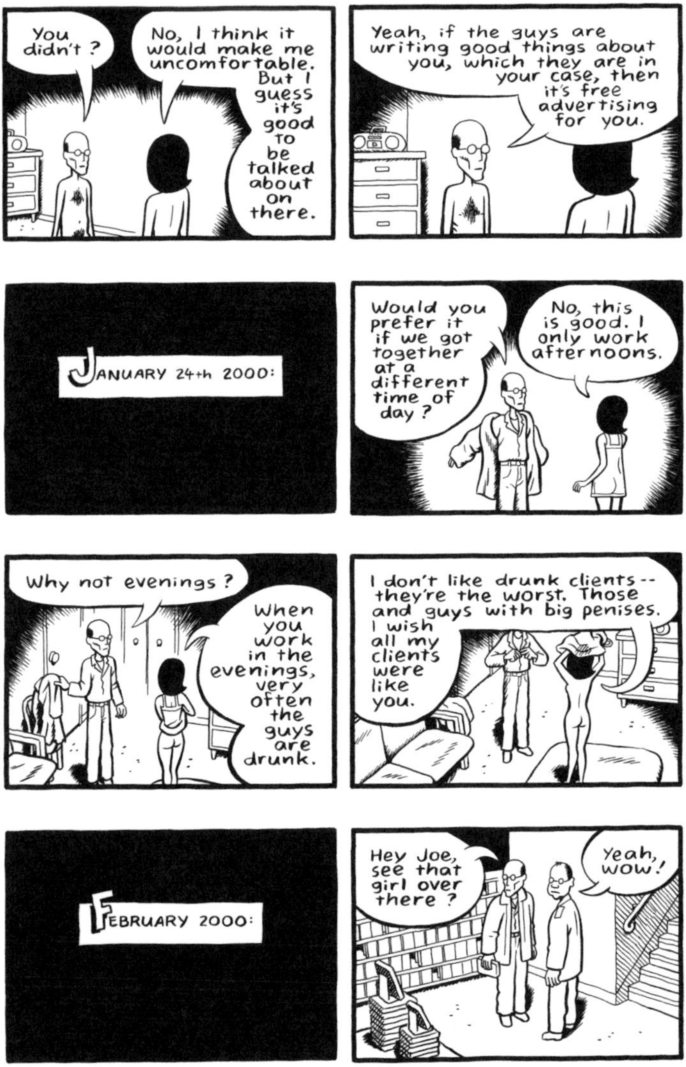
You didn't ?
No, I think it would make me uncomfortable. But I guess it's good to be talked about on there.
Yeah, if the guys are writing good things about you, which they are in your case, then it's free advertising for you.
JANUARY 24th 2000:
Would you prefer it if we got together at a different time of day ?
No, this is good. I only work afternoons.
Why not evenings ?
When you work in the evenings, very often the guys are drunk.
I don't like drunk clients -- they're the worst. Those and guys with big penises. I wish all my clients were like you.
FEBRUARY 2000:
Hey Joe, see that girl over there ?
Yeah, wow!

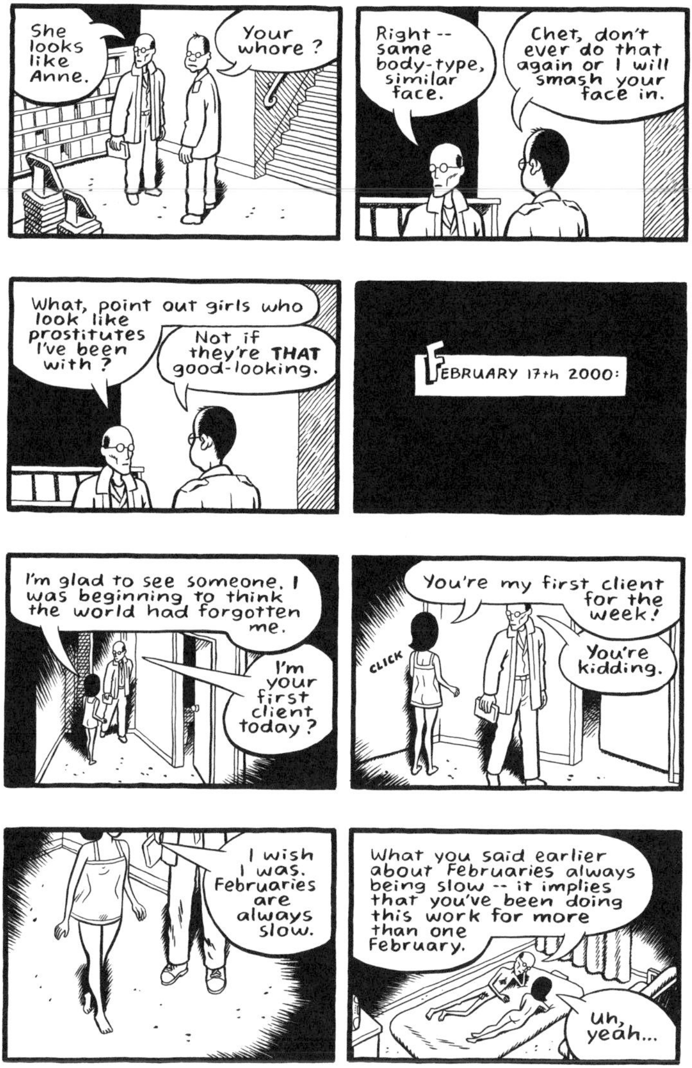
She looks like Anne.
Your whore ?
Right -- same body-type, similar face.
Chet, don't ever do that again or I will smash your face in.
What, point out girls who look like prostitutes I've been with ?
Not if they're THAT good-looking.
FEBRUARY 17th 2000:
I'm glad to see someone. I was beginning to think the world had forgotten me.
I'm your first client today ?
You're my first client for the week!
CLICK
You're kidding.
I wish I was. Februaries are always slow.
What you said earlier about Februaries always being slow -- it implies that you've been doing this work for more than one February.
Uh, yeah...

CHAPTER 10

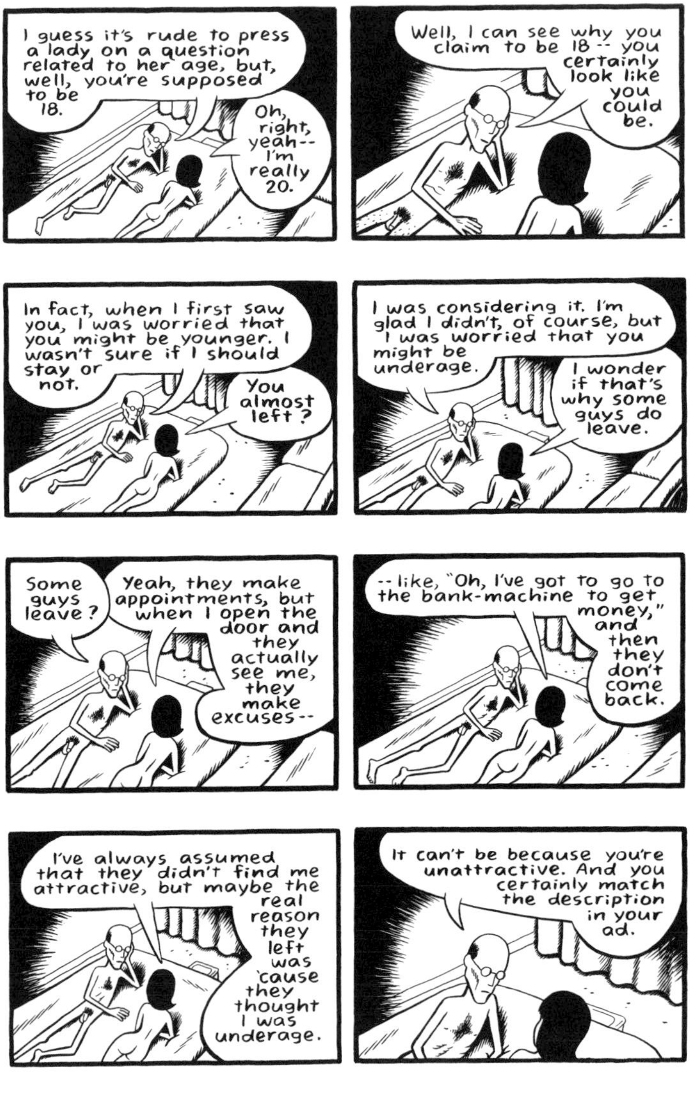
I guess it's rude to press a lady on a question related to her age, but, well, you're supposed to be 18.
Oh, right, yeah-- I'm really 20.
Well, I can see why you claim to be 18 -- you certainly look like you could be.
In fact, when I first saw you, I was worried that you might be younger. I wasn't sure if I should stay or not.
You almost left?
I was considering it. I'm glad I didn't, of course, but I was worried that you might be underage.
I wonder if that's why some guys do leave.
Some guys leave?
Yeah, they make appointments, but when I open the door and they actually see me, they make excuses--
--like, "Oh, I've got to go to the bank-machine to get money," and then they don't come back.
I've always assumed that they didn't find me attractive, but maybe the real reason they left was 'cause they thought I was underage.
It can't be because you're unattractive. And you certainly match the description in your ad.

Those guys MUST think you're underage -- that MUST be why they walk away. That's the only reason that makes sense to me.
That makes me feel better. I know I'm not every guy's type, but you still feel a bit bad when it seems like you're being rejected.

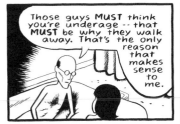

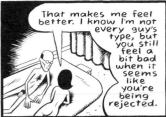

CHAPTER 11

WENDY

MARCH 9th 2000:
Could you give me a description of yourself?
I'm 22, 110 pounds, I've got an athletic body, I look like a model, I'm a very sensual person.
Where are you located?
At E___ and D___.
Can I make an appointment to see you today?
Sure, what time?

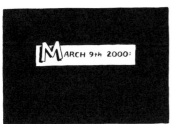

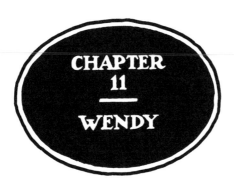

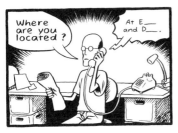

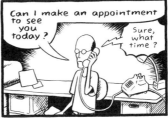

CHAPTER 11

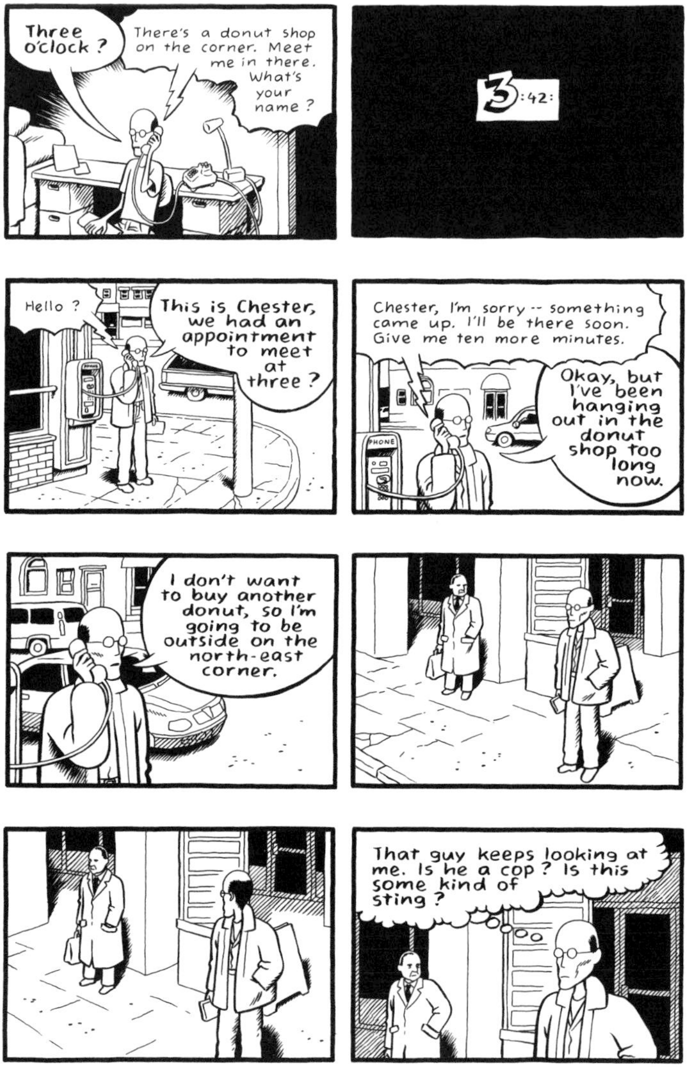
Three o'clock ?
There's a donut shop on the corner. Meet me in there. What's your name ?
3:42:
Hello ?
This is Chester, we had an appointment to meet at three ?
Chester, I'm sorry -- something came up. I'll be there soon. Give me ten more minutes.
Okay, but I've been hanging out in the donut shop too long now.
I don't want to buy another donut, so I'm going to be outside on the north-east corner.
That guy keeps looking at me. Is he a cop ? Is this some kind of sting ?
PHONE

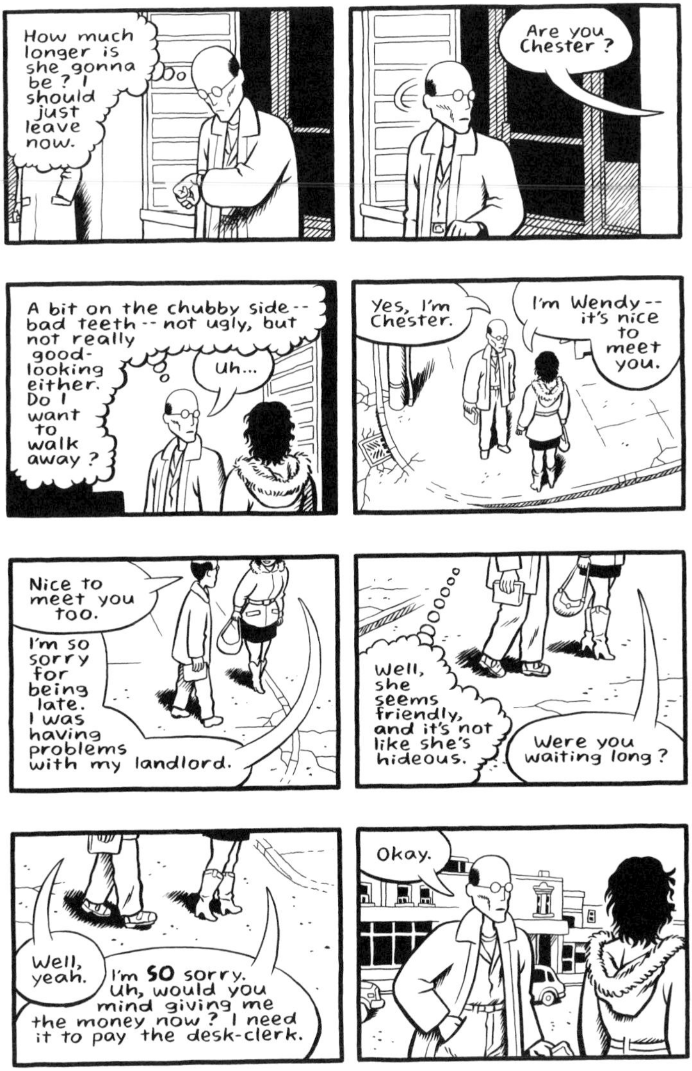
How much longer is she gonna be? I should just leave now.
Are you Chester?
A bit on the chubby side -- bad teeth -- not ugly, but not really good-looking either. Do I want to walk away?
Uh...
Yes, I'm Chester.
I'm Wendy -- it's nice to meet you.
Nice to meet you too.
I'm so sorry for being late. I was having problems with my landlord.
Well, she seems friendly, and it's not like she's hideous.
Were you waiting long?
Well, yeah.
I'm SO sorry. Uh, would you mind giving me the money now? I need it to pay the desk-clerk.
Okay.

CHAPTER 11

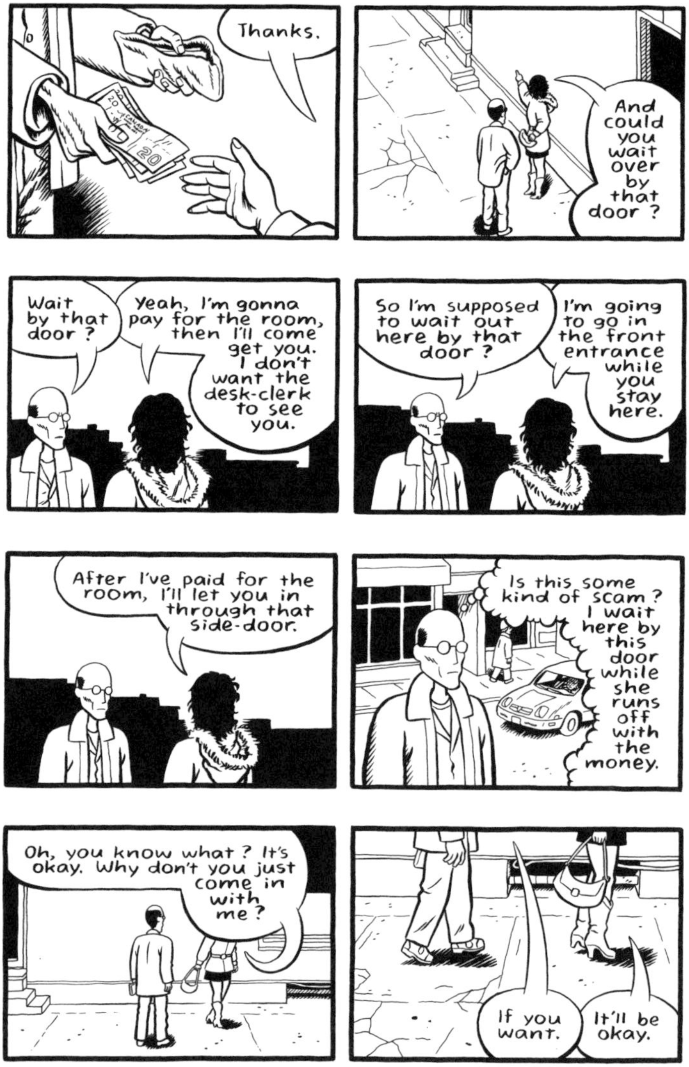

Thanks.
And could you wait over by that door?
Wait by that door?
Yeah, I'm gonna pay for the room, then I'll come get you. I don't want the desk-clerk to see you.
So I'm supposed to wait out here by that door?
I'm going to go in the front entrance while you stay here.
After I've paid for the room, I'll let you in through that side-door.
Is this some kind of scam? I wait here by this door while she runs off with the money.
Oh, you know what? It's okay. Why don't you just come in with me?
If you want.
It'll be okay.

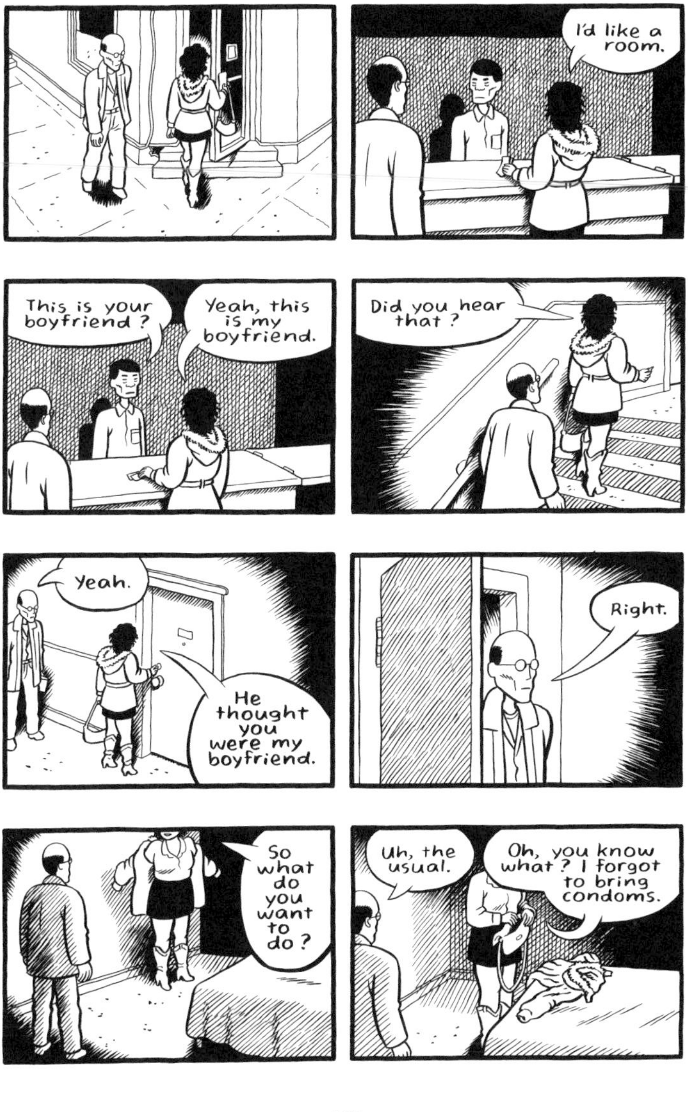
I'd like a room.
This is your boyfriend?
Yeah, this is my boyfriend.
Did you hear that?
Yeah.
He thought you were my boyfriend.
Right.
So what do you want to do?
Uh, the usual.
Oh, you know what? I forgot to bring condoms.

CHAPTER 11

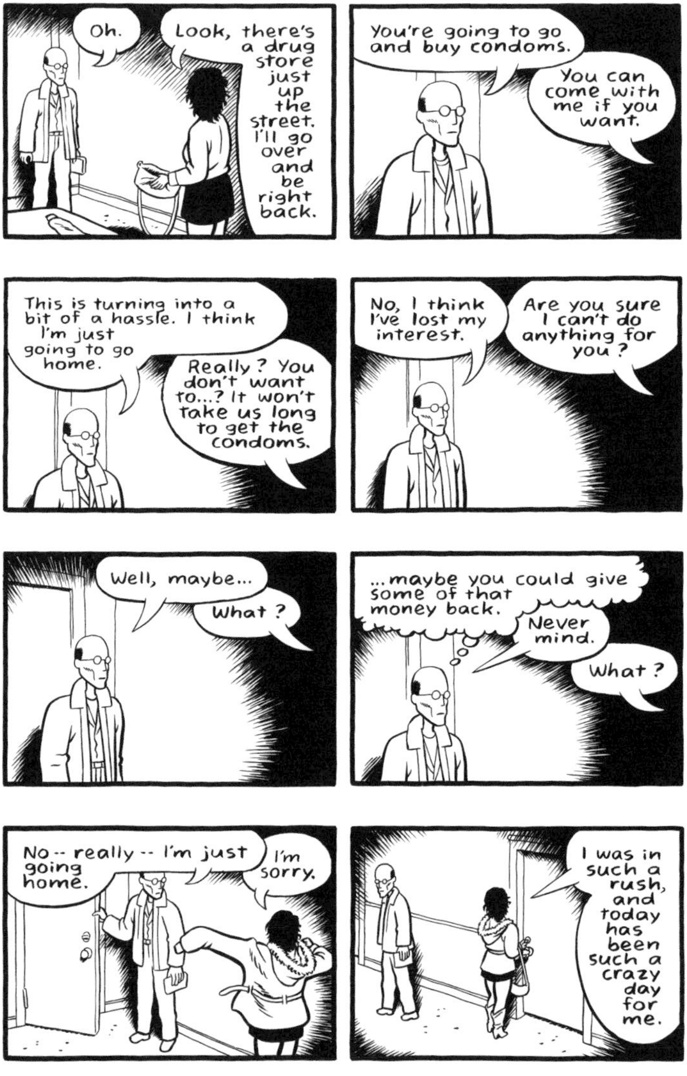

Oh.
Look, there's a drug store just up the street. I'll go over and be right back.
You're going to go and buy condoms.
You can come with me if you want.
This is turning into a bit of a hassle. I think I'm just going to go home.
Really? You don't want to...? It won't take us long to get the condoms.
No, I think I've lost my interest.
Are you sure I can't do anything for you?
Well, maybe...
What?
...maybe you could give some of that money back.
Never mind.
What?
No -- really -- I'm just going home.
I'm sorry.
I was in such a rush, and today has been such a crazy day for me.

Look, give me a call in a few days. I owe you one, okay?
Yeah, sure.
At least I can write a bad review about her on Terb. Let's see, what will I write?

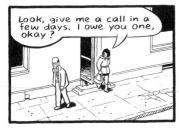

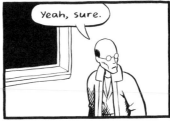

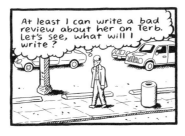

CHAPTER 12
—
BACK TO ANNE

March 10th 2000:

Okay, I'm done.

You're always so quiet when you come. It's hard to tell when you're finished.

CHAPTER 12

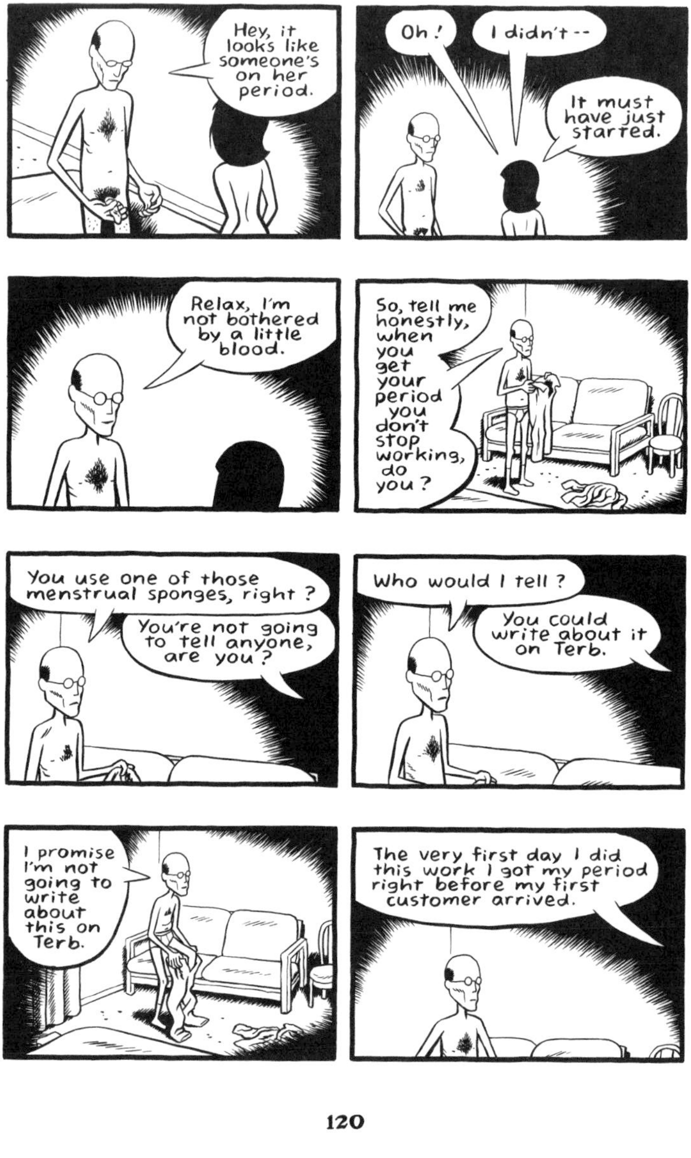
Hey, it looks like someone's on her period.
Oh!
I didn't --
It must have just started.
Relax, I'm not bothered by a little blood.
So, tell me honestly, when you get your period you don't stop working, do you?
You use one of those menstrual sponges, right?
You're not going to tell anyone, are you?
Who would I tell?
You could write about it on Terb.
I promise I'm not going to write about this on Terb.
The very first day I did this work I got my period right before my first customer arrived.

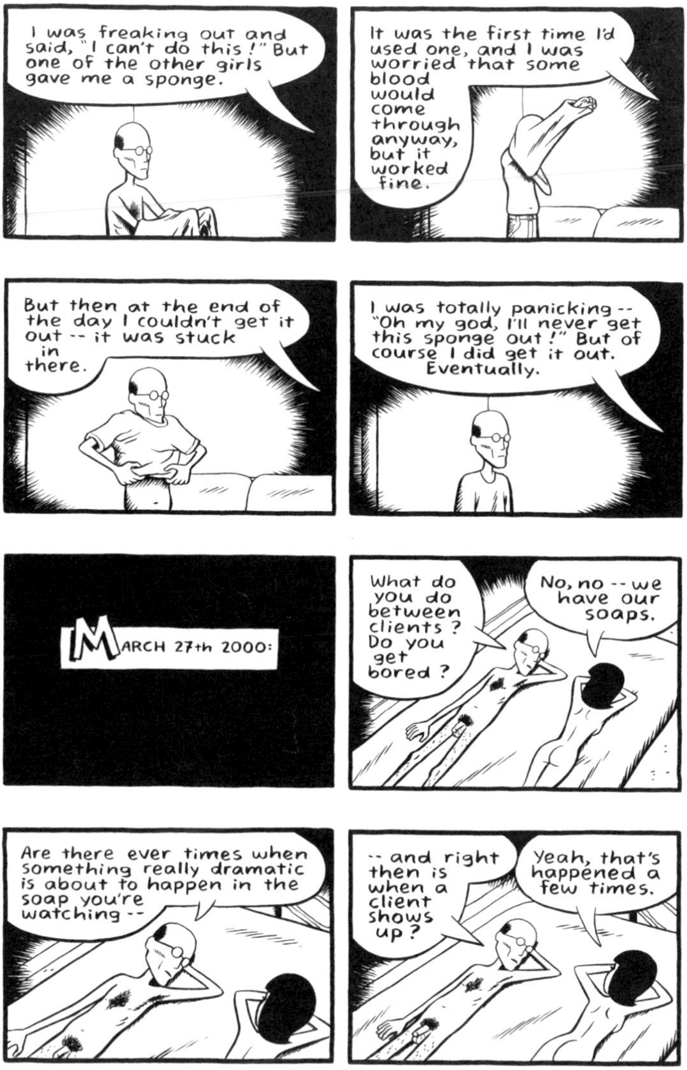
I was freaking out and said, "I can't do this!" But one of the other girls gave me a sponge.
It was the first time I'd used one, and I was worried that some blood would come through anyway, but it worked fine.
But then at the end of the day I couldn't get it out -- it was stuck in there.
I was totally panicking -- "Oh my god, I'll never get this sponge out!" But of course I did get it out. Eventually.
MARCH 27th 2000:
What do you do between clients? Do you get bored?
No, no -- we have our soaps.
Are there ever times when something really dramatic is about to happen in the soap you're watching --
-- and right then is when a client shows up?
Yeah, that's happened a few times.

CHAPTER 12

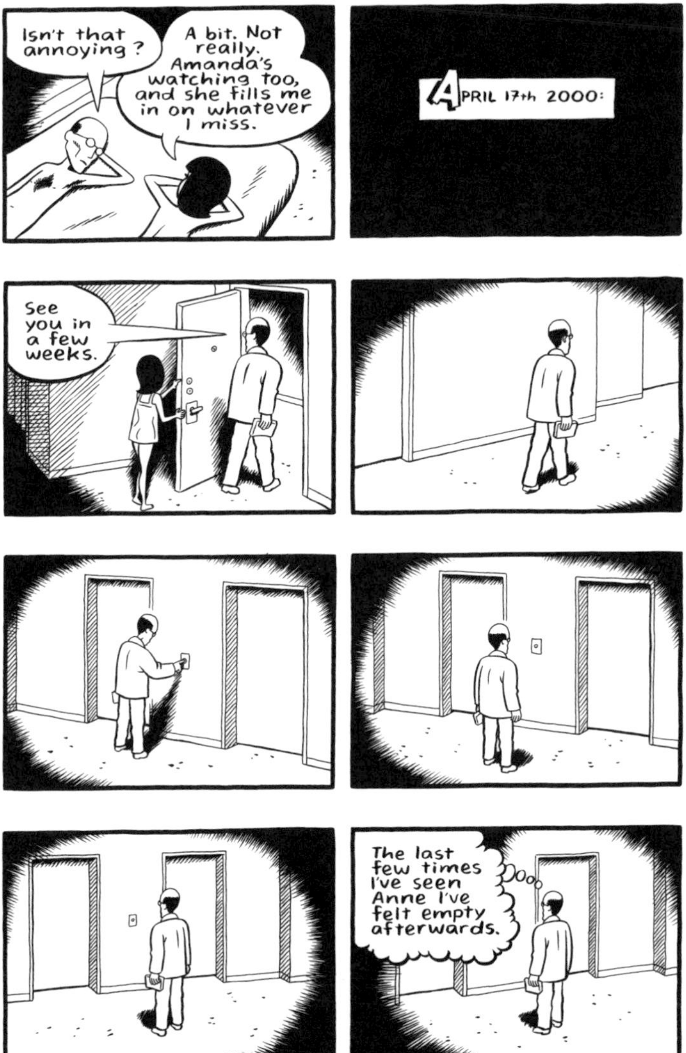
Isn't that annoying?
A bit. Not really. Amanda's watching too, and she fills me in on whatever I miss.
APRIL 17th 2000:
See you in a few weeks.
The last few times I've seen Anne I've felt empty afterwards.

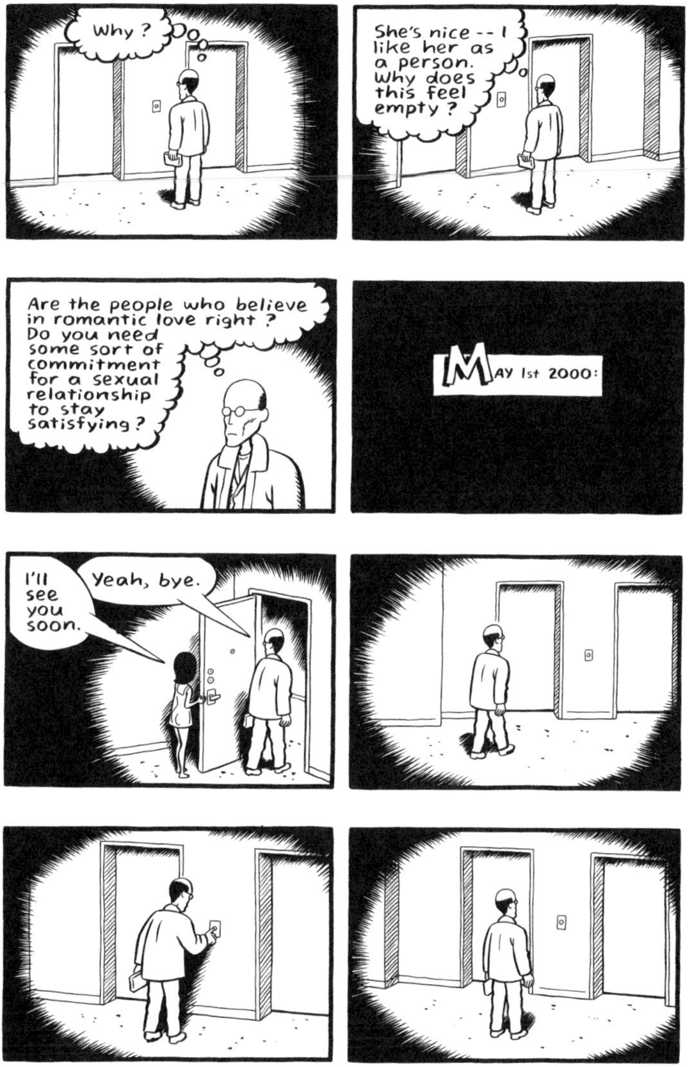
Why?
She's nice -- I like her as a person. Why does this feel empty?
Are the people who believe in romantic love right? Do you need some sort of commitment for a sexual relationship to stay satisfying?
MAY 1st 2000:
I'll see you soon.
Yeah, bye.

CHAPTER 12

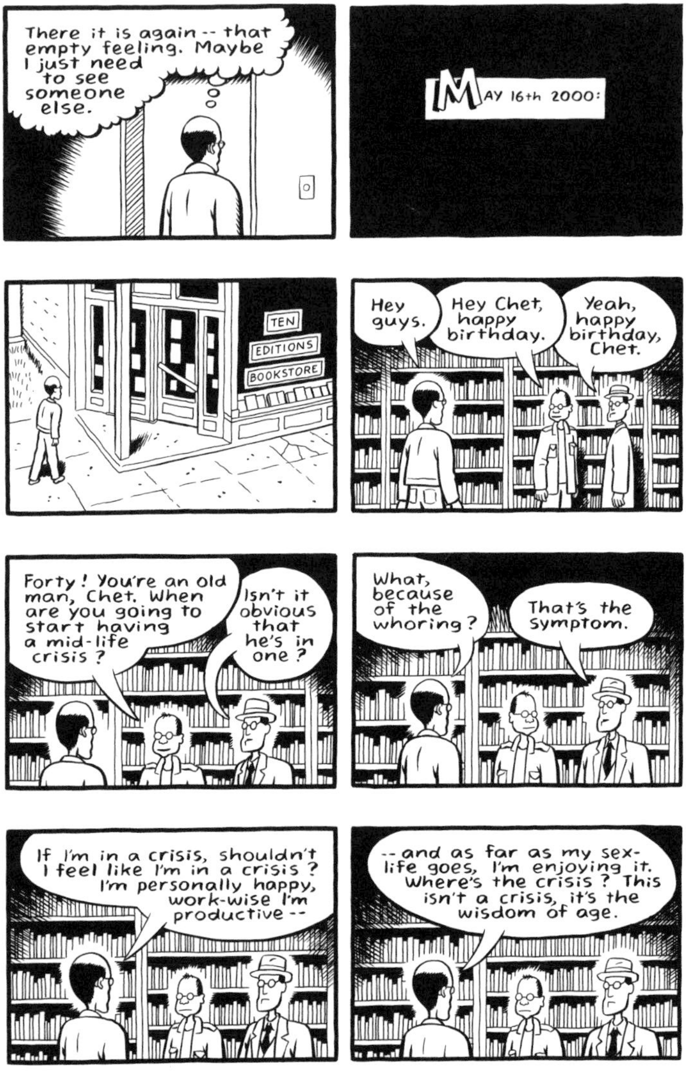
There it is again -- that empty feeling. Maybe I just need to see someone else.
MAY 16th 2000:
TEN
EDITIONS
BOOKSTORE
Hey guys.
Hey Chet, happy birthday.
Yeah, happy birthday, Chet.
Forty! You're an old man, Chet. When are you going to start having a mid-life crisis?
Isn't it obvious that he's in one?
What, because of the whoring?
That's the symptom.
If I'm in a crisis, shouldn't I feel like I'm in a crisis? I'm personally happy, work-wise I'm productive --
-- and as far as my sex-life goes, I'm enjoying it. Where's the crisis? This isn't a crisis, it's the wisdom of age.

After all these years I now recognize what makes me happy and have changed my life accordingly.
Romantic love is bullshit, and I'm not going to waste any more time chasing it.
Touchy, touchy.
This is obviously a delicate subject for SOMEbody.

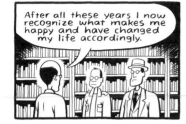

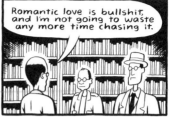

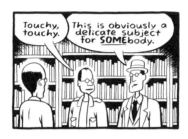

CHAPTER
13
—
DIANE

May 25th 2000:

Hi, I'm Chester.

Hi, I'm... I'm... uh...

Diane.

Yeah... uh... Diane. It's nice to meet... you.

It doesn't sound like you have that name memorized yet. I guess you haven't been working here long.

I haven't? I mean... uh... what?

CHAPTER 13

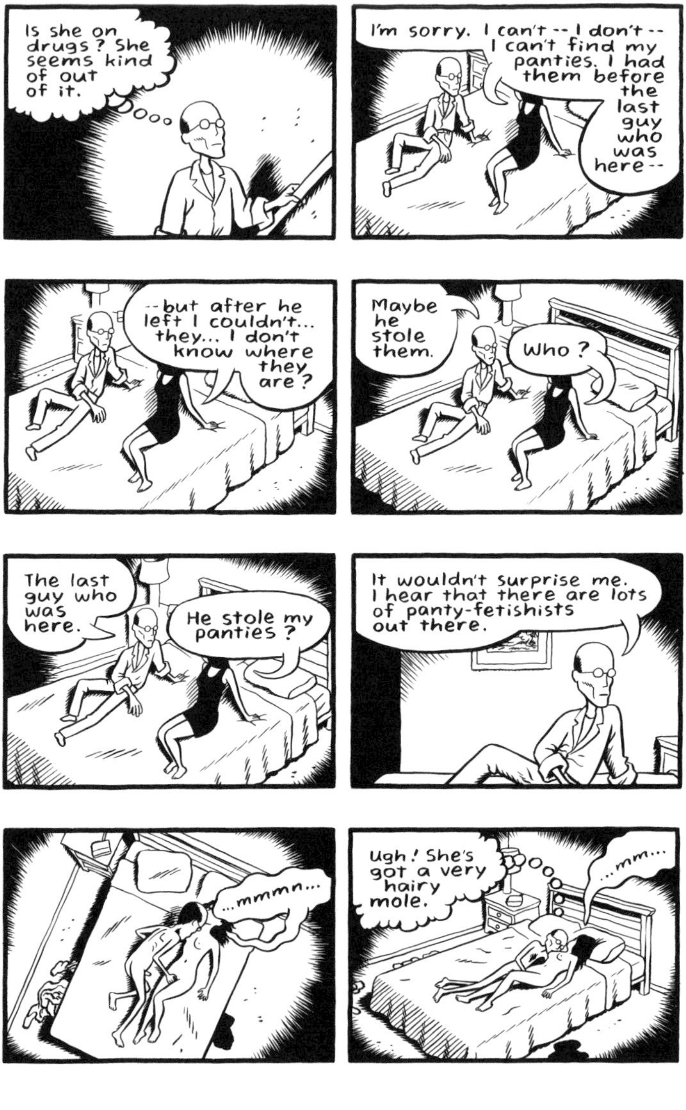

Is she on drugs? She seems kind of out of it.
I'm sorry. I can't -- I don't -- I can't find my panties. I had them before the last guy who was here --
--but after he left I couldn't... they... I don't know where they are?
Maybe he stole them.
Who?
The last guy who was here.
He stole my panties?
It wouldn't surprise me. I hear that there are lots of panty-fetishists out there.
...mmmn...
Ugh! She's got a very hairy mole.
...mm...

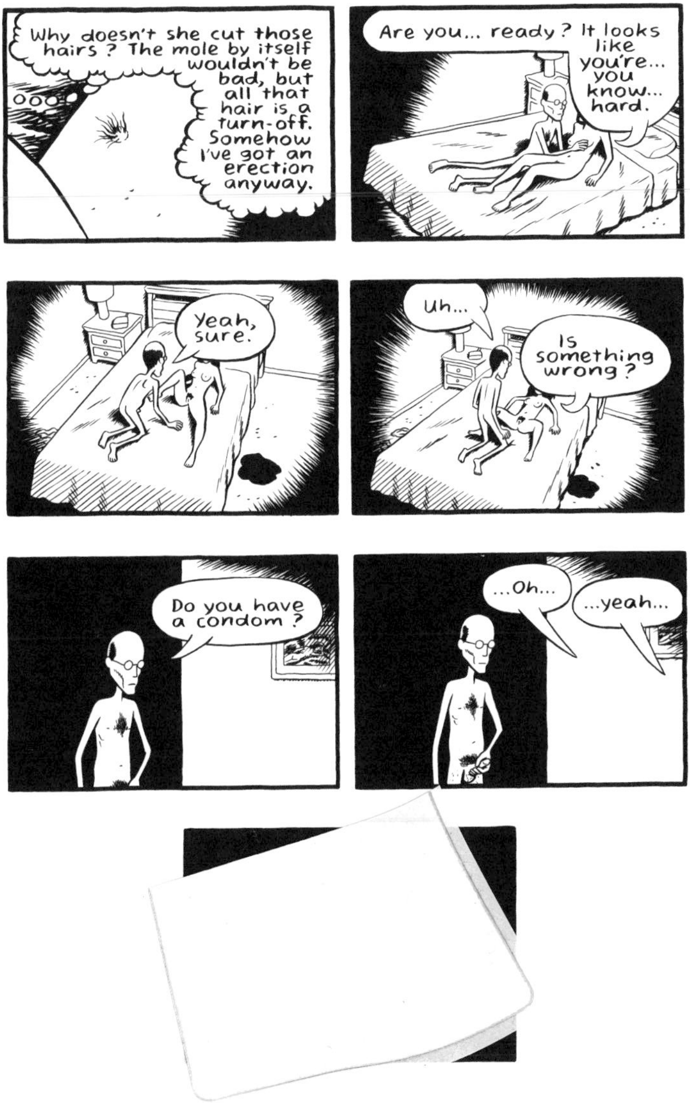
Why doesn't she cut those hairs? The mole by itself wouldn't be bad, but all that hair is a turn-off. Somehow I've got an erection anyway.
Are you... ready? It looks like you're... you know... hard.
Yeah, sure.
Uh...
Is something wrong?
Do you have a condom?
...Oh...
...yeah...

CHAPTER 14
DANIELLE

JUNE 9th 2000:

Danielle's not in today. She'll be in on Monday, but we have several other girls working today.

Thanks, but Danielle's the one I want to see. I'll call back on Monday.

MONDAY -- JUNE 12th 2000:

CHAPTER 14

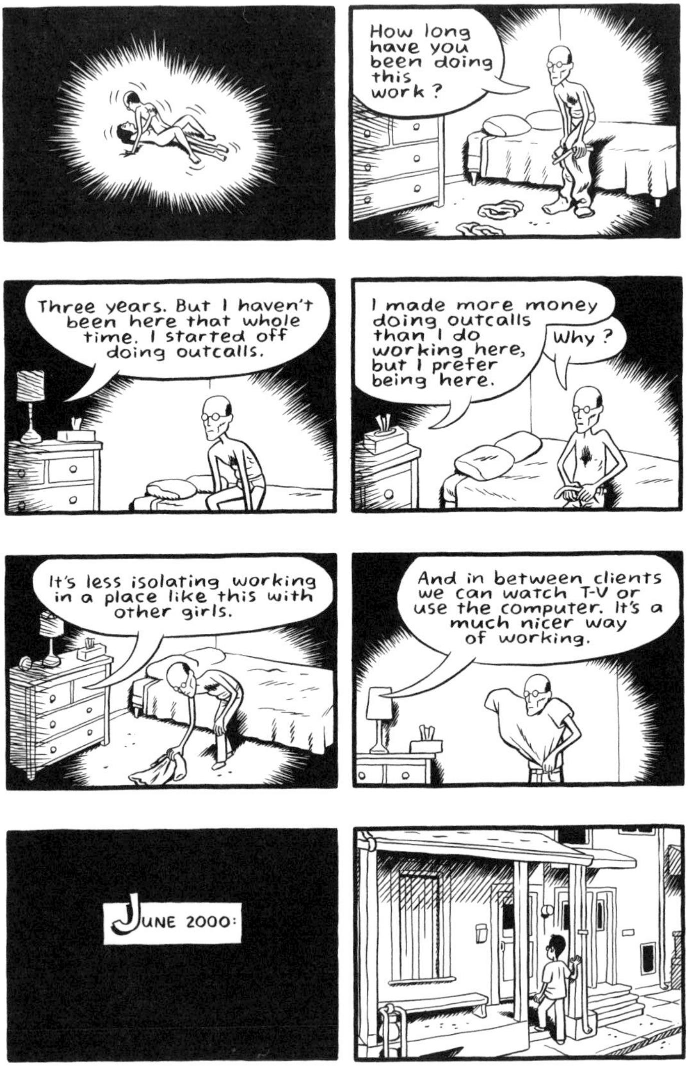
How long have you been doing this work?
Three years. But I haven't been here that whole time. I started off doing outcalls.
I made more money doing outcalls than I do working here, but I prefer being here.
Why?
It's less isolating working in a place like this with other girls.
And in between clients we can watch T-V or use the computer. It's a much nicer way of working.
JUNE 2000:

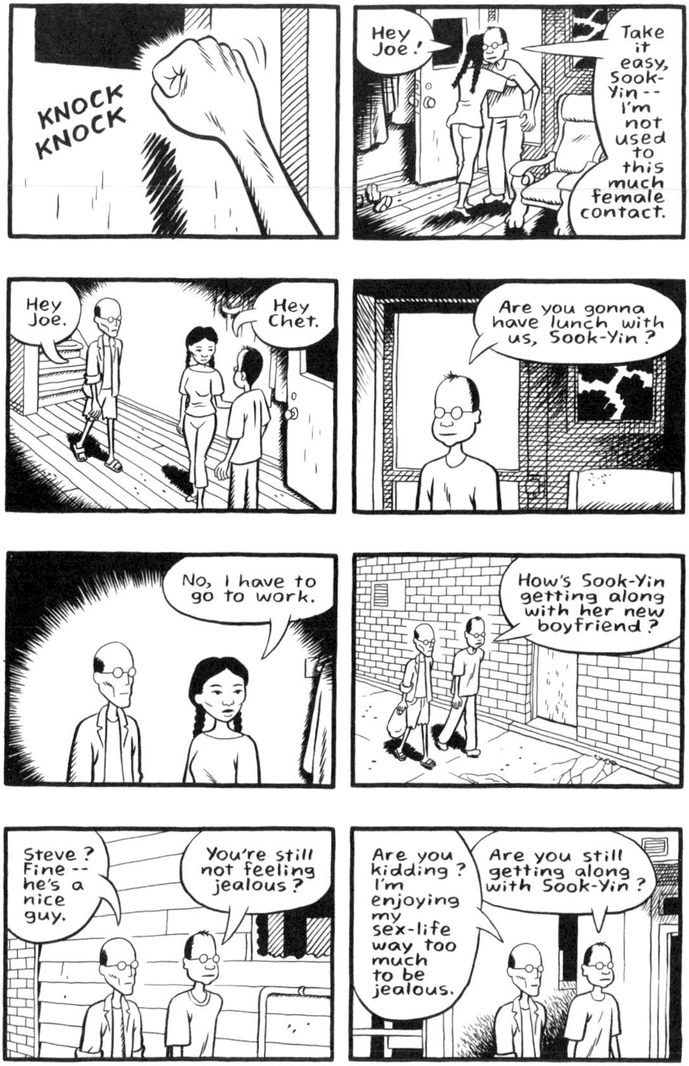
KNOCK KNOCK
Hey Joe!
Take it easy, Sook-Yin -- I'm not used to this much female contact.
Hey Joe.
Hey Chet.
Are you gonna have lunch with us, Sook-Yin?
No, I have to go to work.
How's Sook-Yin getting along with her new boyfriend?
Steve? Fine -- he's a nice guy.
You're still not feeling jealous?
Are you still getting along with Sook-Yin?
Are you kidding? I'm enjoying my sex-life way too much to be jealous.

CHAPTER 14

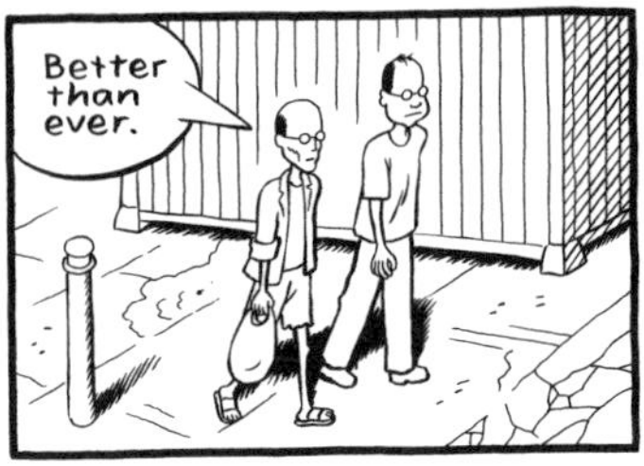
Better than ever.

CHAPTER 15

JOLENE

JULY 2nd 2000:
THIS IS THE BEST BLOW-JOB OF MY LIFE!
This girl was kinda silent and sullen before we got undressed, but now she's going wild!
This is crazy intense.

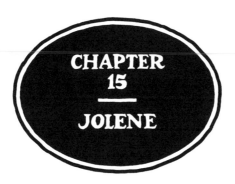

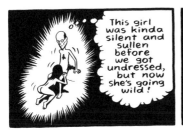

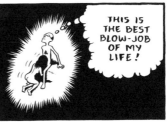

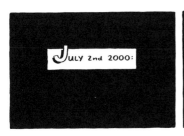

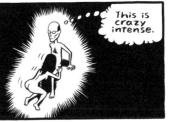

CHAPTER 15

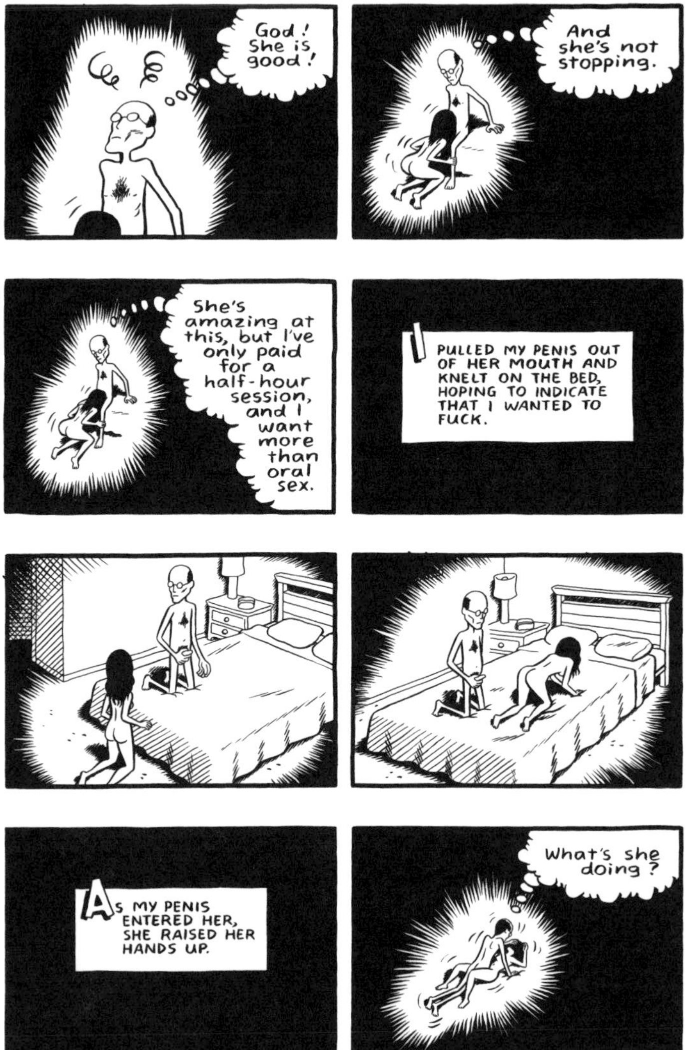
God! She is good!
And she's not stopping.
She's amazing at this, but I've only paid for a half-hour session, and I want more than oral sex.
I PULLED MY PENIS OUT OF HER MOUTH AND KNELT ON THE BED, HOPING TO INDICATE THAT I WANTED TO FUCK.
AS MY PENIS ENTERED HER, SHE RAISED HER HANDS UP.
What's she doing?

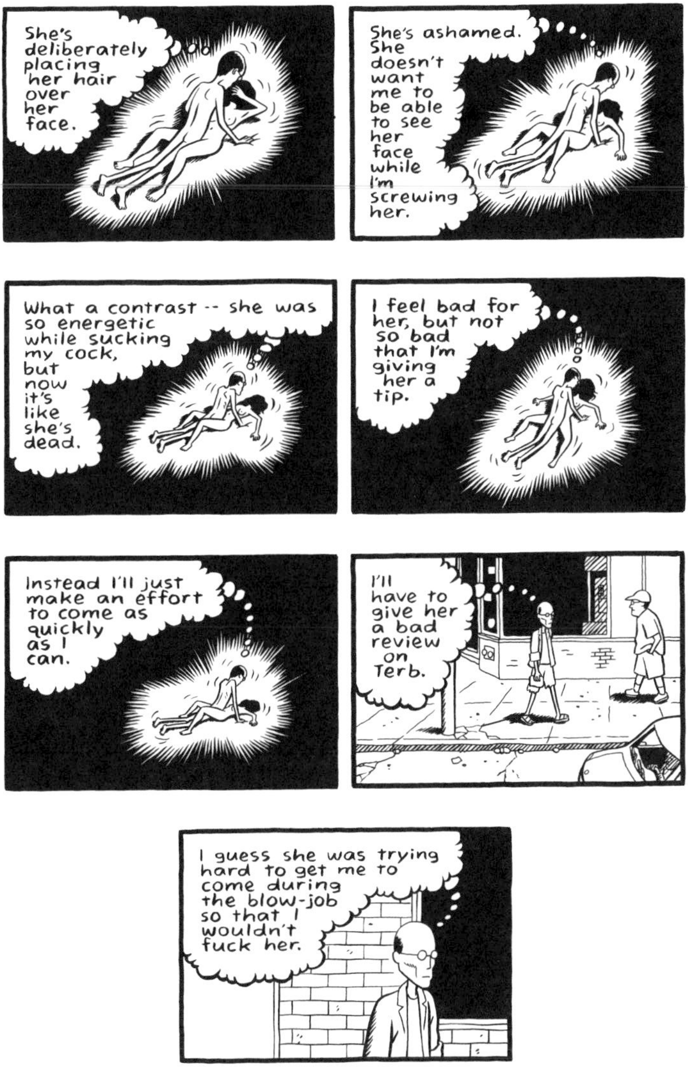
She's deliberately placing her hair over her face.
She's ashamed. She doesn't want me to be able to see her face while I'm screwing her.
What a contrast -- she was so energetic while sucking my cock, but now it's like she's dead.
I feel bad for her, but not so bad that I'm giving her a tip.
Instead I'll just make an effort to come as quickly as I can.
I'll have to give her a bad review on Terb.
I guess she was trying hard to get me to come during the blow-job so that I wouldn't fuck her.

CHAPTER 16

BACK TO ANNE

JULY 17th 2000:

It's been awhile since I saw you.

Yeah, I've been busy with this and that-- work and what-not.

IT HAD BEEN 2 MONTHS SINCE I'D LAST BEEN WITH ANNE, AND IT DID FEEL GOOD TO SEE HER AGAIN.

Maybe the reason I'd been feeling empty after seeing her was that I'd been seeing her too often.

CHAPTER 16

Perhaps this is an absence-makes-the-heart-grow-fonder kind of thing.
BUT AFTER I LEFT THE APARTMENT:
Scratch that theory. I'm feeling empty again.

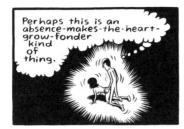

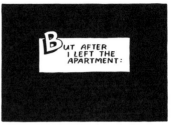

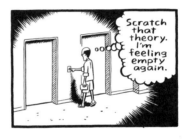

CHAPTER 17
—
YVETTE

AUGUST 18th 2000:

Unfriendly, not very pretty, no blow-job--

-- no tip for this one.

CHAPTER 18

GWENDOLYN

August 28th 2000:

Hello, is this Gwendolyn?

Yes.

Hi, this is Chester -- I have an appointment for twelve?

Oh my god, Chester, I'm sorry -- I know I'm late.

I'm in my car right now, on my way. I'll be there in twenty minutes -- can you wait?

CHAPTER 18

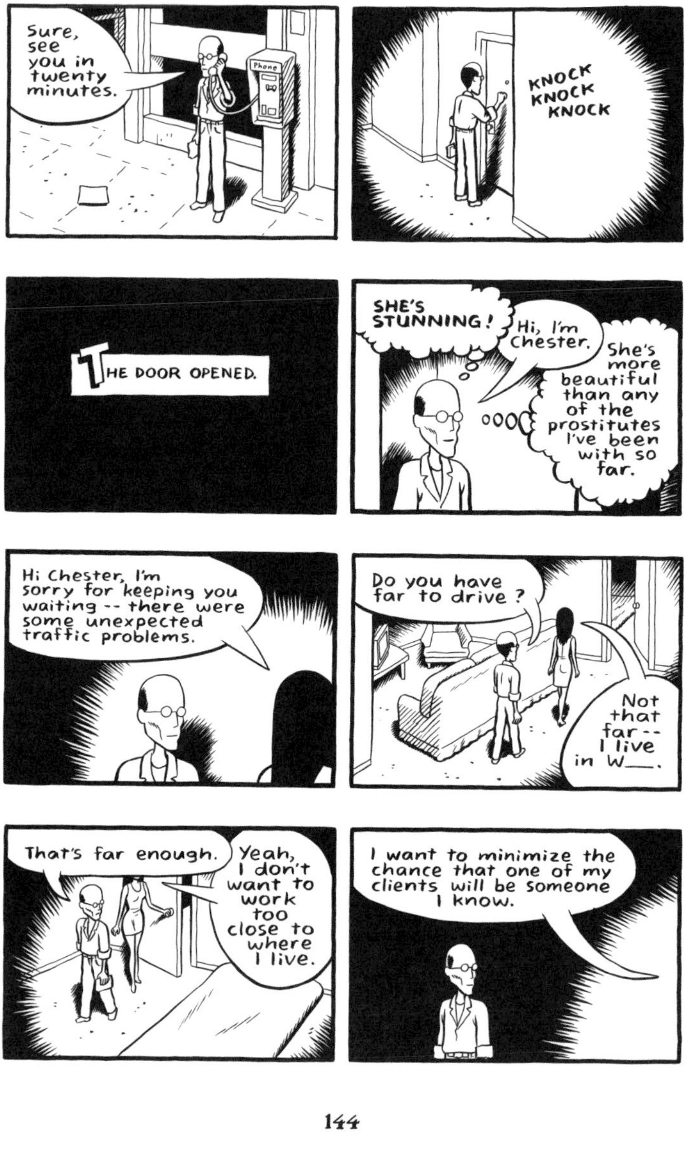

Sure, see you in twenty minutes.
Phone
KNOCK KNOCK KNOCK
THE DOOR OPENED.
SHE'S STUNNING!
Hi, I'm Chester.
She's more beautiful than any of the prostitutes I've been with so far.
Hi Chester, I'm sorry for keeping you waiting -- there were some unexpected traffic problems.
Do you have far to drive?
Not that far -- I live in W___.
That's far enough.
Yeah, I don't want to work too close to where I live.
I want to minimize the chance that one of my clients will be someone I know.

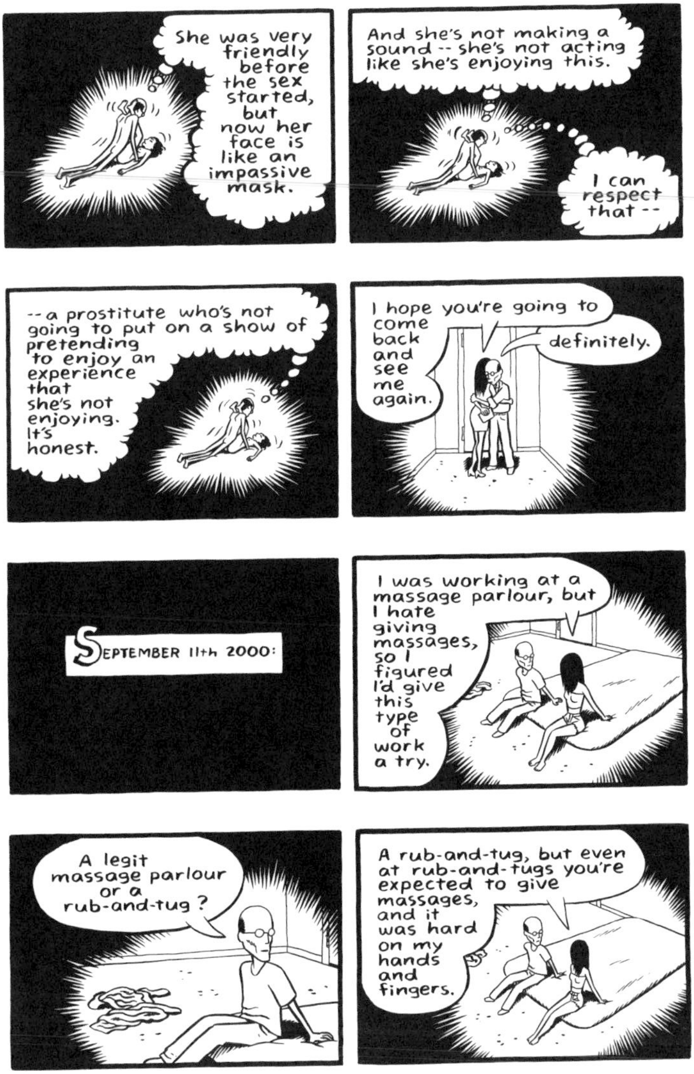
She was very friendly before the sex started, but now her face is like an impassive mask.
And she's not making a sound -- she's not acting like she's enjoying this.
I can respect that --
-- a prostitute who's not going to put on a show of pretending to enjoy an experience that she's not enjoying. It's honest.
I hope you're going to come back and see me again.
definitely.
SEPTEMBER 11th 2000:
I was working at a massage parlour, but I hate giving massages, so I figured I'd give this type of work a try.
A legit massage parlour or a rub-and-tug?
A rub-and-tug, but even at rub-and-tugs you're expected to give massages, and it was hard on my hands and fingers.

CHAPTER 18

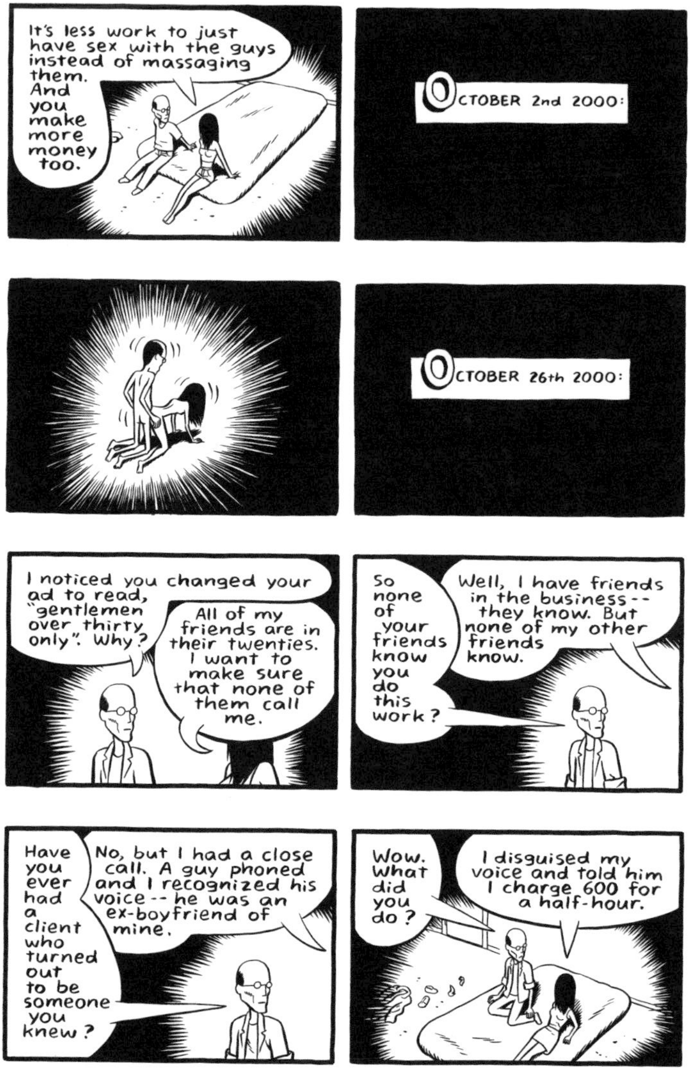

It's less work to just have sex with the guys instead of massaging them. And you make more money too.
OCTOBER 2nd 2000:
OCTOBER 26th 2000:
I noticed you changed your ad to read, "gentlemen over thirty only". Why?
All of my friends are in their twenties. I want to make sure that none of them call me.
So none of your friends know you do this work?
Well, I have friends in the business -- they know. But none of my other friends know.
Have you ever had a client who turned out to be someone you knew?
No, but I had a close call. A guy phoned and I recognized his voice -- he was an ex-boyfriend of mine.
Wow. What did you do?
I disguised my voice and told him I charge 600 for a half-hour.

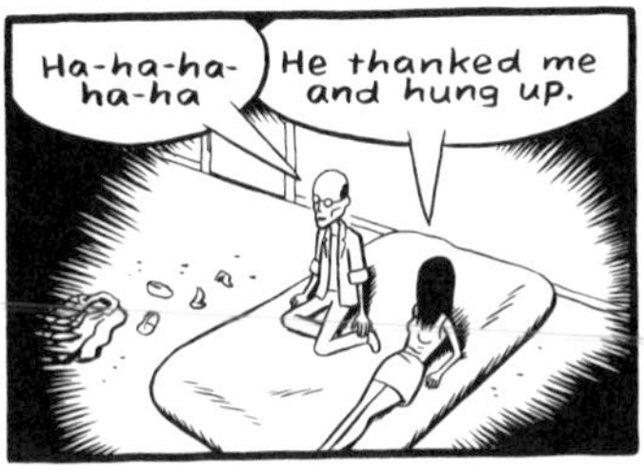
Ha-ha-ha-
ha-ha
He thanked me
and hung up.

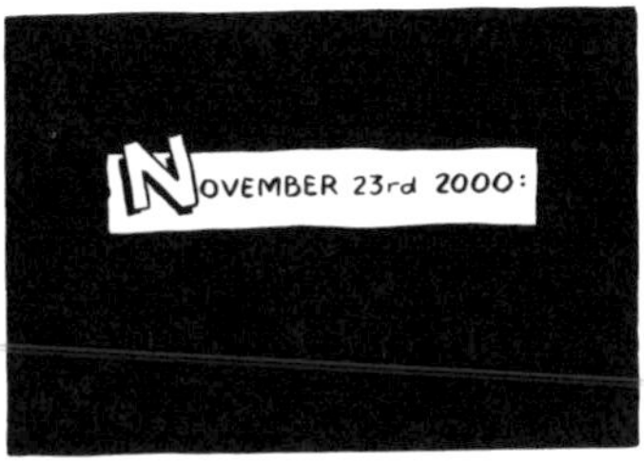
NOVEMBER 23rd 2000:

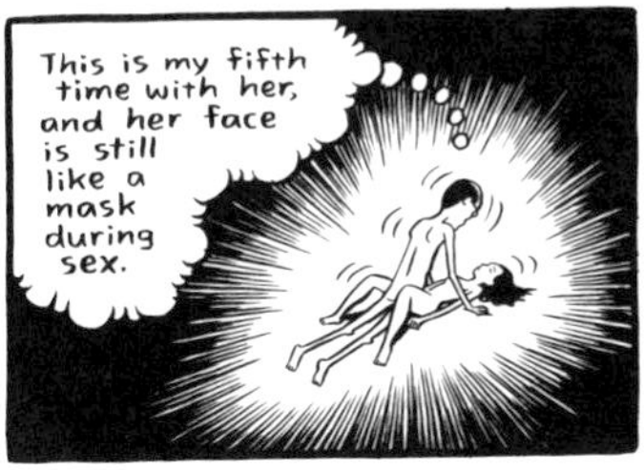
This is my fifth time with her, and her face is still like a mask during sex.

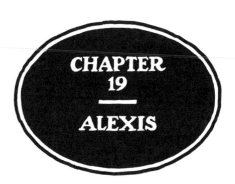

CHAPTER
19
—
ALEXIS

DECEMBER 4th 2000:

Hi, I'm Chester.

Hi, I'm Alexis.

Not as beautiful as Gwendolyn but still attractive, and what a body -- she is stacked!

You brought a book -- what are you reading?

PAUL JOHNSON

A HISTORY OF THE AMERICAN PEOPLE

Oh. Does Johnson think the Civil War started over slavery or tarrifs?

CHAPTER 19

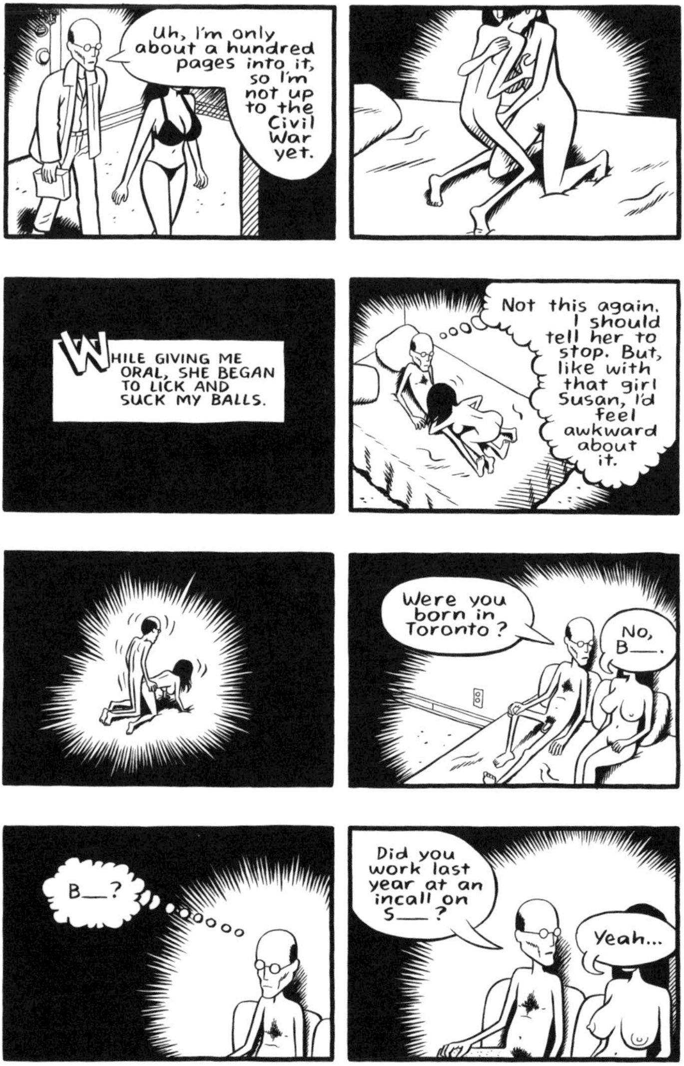

Uh, I'm only about a hundred pages into it, so I'm not up to the Civil War yet.
WHILE GIVING ME ORAL, SHE BEGAN TO LICK AND SUCK MY BALLS.
Not this again. I should tell her to stop. But, like with that girl Susan, I'd feel awkward about it.
Were you born in Toronto?
No, B___.
B___?
Did you work last year at an incall on S___?
Yeah...

And did you use the name Susan when you worked there?
Yeah.
Then this isn't the first time we've had sex.
Really?

CHAPTER 20 — HILLARY

JANUARY 12th 2001:

Here are the rules: no kissing on the mouth--

I don't find her attractive.

--no digging for gold, no dining at the Y--

I should have walked away when I saw what she looks like.

--and we use a condom for everything including the blow-job. Is that fine?

Sure.

153

CHAPTER 20

I'm not getting an erection. This girl just isn't turning me on.
Is it me? You don't find me attractive.
It looks like this isn't working. We might as well give up.
No, it's me. I come too easily, so before I have sex I masturbate so that I'll be able to last longer, but doing that can make it more difficult to get an erection.
If I hadn't jerked off right before coming over here, I'd have gotten an erection easily.
That makes me feel a bit better.
"Digging for gold".

CHAPTER 21

BEATRICE

MARCH 12th 2001:
Is she going to turn the television off?
Darling, I can't live without you.
So, what do you want to do?
Half-and-half?
What's that?

CHAPTER 21

You give me oral, then we have sex.
I don't give oral.
Okay, just the sex then.
I don't have any idea what that means.
She's STILL watching the soap-opera.
Why are you giving me a tip?
Why DID I give her a tip?

CHAPTER 22

MYRA

MAY 1st 2001:
She's cute in an average way but not my type. And this is a very mediocre blow-job.
Thanks for trying, but it looks like I'm not going to be able to get an erection.
Are we... giving up?
Yeah, I think I'll take off.
I feel like I've let you down -- like I didn't do my job properly.

CHAPTER 22

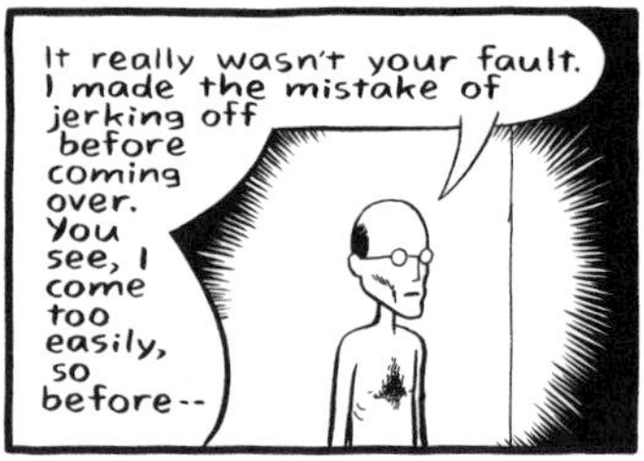
It really wasn't your fault. I made the mistake of jerking off before coming over. You see, I come too easily, so before--

CHAPTER 23

THE MOVE

MAY 2001:

Chester, can we talk?

Sure, what's up?

Well, things are getting serious with Steve--

--and we've been talking about him moving in here. But, you know, it's a small house, and, well... I feel terrible asking this--

CHAPTER 23

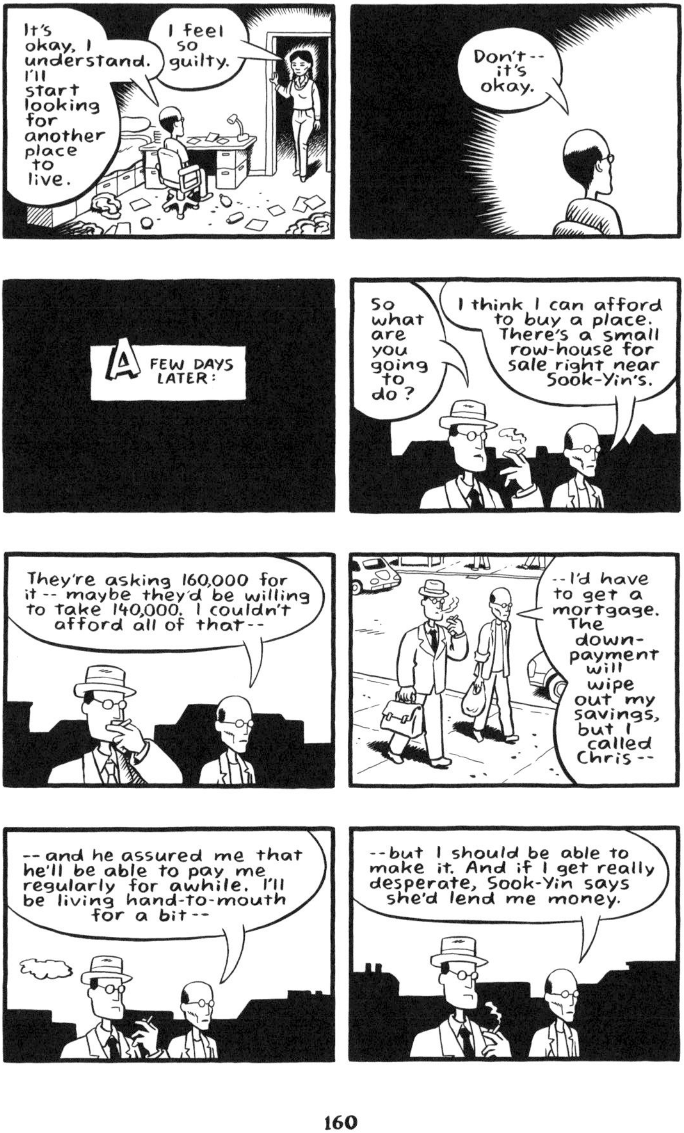
I feel so guilty.
It's okay, I understand. I'll start looking for another place to live.
Don't -- it's okay.
A FEW DAYS LATER:
So what are you going to do?
I think I can afford to buy a place. There's a small row-house for sale right near Sook-Yin's.
They're asking 160,000 for it -- maybe they'd be willing to take 140,000. I couldn't afford all of that--
--I'd have to get a mortgage. The down-payment will wipe out my savings, but I called Chris--
--and he assured me that he'll be able to pay me regularly for awhile. I'll be living hand-to-mouth for a bit--
--but I should be able to make it. And if I get really desperate, Sook-Yin says she'd lend me money.

THE MOVE

That's the least she could do.

The least she could do? It's not like she's done anything wrong here.

Because she was my girlfriend for a few years she owes me a place to live for the rest of my life?

It's completely understandable that she would want to live in her own house with her new boyfriend and WITHOUT an ex-boyfriend hanging around all the time.

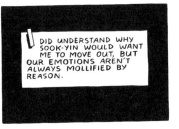

I DID UNDERSTAND WHY SOOK-YIN WOULD WANT ME TO MOVE OUT, BUT OUR EMOTIONS AREN'T ALWAYS MOLLIFIED BY REASON.

FOR MANY DAYS I MANAGED TO HOLD MYSELF TOGETHER.

I called you yesterday about arranging a mortgage--

THEN SOOK-YIN AND STEVE WENT UP NORTH FOR A WEEKEND, AND I WAS LEFT TO MYSELF IN THE HOUSE.

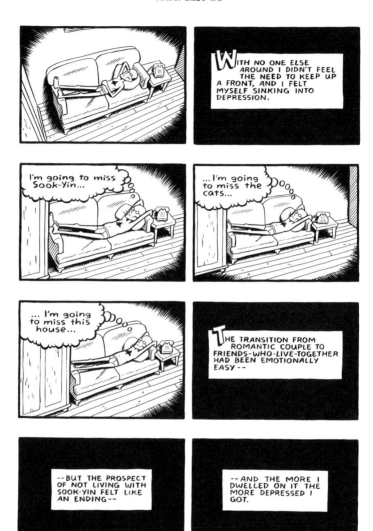

WITH NO ONE ELSE AROUND I DIDN'T FEEL THE NEED TO KEEP UP A FRONT, AND I FELT MYSELF SINKING INTO DEPRESSION.

I'm going to miss Sook-Yin...

...I'm going to miss the cats...

... I'm going to miss this house...

THE TRANSITION FROM ROMANTIC COUPLE TO FRIENDS-WHO-LIVE-TOGETHER HAD BEEN EMOTIONALLY EASY --

--BUT THE PROSPECT OF NOT LIVING WITH SOOK-YIN FELT LIKE AN ENDING--

--AND THE MORE I DWELLED ON IT THE MORE DEPRESSED I GOT.

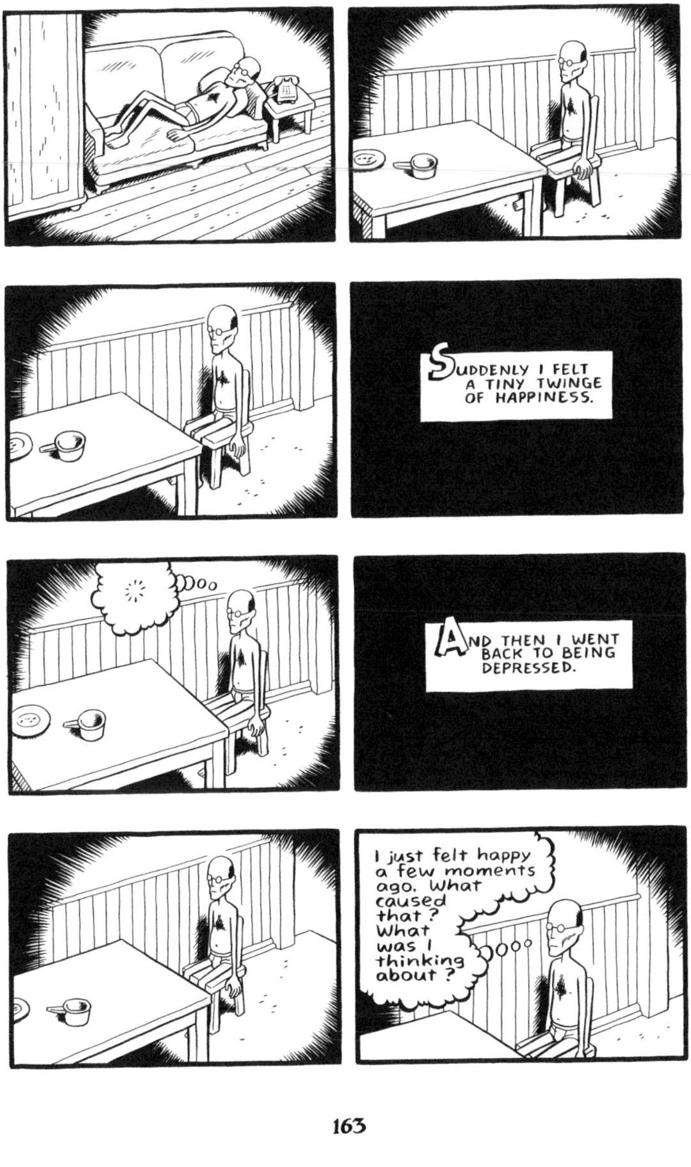
SUDDENLY I FELT A TINY TWINGE OF HAPPINESS.
AND THEN I WENT BACK TO BEING DEPRESSED.
I just felt happy a few moments ago. What caused that? What was I thinking about?

CHAPTER 23

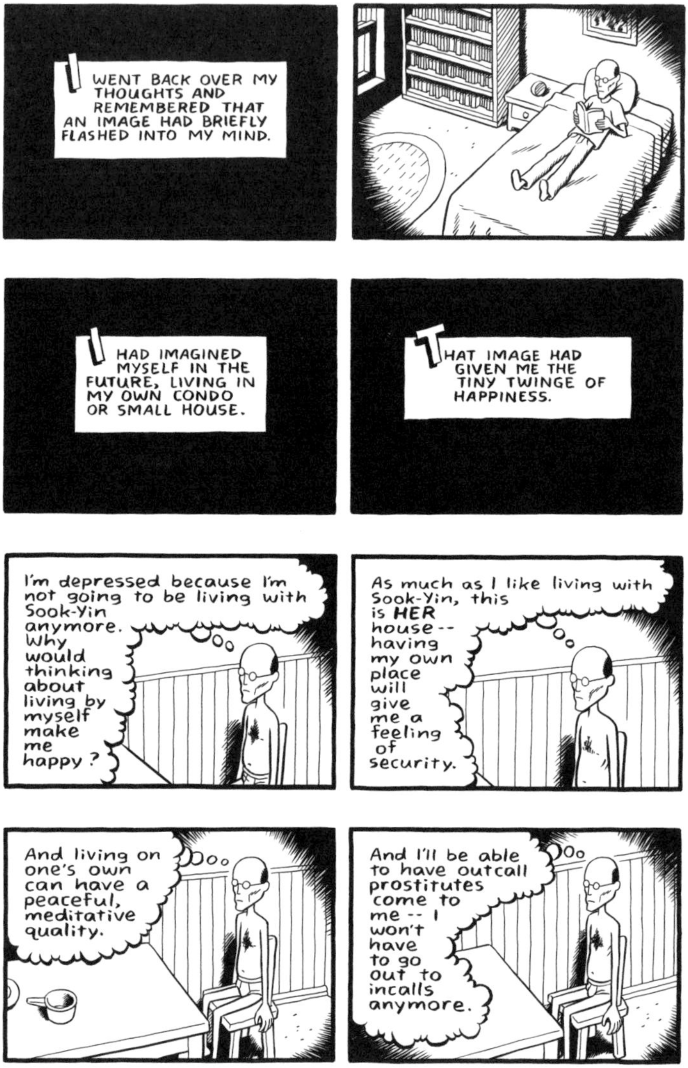
I WENT BACK OVER MY THOUGHTS AND REMEMBERED THAT AN IMAGE HAD BRIEFLY FLASHED INTO MY MIND.
I HAD IMAGINED MYSELF IN THE FUTURE, LIVING IN MY OWN CONDO OR SMALL HOUSE.
THAT IMAGE HAD GIVEN ME THE TINY TWINGE OF HAPPINESS.
I'm depressed because I'm not going to be living with Sook-Yin anymore. Why would thinking about living by myself make me happy?
As much as I like living with Sook-Yin, this is HER house -- having my own place will give me a feeling of security.
And living on one's own can have a peaceful, meditative quality.
And I'll be able to have outcall prostitutes come to me -- I won't have to go out to incalls anymore.

THE MOVE

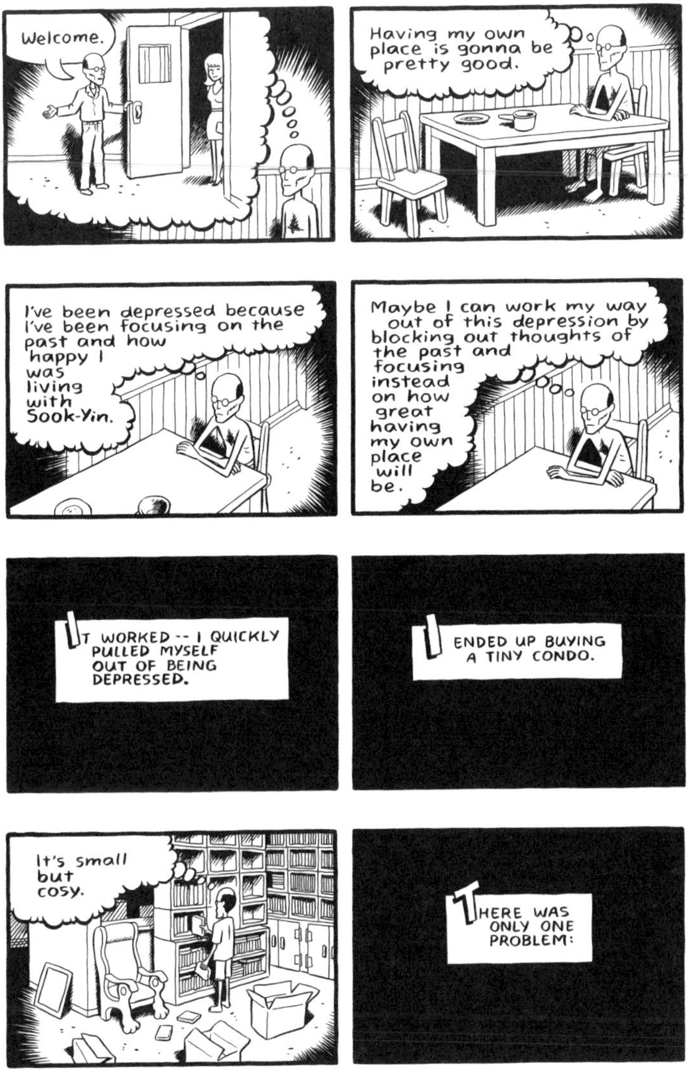

Welcome.
Having my own place is gonna be pretty good.
I've been depressed because I've been focusing on the past and how happy I was living with Sook-Yin.
Maybe I can work my way out of this depression by blocking out thoughts of the past and focusing instead on how great having my own place will be.
IT WORKED -- I QUICKLY PULLED MYSELF OUT OF BEING DEPRESSED.
I ENDED UP BUYING A TINY CONDO.
It's small but cosy.
THERE WAS ONLY ONE PROBLEM:

CHAPTER 23

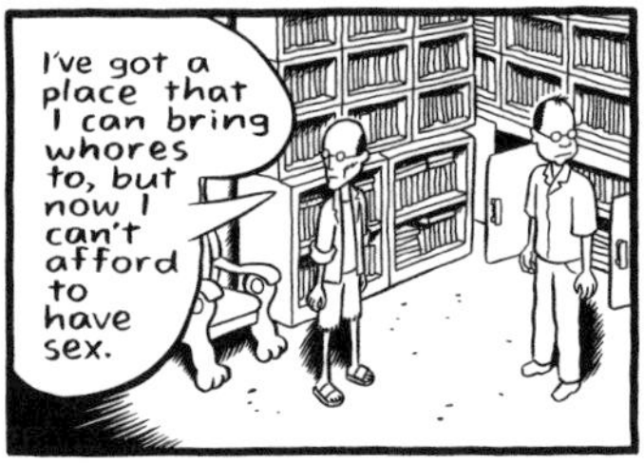
I've got a place that I can bring whores to, but now I can't afford to have sex.

CHAPTER
24
—
JENNA

ABOUT A HALF-YEAR LATER, IN LATE JANUARY 2002:

I think I can afford to start seeing prostitutes again.

I wonder if Gwendolyn would do outcall sessions?

This number is no longer in service.

I guess I'll have to see someone else.

167

CHAPTER 24

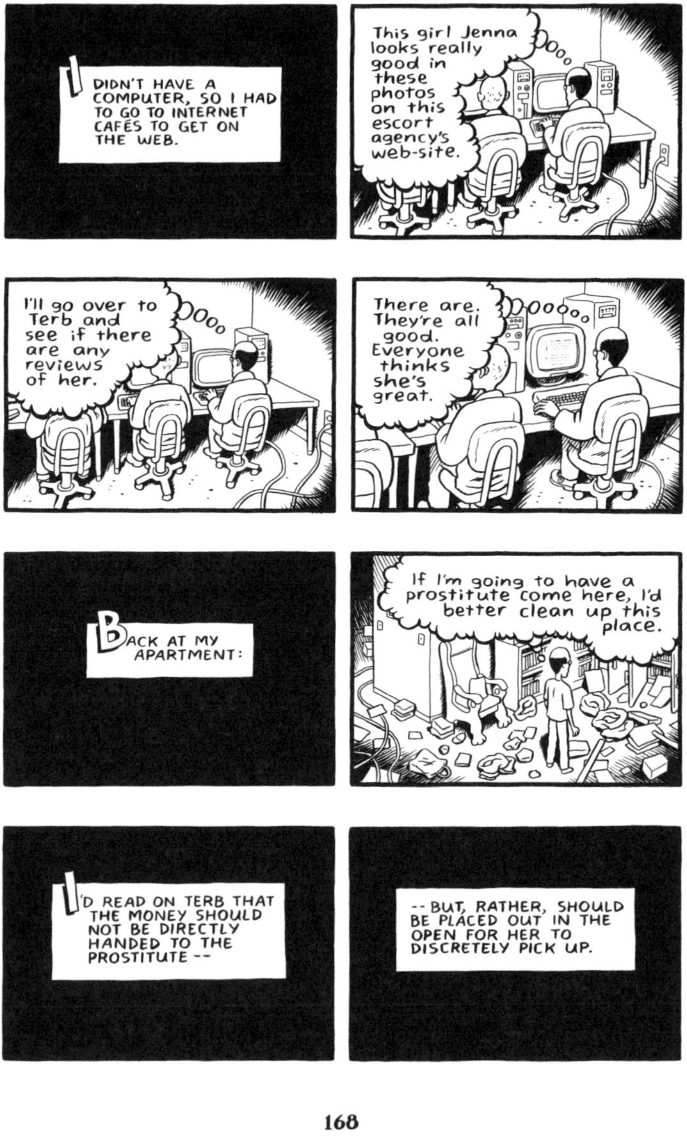
I DIDN'T HAVE A COMPUTER, SO I HAD TO GO TO INTERNET CAFÉS TO GET ON THE WEB.
This girl Jenna looks really good in these photos on this escort agency's web-site.
I'll go over to Terb and see if there are any reviews of her.
There are. They're all good. Everyone thinks she's great.
BACK AT MY APARTMENT:
If I'm going to have a prostitute come here, I'd better clean up this place.
I'D READ ON TERB THAT THE MONEY SHOULD NOT BE DIRECTLY HANDED TO THE PROSTITUTE --
-- BUT, RATHER, SHOULD BE PLACED OUT IN THE OPEN FOR HER TO DISCRETELY PICK UP.

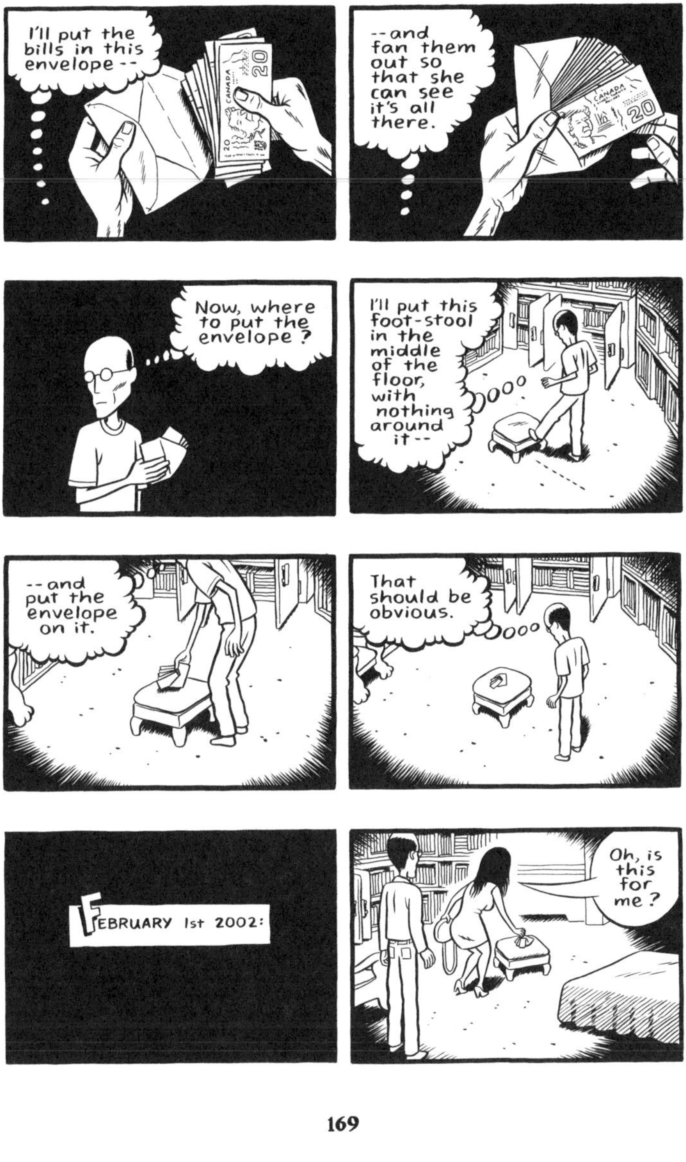
I'll put the bills in this envelope --
-- and fan them out so that she can see it's all there.
Now, where to put the envelope?
I'll put this foot-stool in the middle of the floor, with nothing around it --
-- and put the envelope on it.
That should be obvious.
FEBRUARY 1st 2002:
Oh, is this for me?

CHAPTER 24

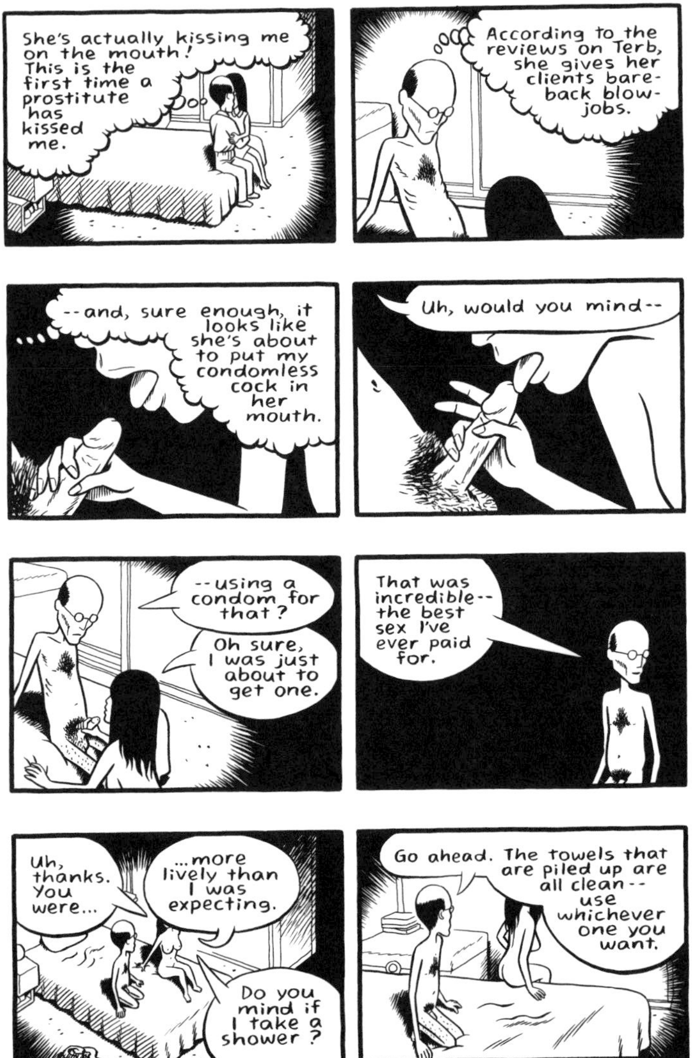
She's actually kissing me on the mouth! This is the first time a prostitute has kissed me.
According to the reviews on Terb, she gives her clients bare-back blow-jobs.
--and, sure enough, it looks like she's about to put my condomless cock in her mouth.
Uh, would you mind--
--using a condom for that?
Oh sure, I was just about to get one.
That was incredible--the best sex I've ever paid for.
Uh, thanks. You were...
...more lively than I was expecting.
Do you mind if I take a shower?
Go ahead. The towels that are piled up are all clean--use whichever one you want.

I hope I'll see you again.
You definitely will.
I feel all giddy and excited.

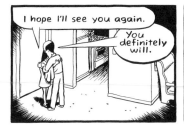

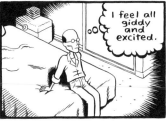

CHAPTER 25

KITTY

APRIL 2002:

I thought I was going to see Jenna again, but this girl Kitty has been getting really good reviews, and she's a lot less expensive than Jenna.

I SAW KITTY ON APRIL 10th.

CHAPTER 25

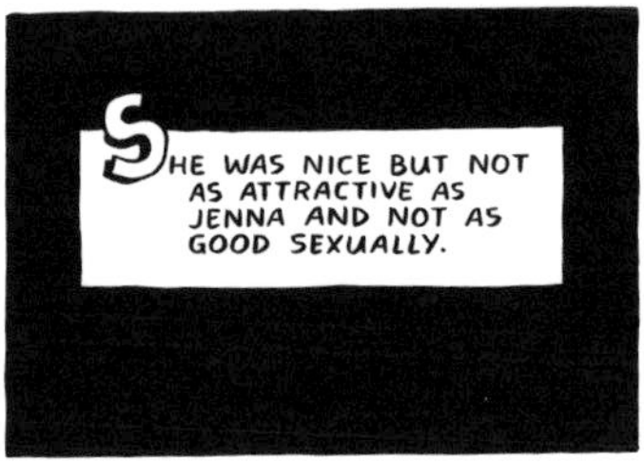
SHE WAS NICE BUT NOT AS ATTRACTIVE AS JENNA AND NOT AS GOOD SEXUALLY.

CHAPTER
26

LARISSA

MAY 9th 2002:

230 for an hour, 180 for a half-hour. So would you like to see me?

She has such a cute voice.

Uh, I'm thinking about it.

Come on, I'm worth it. I promise you won't be disappointed.

Uh... okay -- for a half-hour.

SHE CAME OVER THAT EVENING.

CHAPTER 26

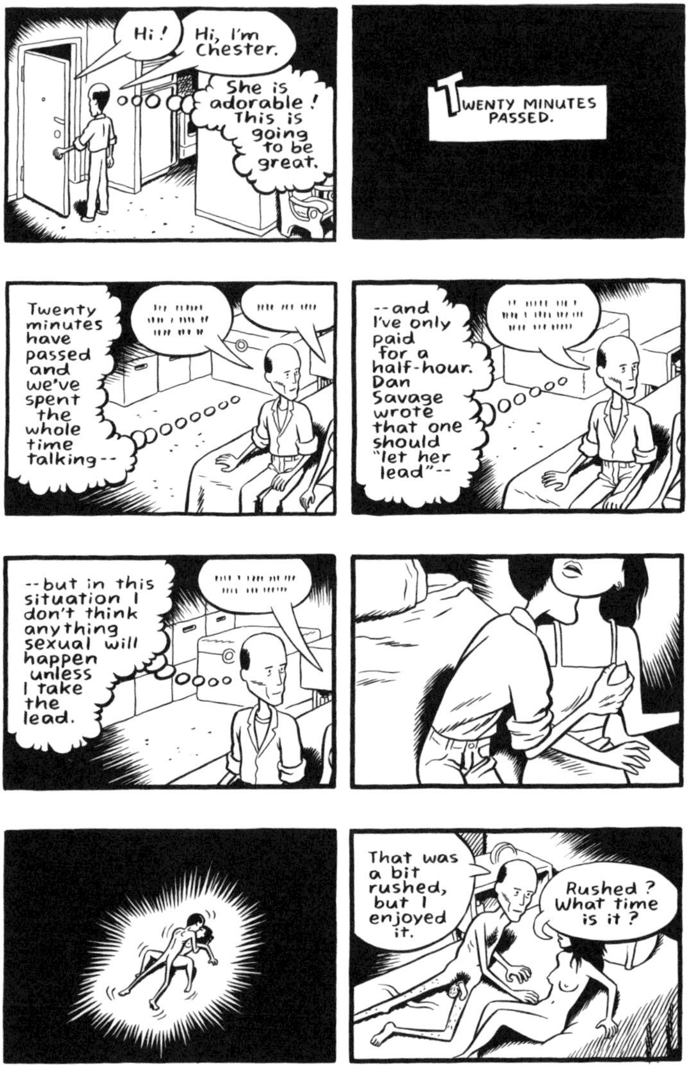
Hi!
Hi, I'm Chester.
She is adorable! This is going to be great.
TWENTY MINUTES PASSED.
Twenty minutes have passed and we've spent the whole time talking--
--and I've only paid for a half-hour. Dan Savage wrote that one should "let her lead"--
--but in this situation I don't think anything sexual will happen unless I take the lead.
That was a bit rushed, but I enjoyed it.
Rushed? What time is it?

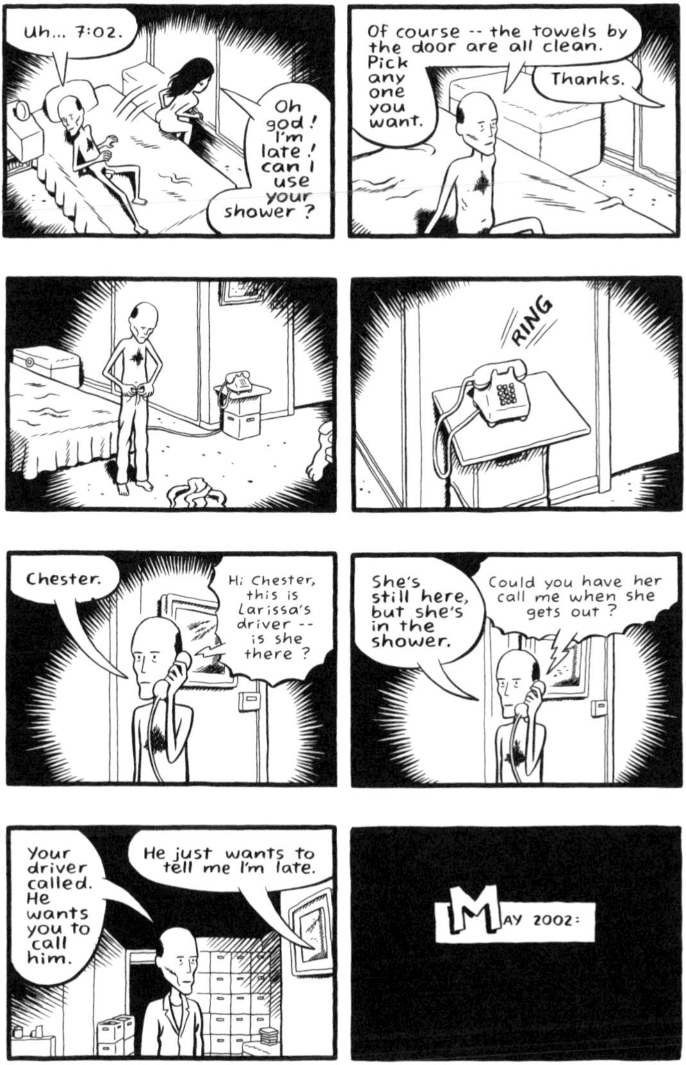
Uh... 7:02.
Oh god! I'm late! can I use your shower?
Of course -- the towels by the door are all clean. Pick any one you want.
Thanks.
RING
Chester.
Hi Chester, this is Larissa's driver -- is she there?
She's still here, but she's in the shower.
Could you have her call me when she gets out?
Your driver called. He wants you to call him.
He just wants to tell me I'm late.
MAY 2002:

CHAPTER 26

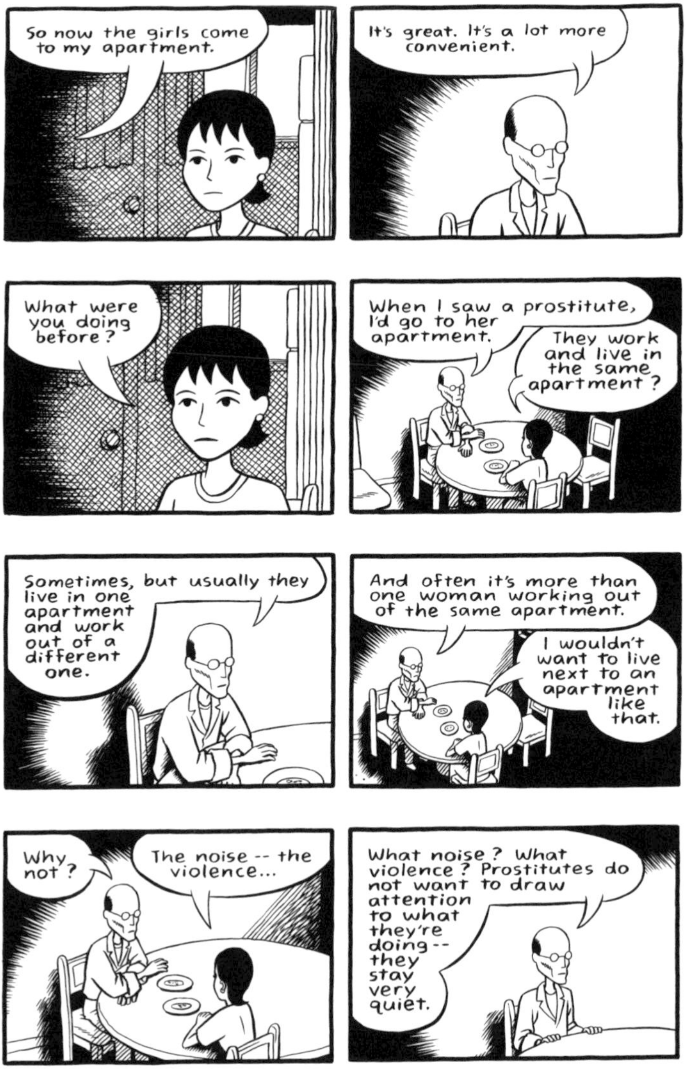
So now the girls come to my apartment.
It's great. It's a lot more convenient.
What were you doing before?
When I saw a prostitute, I'd go to her apartment.
They work and live in the same apartment?
Sometimes, but usually they live in one apartment and work out of a different one.
And often it's more than one woman working out of the same apartment.
I wouldn't want to live next to an apartment like that.
Why not?
The noise -- the violence...
What noise? What violence? Prostitutes do not want to draw attention to what they're doing -- they stay very quiet.

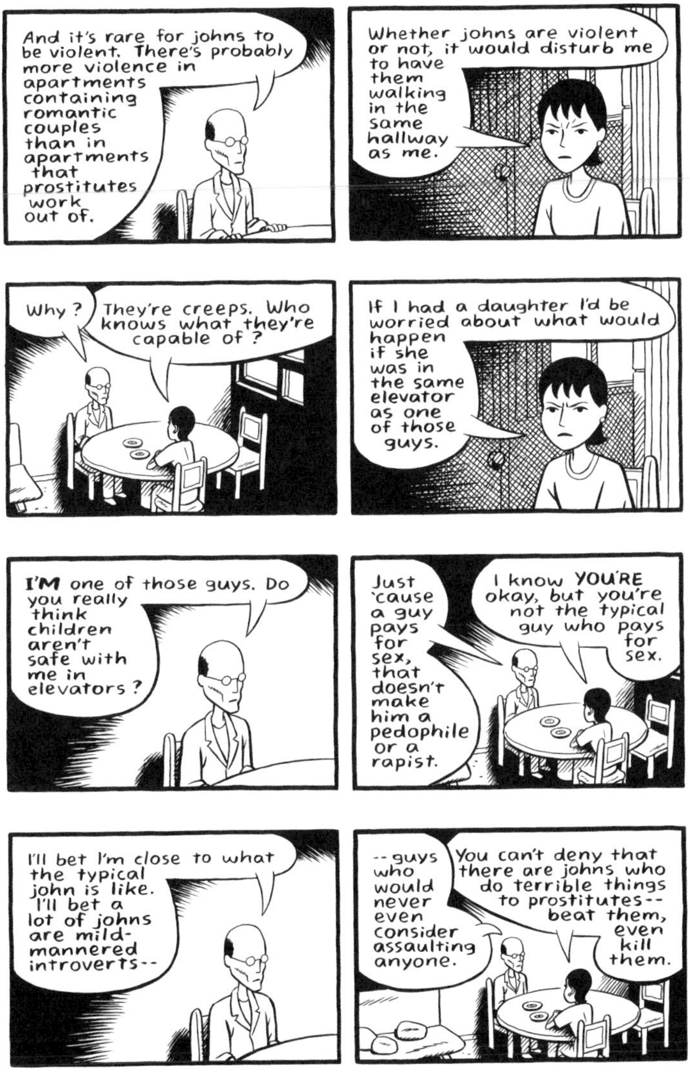
And it's rare for johns to be violent. There's probably more violence in apartments containing romantic couples than in apartments that prostitutes work out of.
Whether johns are violent or not, it would disturb me to have them walking in the same hallway as me.
Why?
They're creeps. Who knows what they're capable of?
If I had a daughter I'd be worried about what would happen if she was in the same elevator as one of those guys.
I'M one of those guys. Do you really think children aren't safe with me in elevators?
Just 'cause a guy pays for sex, that doesn't make him a pedophile or a rapist.
I know YOU'RE okay, but you're not the typical guy who pays for sex.
I'll bet I'm close to what the typical john is like. I'll bet a lot of johns are mild-mannered introverts--
--guys who would never even consider assaulting anyone.
You can't deny that there are johns who do terrible things to prostitutes--beat them, even kill them.

CHAPTER 26

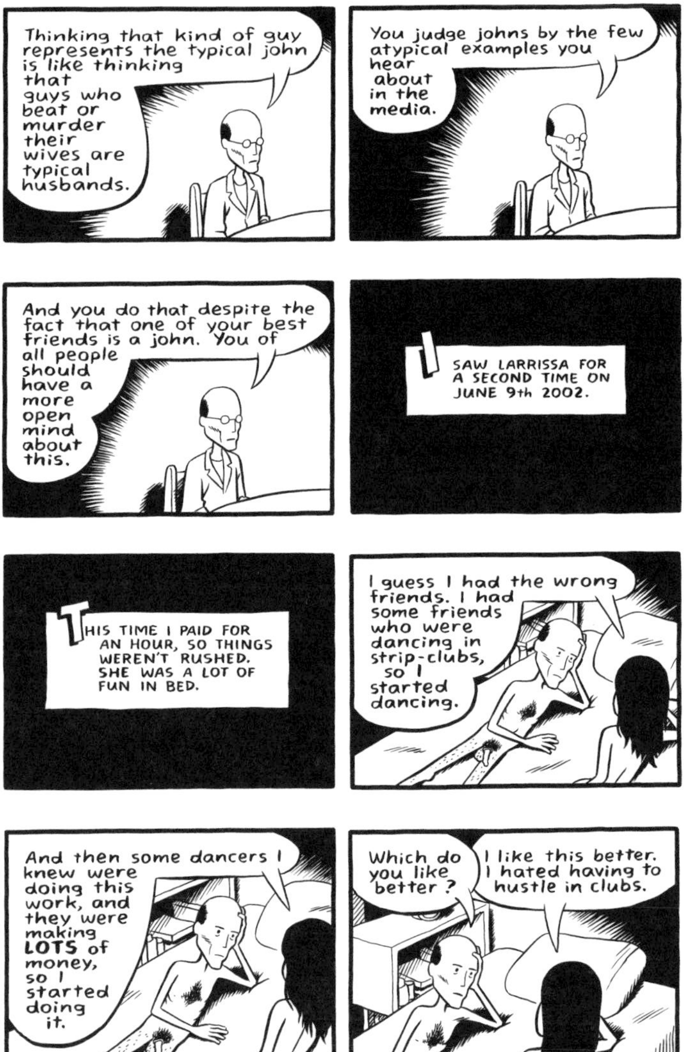
Thinking that kind of guy represents the typical john is like thinking that guys who beat or murder their wives are typical husbands.
You judge johns by the few atypical examples you hear about in the media.
And you do that despite the fact that one of your best friends is a john. You of all people should have a more open mind about this.
I SAW LARRISSA FOR A SECOND TIME ON JUNE 9th 2002.
THIS TIME I PAID FOR AN HOUR, SO THINGS WEREN'T RUSHED. SHE WAS A LOT OF FUN IN BED.
I guess I had the wrong friends. I had some friends who were dancing in strip-clubs, so I started dancing.
And then some dancers I knew were doing this work, and they were making **LOTS** of money, so I started doing it.
Which do you like better?
I like this better. I hated having to hustle in clubs.

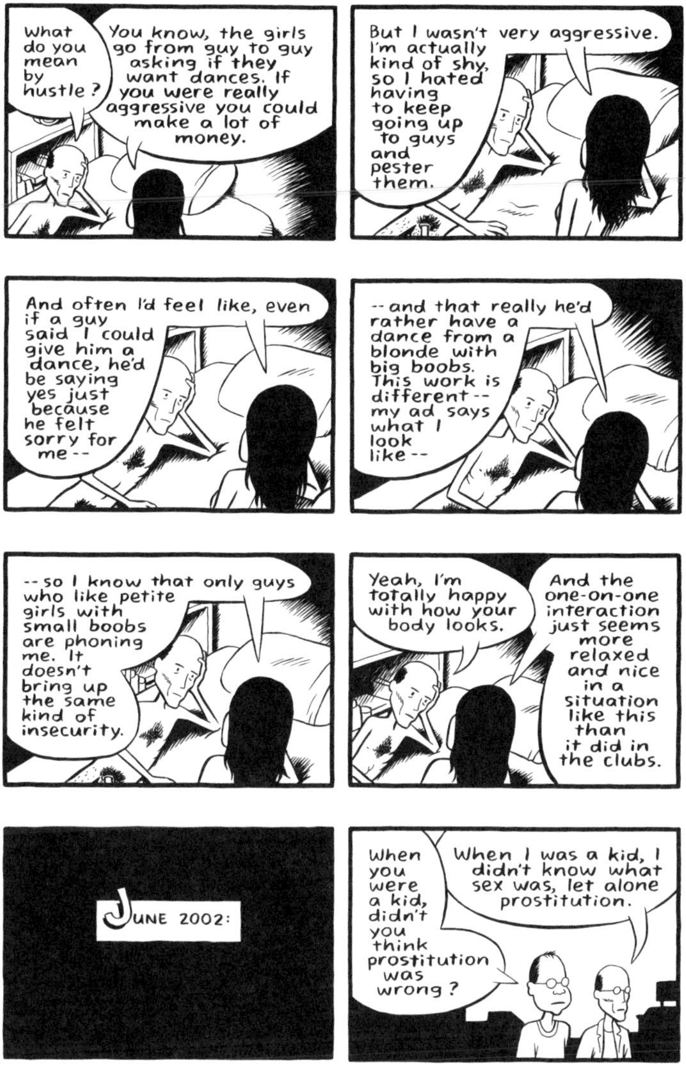
What do you mean by hustle?
You know, the girls go from guy to guy asking if they want dances. If you were really aggressive you could make a lot of money.
But I wasn't very aggressive. I'm actually kind of shy, so I hated having to keep going up to guys and pester them.
And often I'd feel like, even if a guy said I could give him a dance, he'd be saying yes just because he felt sorry for me--
--and that really he'd rather have a dance from a blonde with big boobs. This work is different--my ad says what I look like--
--so I know that only guys who like petite girls with small boobs are phoning me. It doesn't bring up the same kind of insecurity.
Yeah, I'm totally happy with how your body looks.
And the one-on-one interaction just seems more relaxed and nice in a situation like this than it did in the clubs.
JUNE 2002:
When you were a kid, didn't you think prostitution was wrong?
When I was a kid, I didn't know what sex was, let alone prostitution.

CHAPTER 26

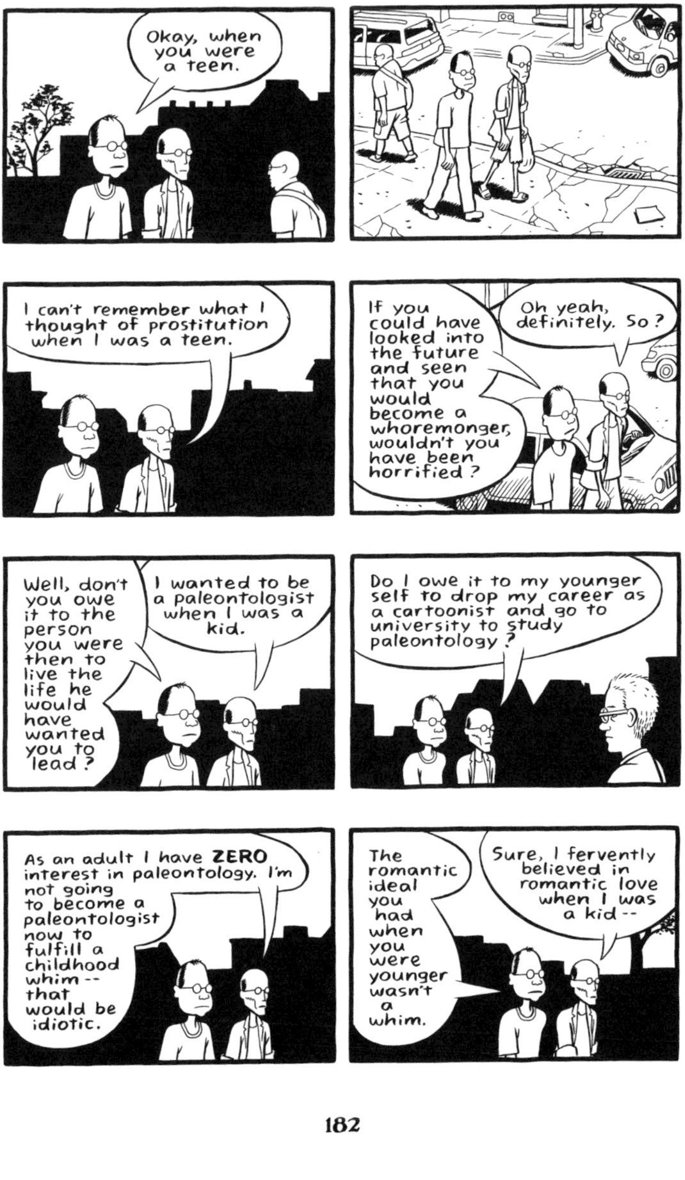
Okay, when you were a teen.
I can't remember what I thought of prostitution when I was a teen.
If you could have looked into the future and seen that you would become a whoremonger, wouldn't you have been horrified?
Oh yeah, definitely. So?
Well, don't you owe it to the person you were then to live the life he would have wanted you to lead?
I wanted to be a paleontologist when I was a kid.
Do I owe it to my younger self to drop my career as a cartoonist and go to university to study paleontology?
As an adult I have ZERO interest in paleontology. I'm not going to become a paleontologist now to fulfill a childhood whim -- that would be idiotic.
The romantic ideal you had when you were younger wasn't a whim.
Sure, I fervently believed in romantic love when I was a kid --

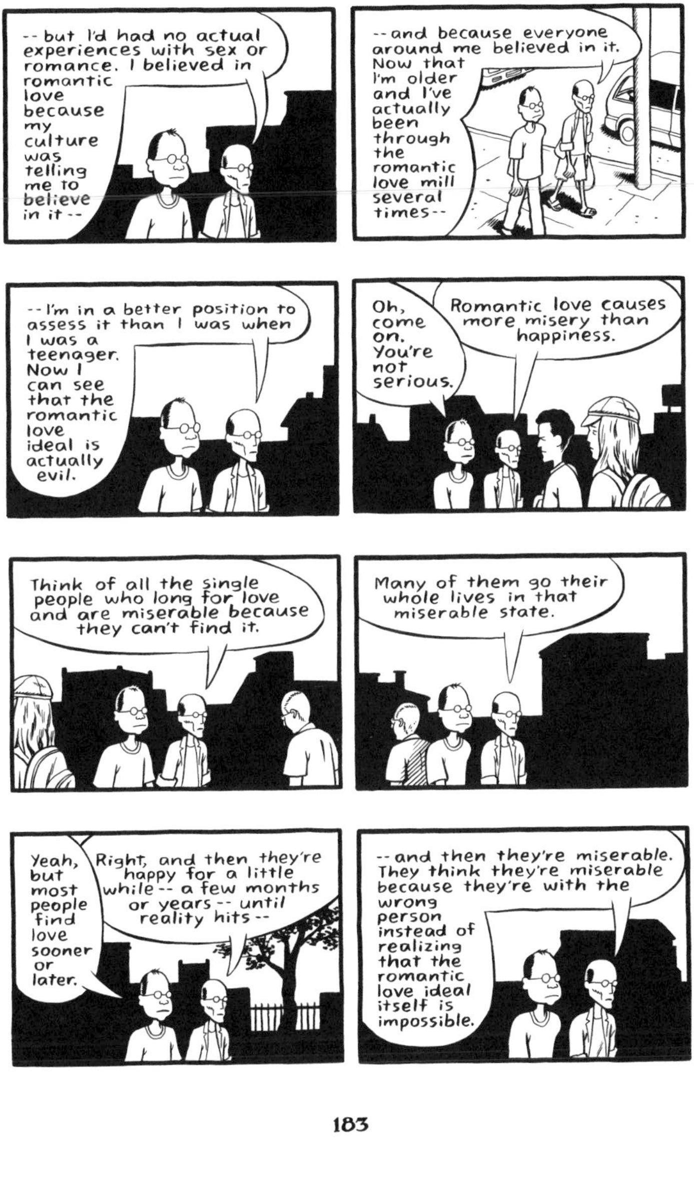
--but I'd had no actual experiences with sex or romance. I believed in romantic love because my culture was telling me to believe in it--
--and because everyone around me believed in it. Now that I'm older and I've actually been through the romantic love mill several times--
--I'm in a better position to assess it than I was when I was a teenager. Now I can see that the romantic love ideal is actually evil.
Romantic love causes more misery than happiness.
Oh, come on. You're not serious.
Think of all the single people who long for love and are miserable because they can't find it.
Many of them go their whole lives in that miserable state.
Yeah, but most people find love sooner or later.
Right, and then they're happy for a little while -- a few months or years -- until reality hits --
--and then they're miserable. They think they're miserable because they're with the wrong person instead of realizing that the romantic love ideal itself is impossible.

CHAPTER 26

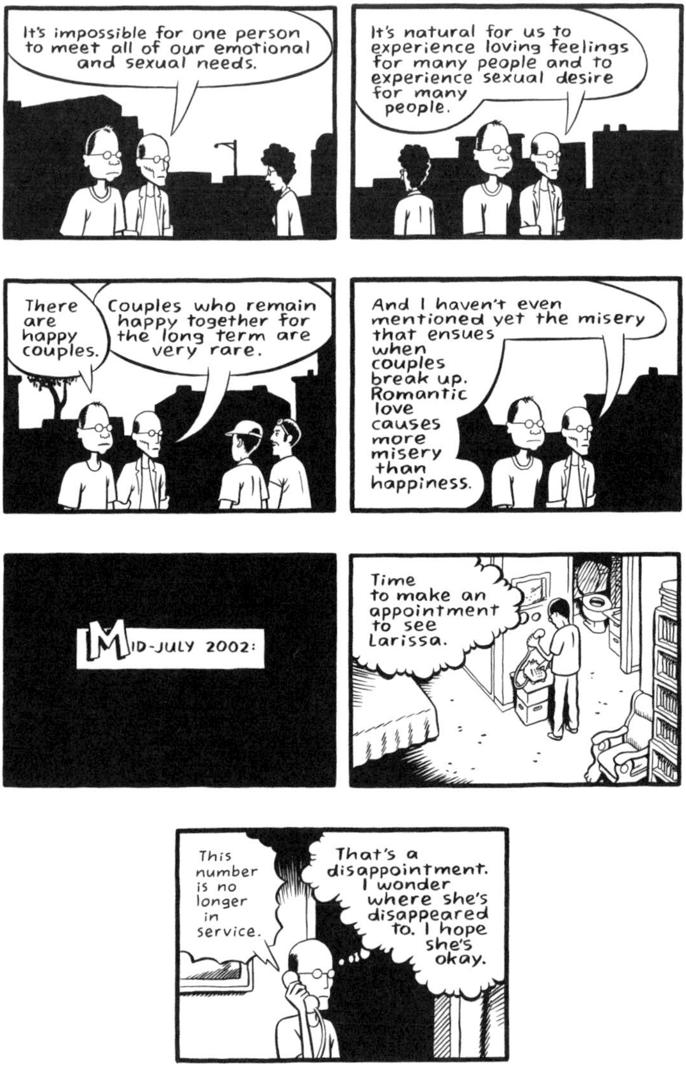

It's impossible for one person to meet all of our emotional and sexual needs.
It's natural for us to experience loving feelings for many people and to experience sexual desire for many people.
There are happy couples.
Couples who remain happy together for the long term are very rare.
And I haven't even mentioned yet the misery that ensues when couples break up. Romantic love causes more misery than happiness.
MID-JULY 2002:
Time to make an appointment to see Larissa.
This number is no longer in service.
That's a disappointment. I wonder where she's disappeared to. I hope she's okay.

CHAPTER
27
—
ARLENE

MID-JULY 2002:

The photo of this girl Arlene looks great, but there are no reviews of her on Terb.

JULY 17th 2002:

I'm calling about Arlene?

You'd like to see her?

CHAPTER 27

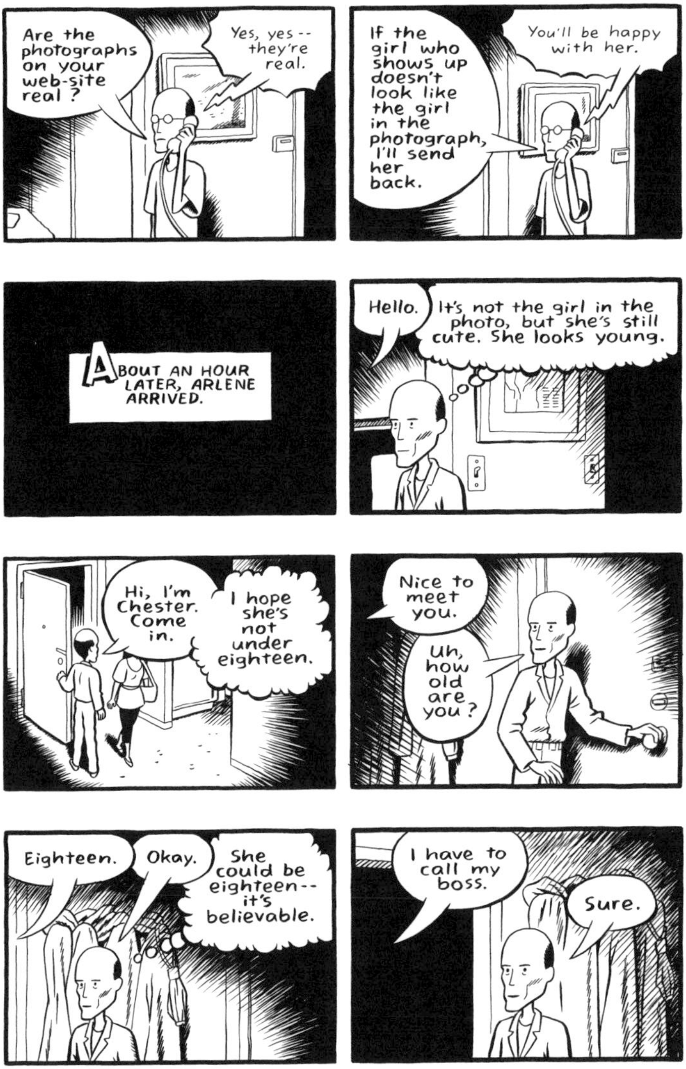

Are the photographs on your web-site real ?
Yes, yes -- they're real.
If the girl who shows up doesn't look like the girl in the photograph, I'll send her back.
You'll be happy with her.
ABOUT AN HOUR LATER, ARLENE ARRIVED.
Hello.
It's not the girl in the photo, but she's still cute. She looks young.
Hi, I'm Chester. Come in.
I hope she's not under eighteen.
Nice to meet you.
Uh, how old are you ?
Eighteen.
Okay.
She could be eighteen-- it's believable.
I have to call my boss.
Sure.

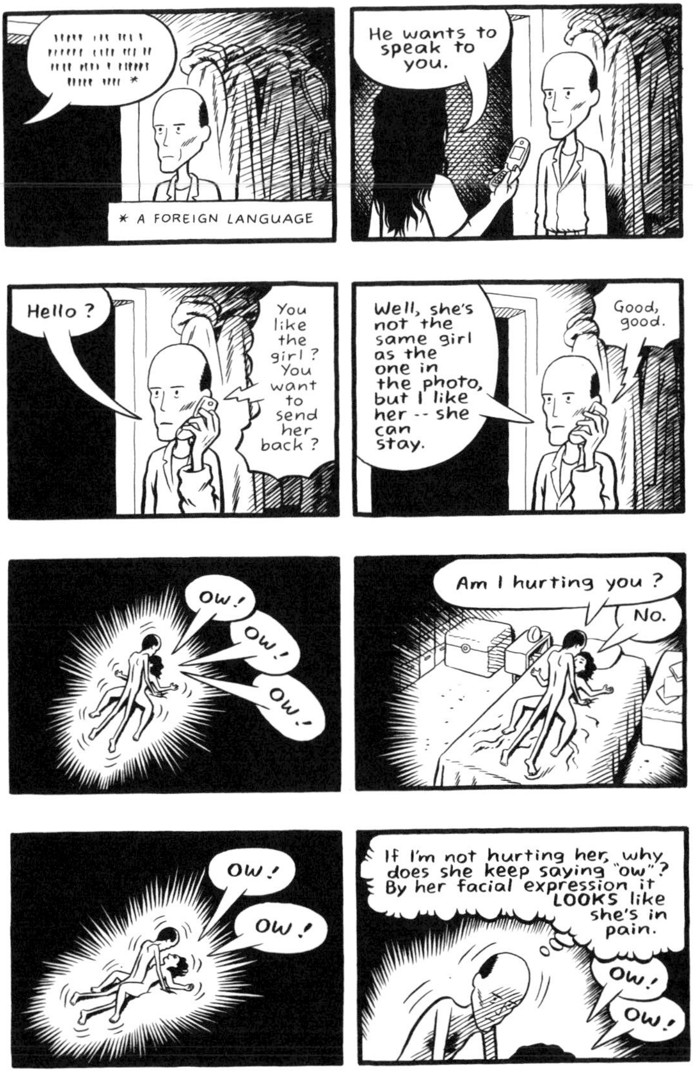
* A FOREIGN LANGUAGE
He wants to speak to you.
Hello?
You like the girl? You want to send her back?
Well, she's not the same girl as the one in the photo, but I like her -- she can stay.
Good, good.
OW!
OW!
OW!
Am I hurting you?
No.
OW!
OW!
If I'm not hurting her, why does she keep saying "ow"? By her facial expression it LOOKS like she's in pain.
OW!
OW!

CHAPTER 27

Are you really eighteen ?
Yes. Why ?
No reason.
Ow!
Ow!
That she seems to be in pain is kind of a turn-on for me, but I also feel bad for her.
I'm gonna cut this short and come quickly.
Ow!
Ow

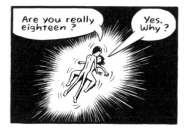

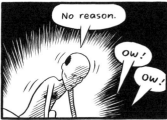

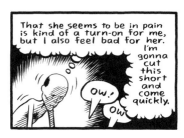

CHAPTER 28

EDITH

AUGUST 22nd 2002:
Hi! You're my fifth client.
oooooooo
She's gorgeous! what a doll!
Are you going to be keeping your bra on?
I'd rather keep it on.
I'd like it if you took it off.
I'm just really self-conscious about my breasts.

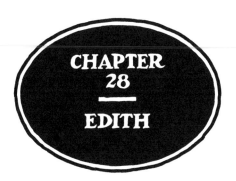

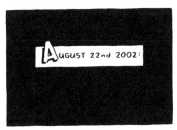

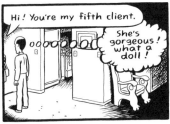

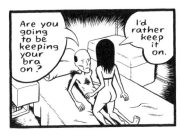

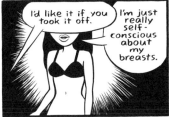

CHAPTER 28

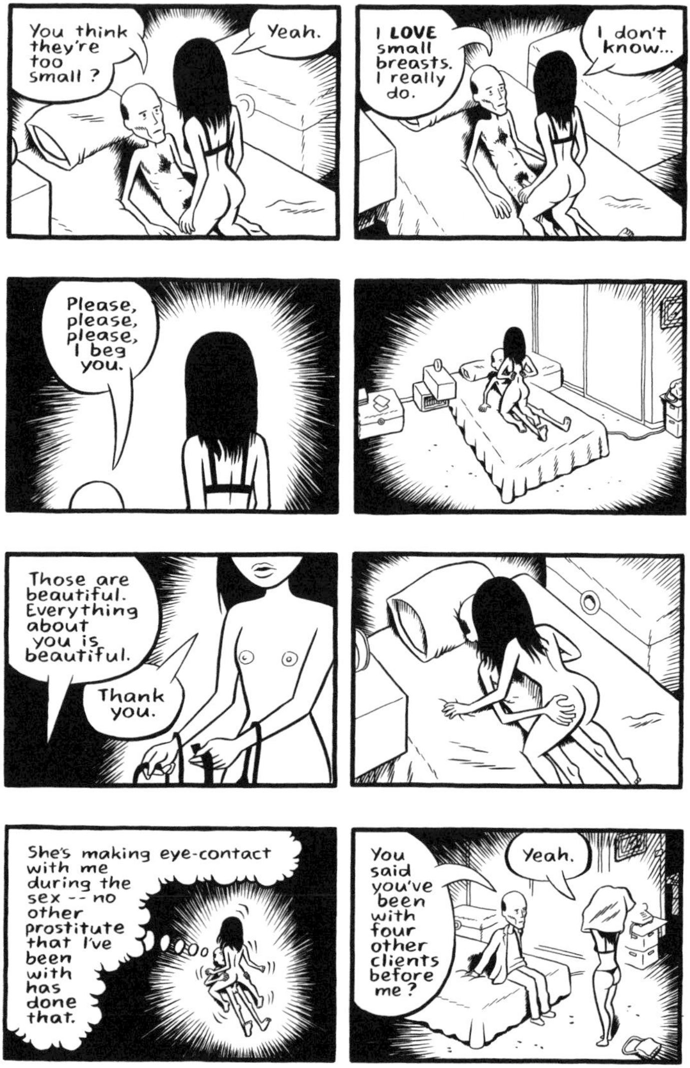
You think they're too small ?
Yeah.
I LOVE small breasts. I really do.
I don't know...
Please, please, please, I beg you.
Those are beautiful. Everything about you is beautiful.
Thank you.
She's making eye-contact with me during the sex -- no other prostitute that I've been with has done that.
You said you've been with four other clients before me ?
Yeah.

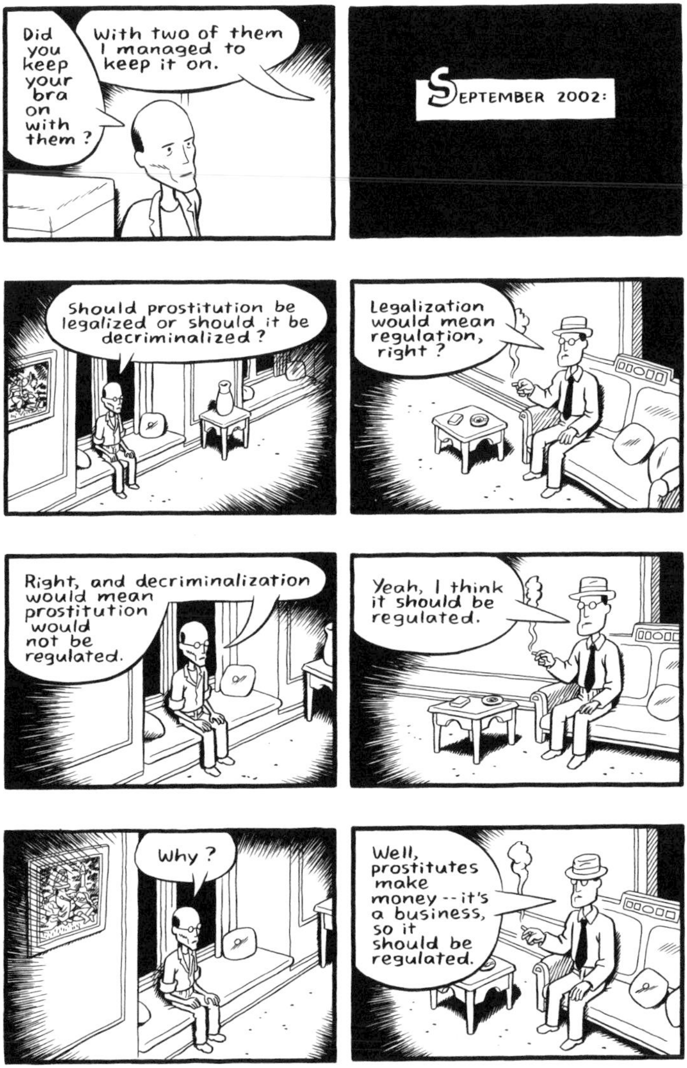
Did you keep your bra on with them?
With two of them I managed to keep it on.
SEPTEMBER 2002:
Should prostitution be legalized or should it be decriminalized?
Legalization would mean regulation, right?
Right, and decriminalization would mean prostitution would not be regulated.
Yeah, I think it should be regulated.
Why?
Well, prostitutes make money -- it's a business, so it should be regulated.

CHAPTER 28

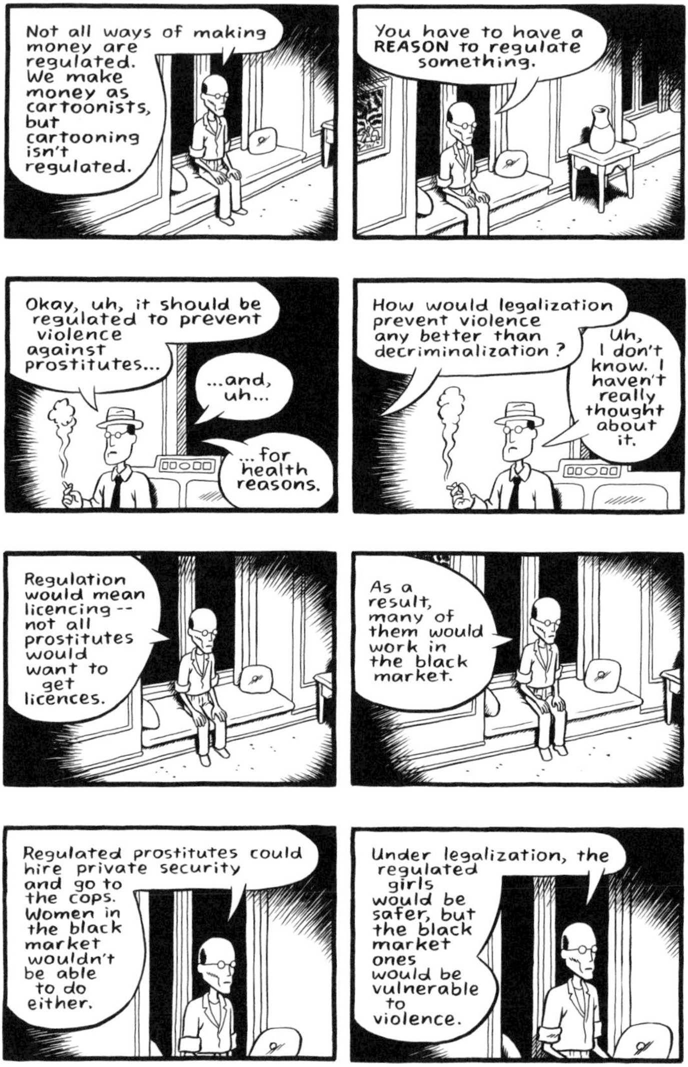
Not all ways of making money are regulated. We make money as cartoonists, but cartooning isn't regulated.
You have to have a REASON to regulate something.
Okay, uh, it should be regulated to prevent violence against prostitutes...
...and, uh...
...for health reasons.
How would legalization prevent violence any better than decriminalization?
Uh, I don't know. I haven't really thought about it.
Regulation would mean licencing -- not all prostitutes would want to get licences.
As a result, many of them would work in the black market.
Regulated prostitutes could hire private security and go to the cops. Women in the black market wouldn't be able to do either.
Under legalization, the regulated girls would be safer, but the black market ones would be vulnerable to violence.

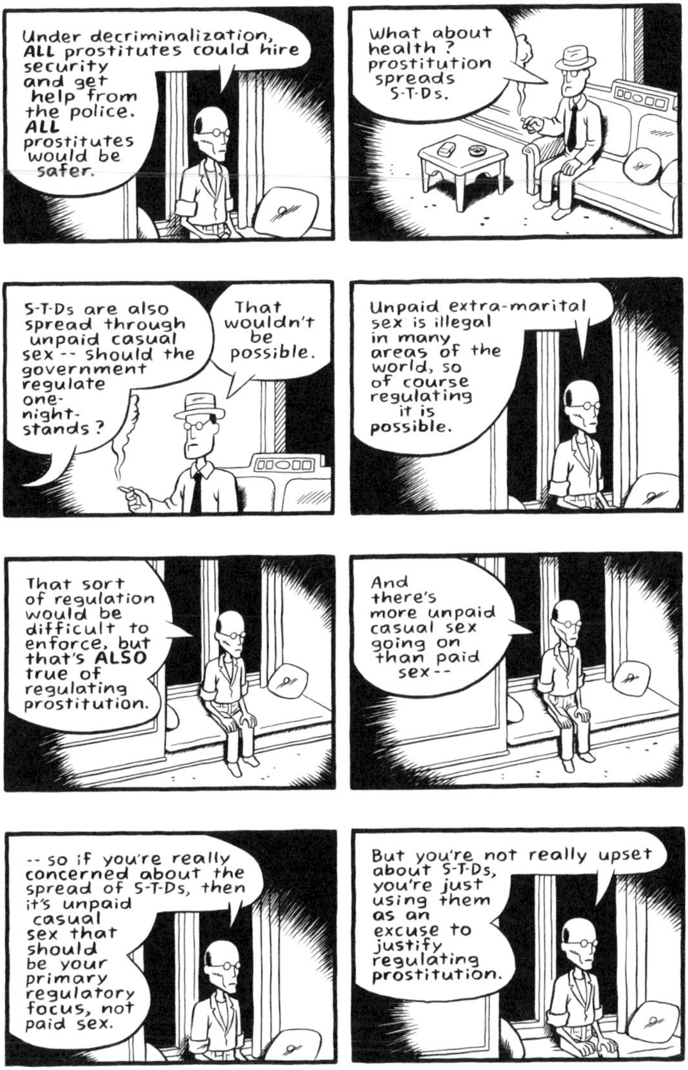
Under decriminalization, ALL prostitutes could hire security and get help from the police. ALL prostitutes would be safer.
What about health? prostitution spreads S-T-Ds.
S-T-Ds are also spread through unpaid casual sex -- should the government regulate one-night-stands?
That wouldn't be possible.
Unpaid extra-marital sex is illegal in many areas of the world, so of course regulating it is possible.
That sort of regulation would be difficult to enforce, but that's ALSO true of regulating prostitution.
And there's more unpaid casual sex going on than paid sex--
-- so if you're really concerned about the spread of S-T-Ds, then it's unpaid casual sex that should be your primary regulatory focus, not paid sex.
But you're not really upset about S-T-Ds, you're just using them as an excuse to justify regulating prostitution.

CHAPTER 28

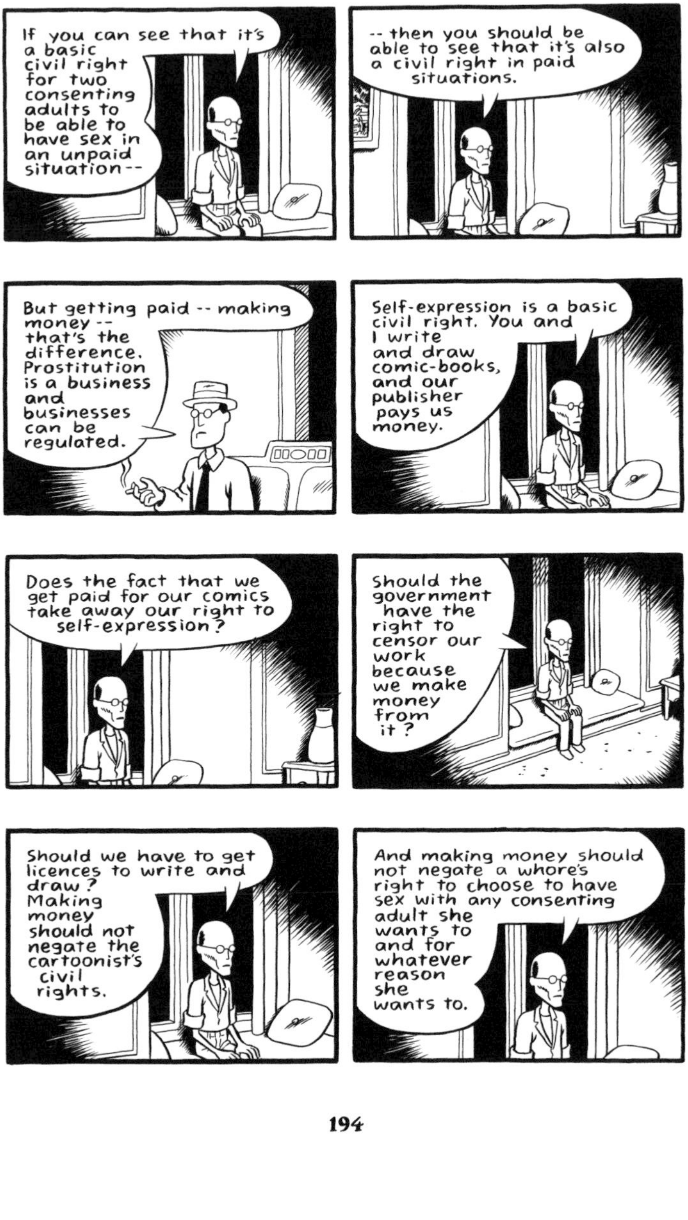
If you can see that it's a basic civil right for two consenting adults to be able to have sex in an unpaid situation--
-- then you should be able to see that it's also a civil right in paid situations.
But getting paid -- making money -- that's the difference. Prostitution is a business and businesses can be regulated.
Self-expression is a basic civil right. You and I write and draw comic-books, and our publisher pays us money.
Does the fact that we get paid for our comics take away our right to self-expression?
Should the government have the right to censor our work because we make money from it?
Should we have to get licences to write and draw? Making money should not negate the cartoonist's civil rights.
And making money should not negate a whore's right to choose to have sex with any consenting adult she wants to and for whatever reason she wants to.

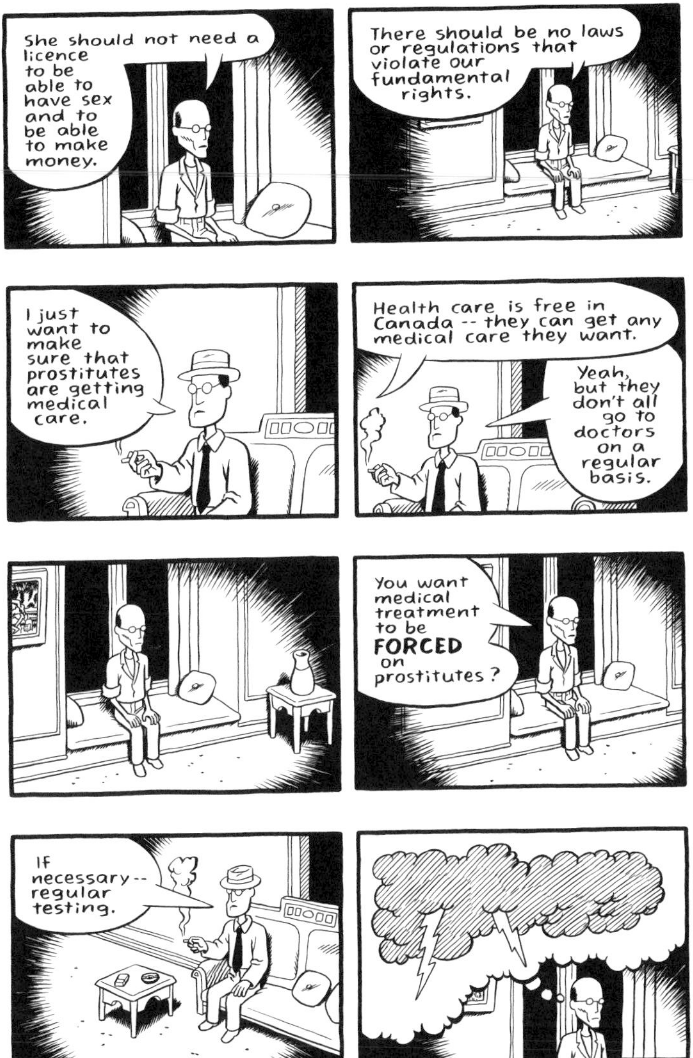
She should not need a licence to be able to have sex and to be able to make money.
There should be no laws or regulations that violate our fundamental rights.
I just want to make sure that prostitutes are getting medical care.
Health care is free in Canada -- they can get any medical care they want.
Yeah, but they don't all go to doctors on a regular basis.
You want medical treatment to be FORCED on prostitutes?
If necessary -- regular testing.

CHAPTER 28

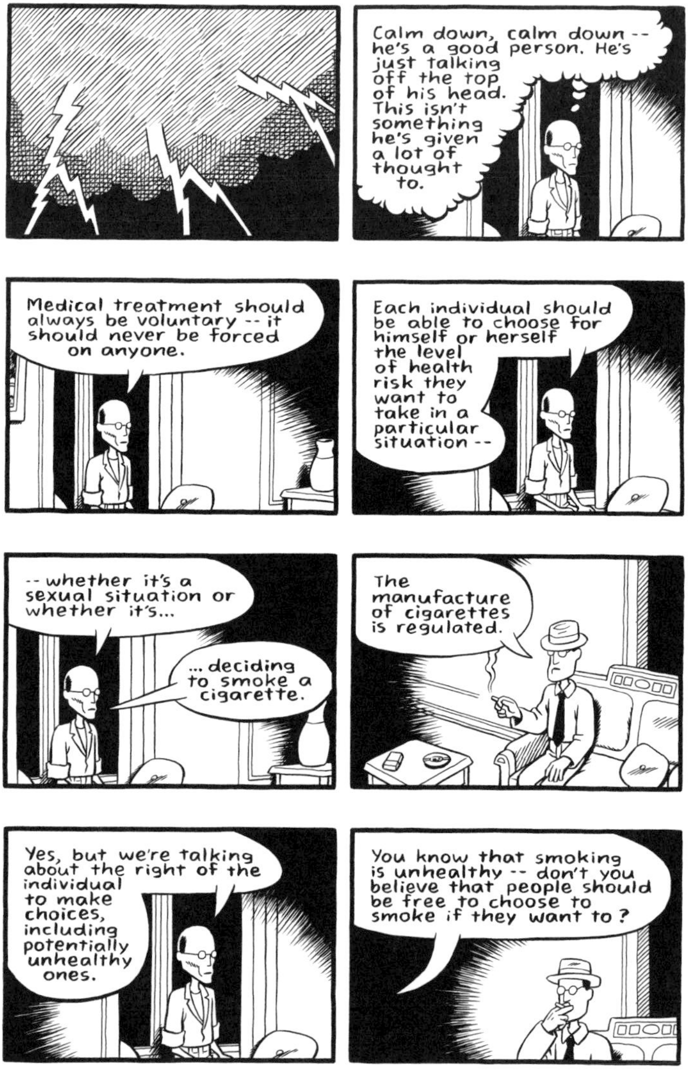

Calm down, calm down -- he's a good person. He's just talking off the top of his head. This isn't something he's given a lot of thought to.
Medical treatment should always be voluntary -- it should never be forced on anyone.
Each individual should be able to choose for himself or herself the level of health risk they want to take in a particular situation --
-- whether it's a sexual situation or whether it's...
... deciding to smoke a cigarette.
The manufacture of cigarettes is regulated.
Yes, but we're talking about the right of the individual to make choices, including potentially unhealthy ones.
You know that smoking is unhealthy -- don't you believe that people should be free to choose to smoke if they want to?

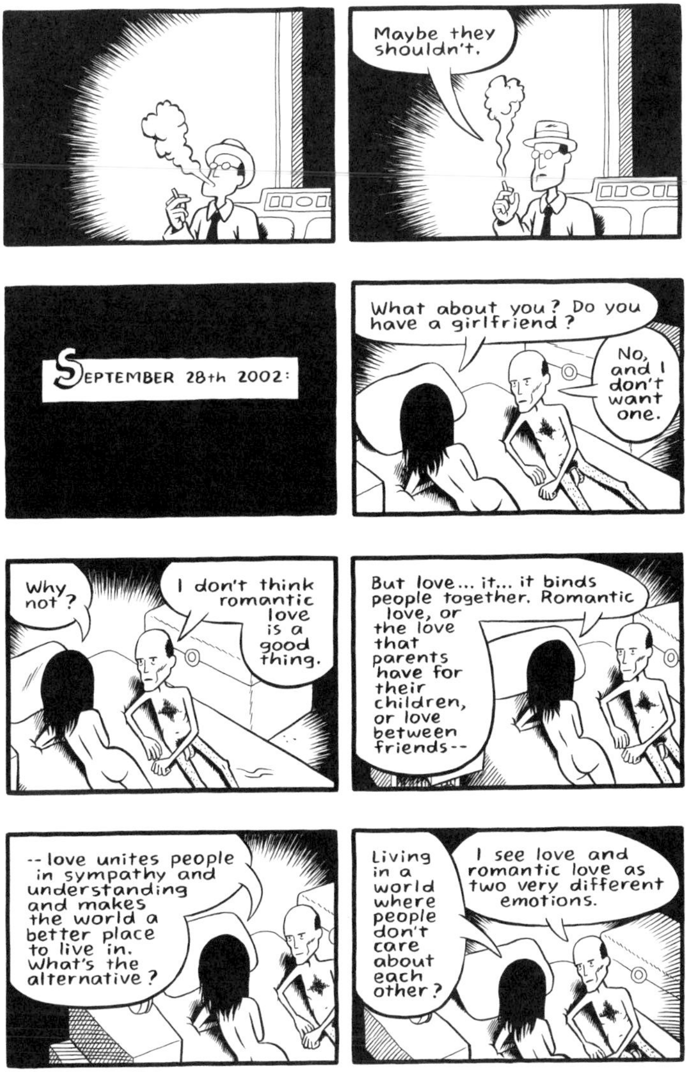
Maybe they shouldn't.
SEPTEMBER 28th 2002:
What about you? Do you have a girlfriend?
No, and I don't want one.
Why not?
I don't think romantic love is a good thing.
But love... it... it binds people together. Romantic love, or the love that parents have for their children, or love between friends--
--love unites people in sympathy and understanding and makes the world a better place to live in. What's the alternative?
Living in a world where people don't care about each other?
I see love and romantic love as two very different emotions.

CHAPTER 28

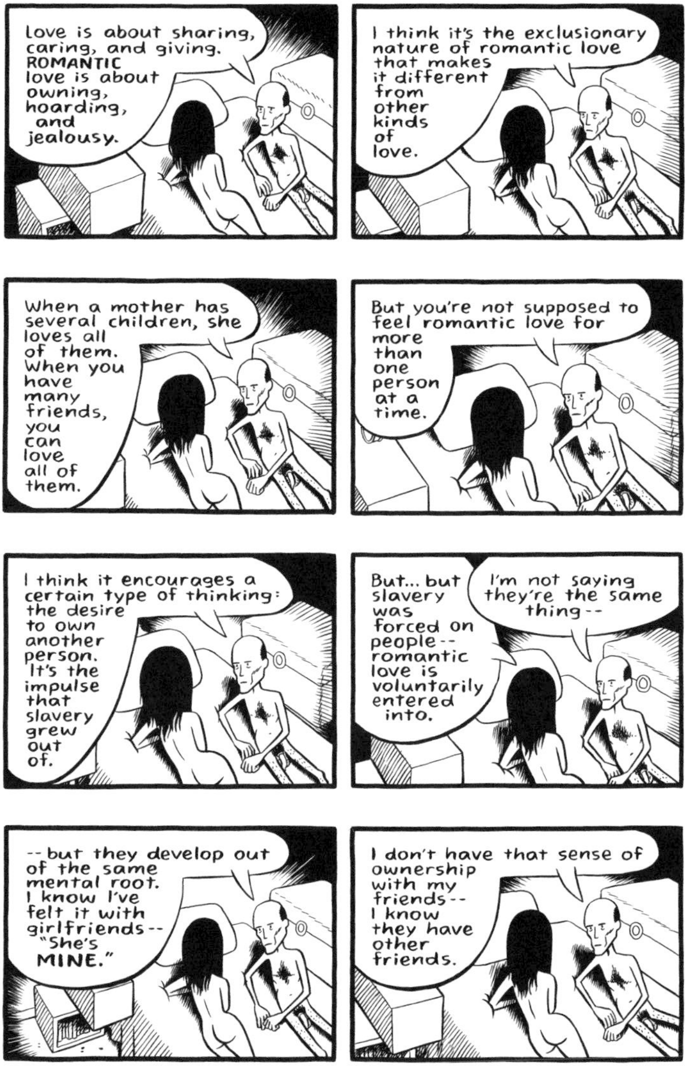
Love is about sharing, caring, and giving. ROMANTIC love is about owning, hoarding, and jealousy.
I think it's the exclusionary nature of romantic love that makes it different from other kinds of love.
When a mother has several children, she loves all of them. When you have many friends, you can love all of them.
But you're not supposed to feel romantic love for more than one person at a time.
I think it encourages a certain type of thinking: the desire to own another person. It's the impulse that slavery grew out of.
But... but slavery was forced on people -- romantic love is voluntarily entered into.
I'm not saying they're the same thing --
-- but they develop out of the same mental root. I know I've felt it with girlfriends -- "She's MINE."
I don't have that sense of ownership with my friends -- I know they have other friends.

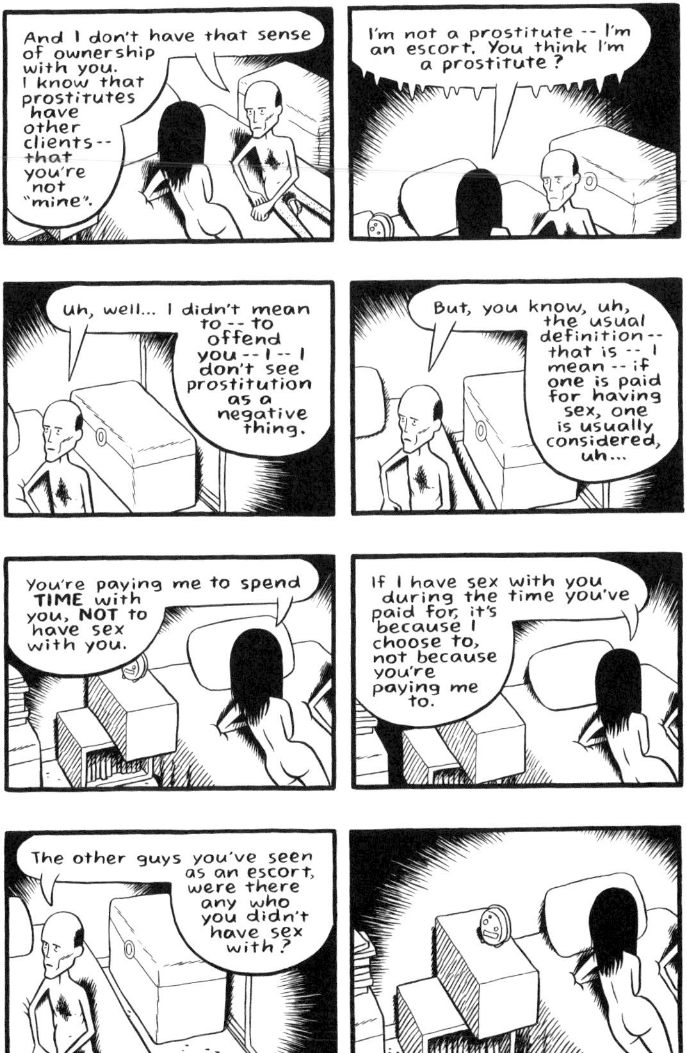
And I don't have that sense of ownership with you. I know that prostitutes have other clients-- that you're not "mine".
I'm not a prostitute -- I'm an escort. You think I'm a prostitute?
Uh, well... I didn't mean to -- to offend you -- I -- I don't see prostitution as a negative thing.
But, you know, uh, the usual definition -- that is -- I mean -- if one is paid for having sex, one is usually considered, uh...
You're paying me to spend TIME with you, NOT to have sex with you.
If I have sex with you during the time you've paid for, it's because I choose to, not because you're paying me to.
The other guys you've seen as an escort, were there any who you didn't have sex with?

CHAPTER 28

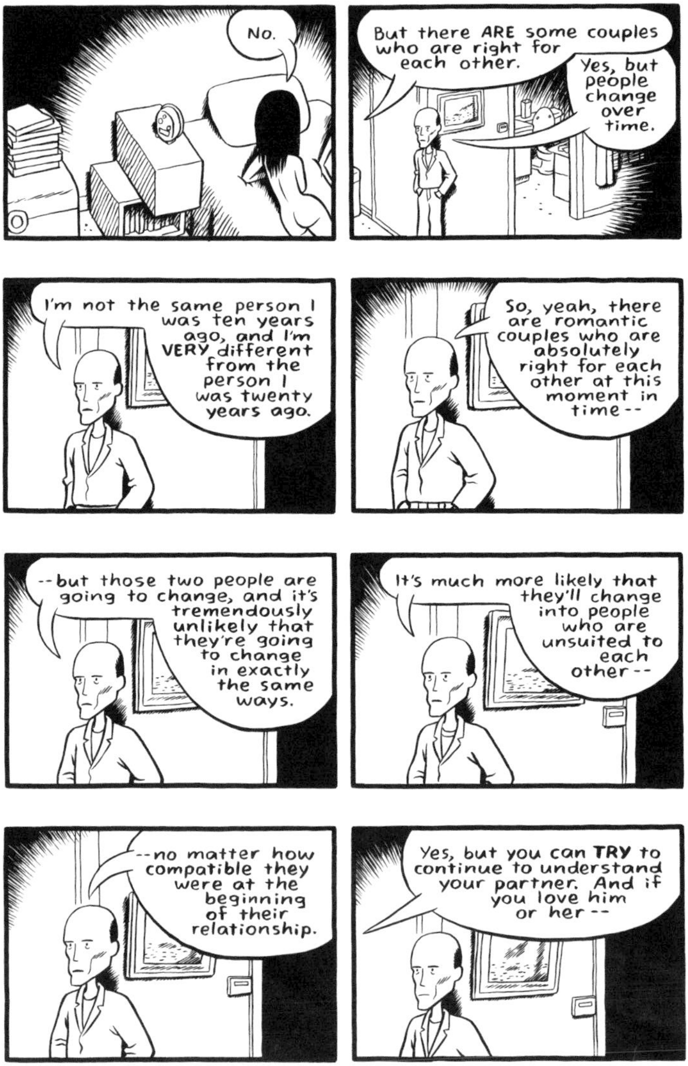
No.
But there ARE some couples who are right for each other.
Yes, but people change over time.
I'm not the same person I was ten years ago, and I'm VERY different from the person I was twenty years ago.
So, yeah, there are romantic couples who are absolutely right for each other at this moment in time --
-- but those two people are going to change, and it's tremendously unlikely that they're going to change in exactly the same ways.
It's much more likely that they'll change into people who are unsuited to each other --
-- no matter how compatible they were at the beginning of their relationship.
Yes, but you can TRY to continue to understand your partner. And if you love him or her --

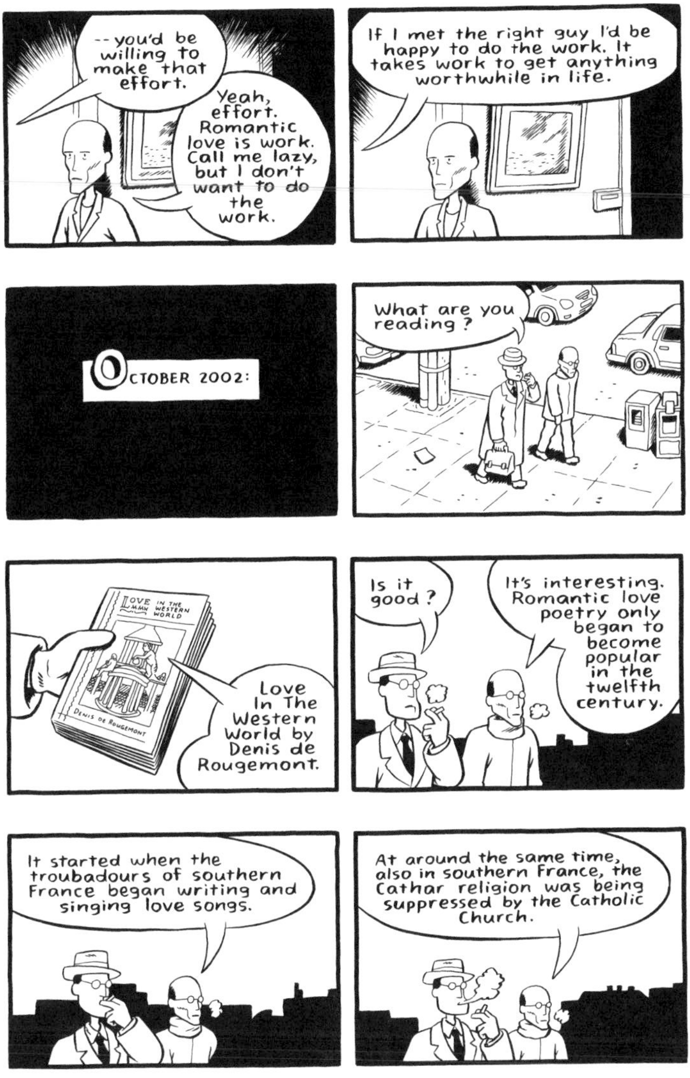
--you'd be willing to make that effort.
Yeah, effort. Romantic love is work. Call me lazy, but I don't want to do the work.
If I met the right guy I'd be happy to do the work. It takes work to get anything worthwhile in life.
OCTOBER 2002:
What are you reading?
LOVE IN THE WESTERN WORLD
DENIS DE ROUGEMONT
Love In The Western World by Denis de Rougemont.
Is it good?
It's interesting. Romantic love poetry only began to become popular in the twelfth century.
It started when the troubadours of southern France began writing and singing love songs.
At around the same time, also in southern France, the Cathar religion was being suppressed by the Catholic Church.

CHAPTER 28

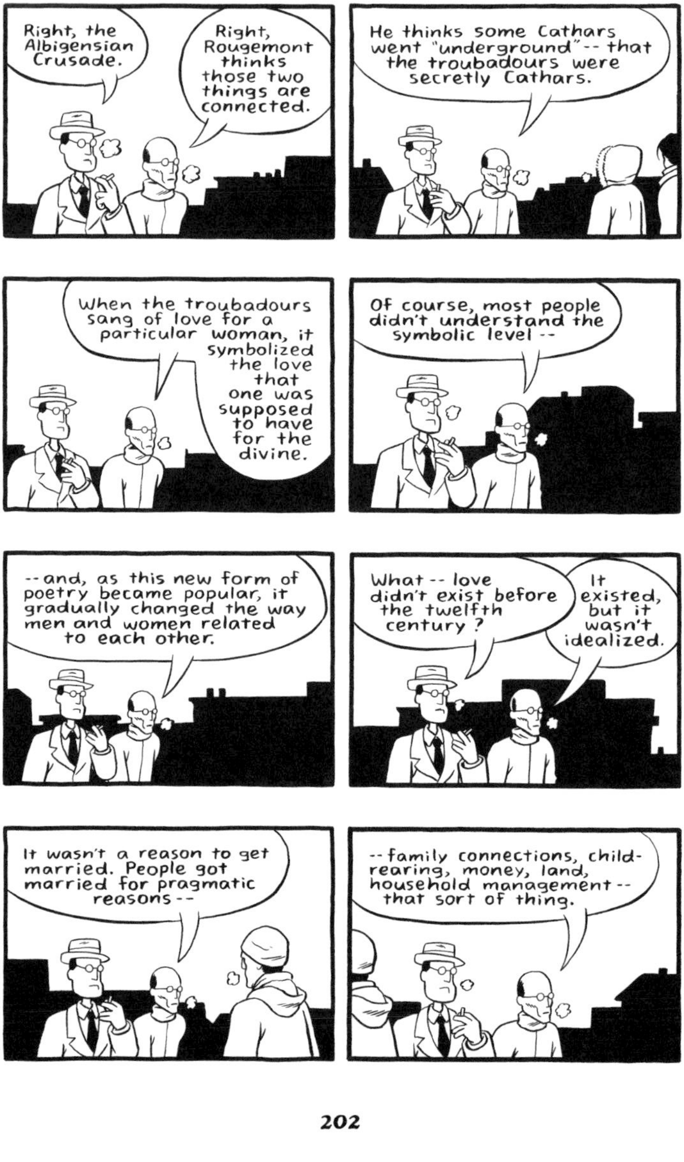
Right, the Albigensian Crusade.
Right, Rougemont thinks those two things are connected.
He thinks some Cathars went "underground" -- that the troubadours were secretly Cathars.
When the troubadours sang of love for a particular woman, it symbolized the love that one was supposed to have for the divine.
Of course, most people didn't understand the symbolic level --
--and, as this new form of poetry became popular, it gradually changed the way men and women related to each other.
What -- love didn't exist before the twelfth century?
It existed, but it wasn't idealized.
It wasn't a reason to get married. People got married for pragmatic reasons --
--family connections, child-rearing, money, land, household management -- that sort of thing.

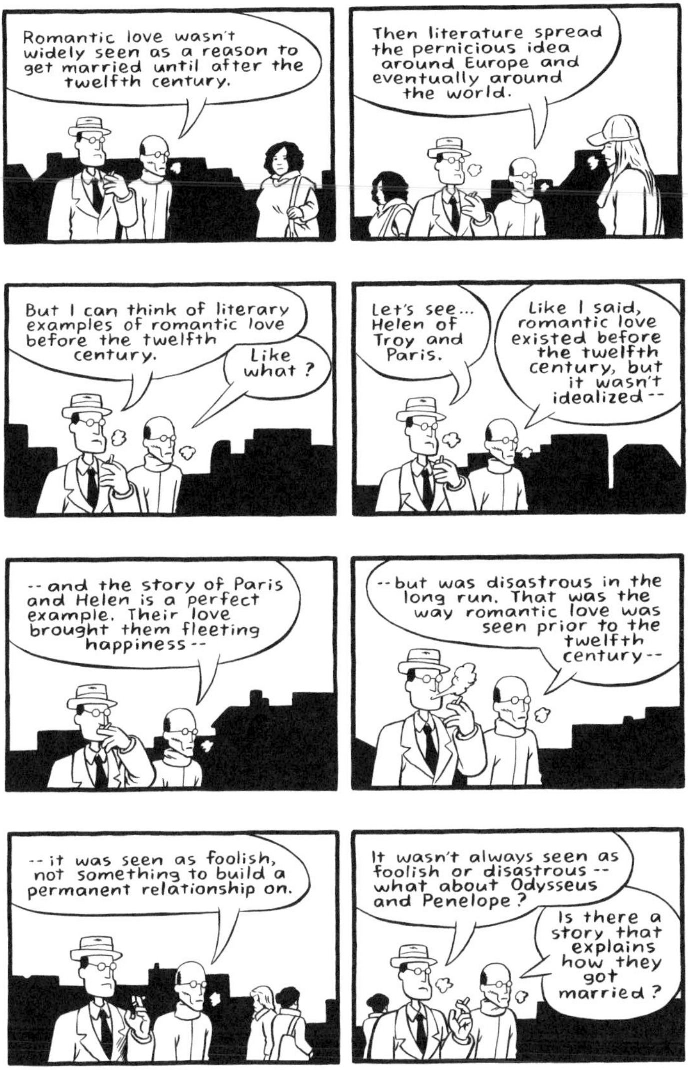
Romantic love wasn't widely seen as a reason to get married until after the twelfth century.
Then literature spread the pernicious idea around Europe and eventually around the world.
But I can think of literary examples of romantic love before the twelfth century.
Like what?
Let's see... Helen of Troy and Paris.
Like I said, romantic love existed before the twelfth century, but it wasn't idealized --
-- and the story of Paris and Helen is a perfect example. Their love brought them fleeting happiness --
-- but was disastrous in the long run. That was the way romantic love was seen prior to the twelfth century --
-- it was seen as foolish, not something to build a permanent relationship on.
It wasn't always seen as foolish or disastrous -- what about Odysseus and Penelope?
Is there a story that explains how they got married?

CHAPTER 28

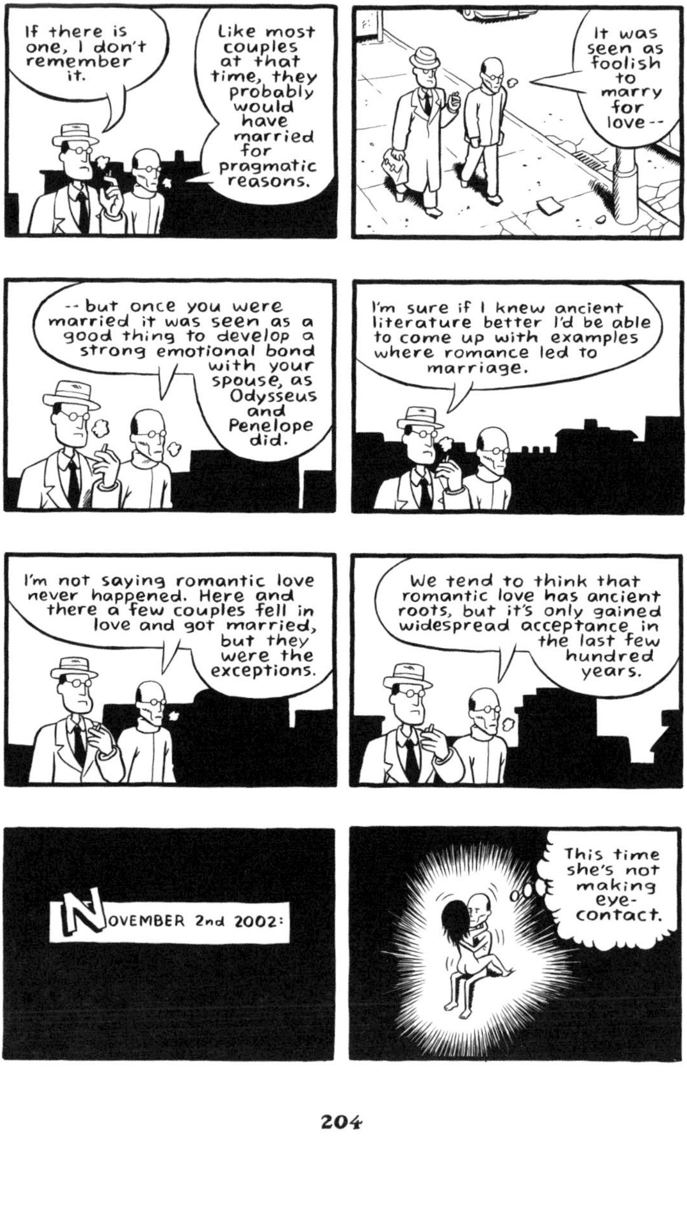

If there is one, I don't remember it.
Like most couples at that time, they probably would have married for pragmatic reasons.
It was seen as foolish to marry for love --
-- but once you were married it was seen as a good thing to develop a strong emotional bond with your spouse, as Odysseus and Penelope did.
I'm sure if I knew ancient literature better I'd be able to come up with examples where romance led to marriage.
I'm not saying romantic love never happened. Here and there a few couples fell in love and got married, but they were the exceptions.
We tend to think that romantic love has ancient roots, but it's only gained widespread acceptance in the last few hundred years.
NOVEMBER 2nd 2002:
This time she's not making eye-contact.

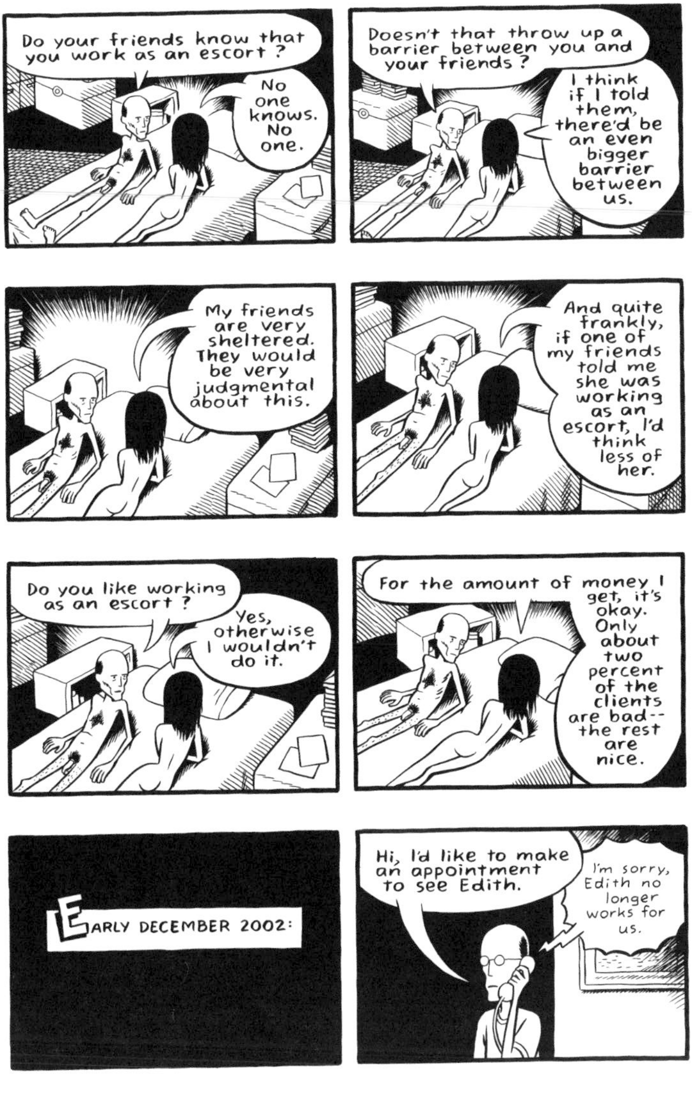
Do your friends know that you work as an escort ?
No one knows. No one.
Doesn't that throw up a barrier between you and your friends ?
I think if I told them, there'd be an even bigger barrier between us.
My friends are very sheltered. They would be very judgmental about this.
And quite frankly, if one of my friends told me she was working as an escort, I'd think less of her.
Do you like working as an escort ?
Yes, otherwise I wouldn't do it.
For the amount of money I get, it's okay. Only about two percent of the clients are bad -- the rest are nice.
EARLY DECEMBER 2002:
Hi, I'd like to make an appointment to see Edith.
I'm sorry, Edith no longer works for us.

CHAPTER 29
—
LAURA

DECEMBER 12th 2002:

She's older than I'd been hoping for -- probably early thirties -- but she's attractive enough.

Passionless kissing.

THINGS GOT BETTER AFTER THE KISSING, BUT NOT SO MUCH BETTER THAT I WANTED TO SEE HER AGAIN.

CHAPTER 29

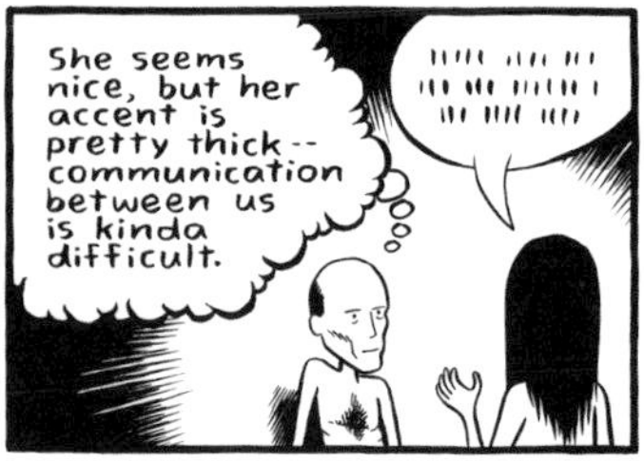
She seems nice, but her accent is pretty thick-- communication between us is kinda difficult.

CHAPTER 30
—
DENISE

JANUARY 8th 2003:

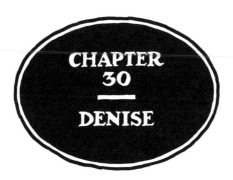

Hi, I'm Denise.

This one's older too, but she's prettier than the last one, and she's got a sweet smile.

I'm Chester. Here, let me take your coat. Do you want something to drink? I've got juice or soft drinks.

Thanks, uh, Pepsi or Coke.

CHAPTER 30

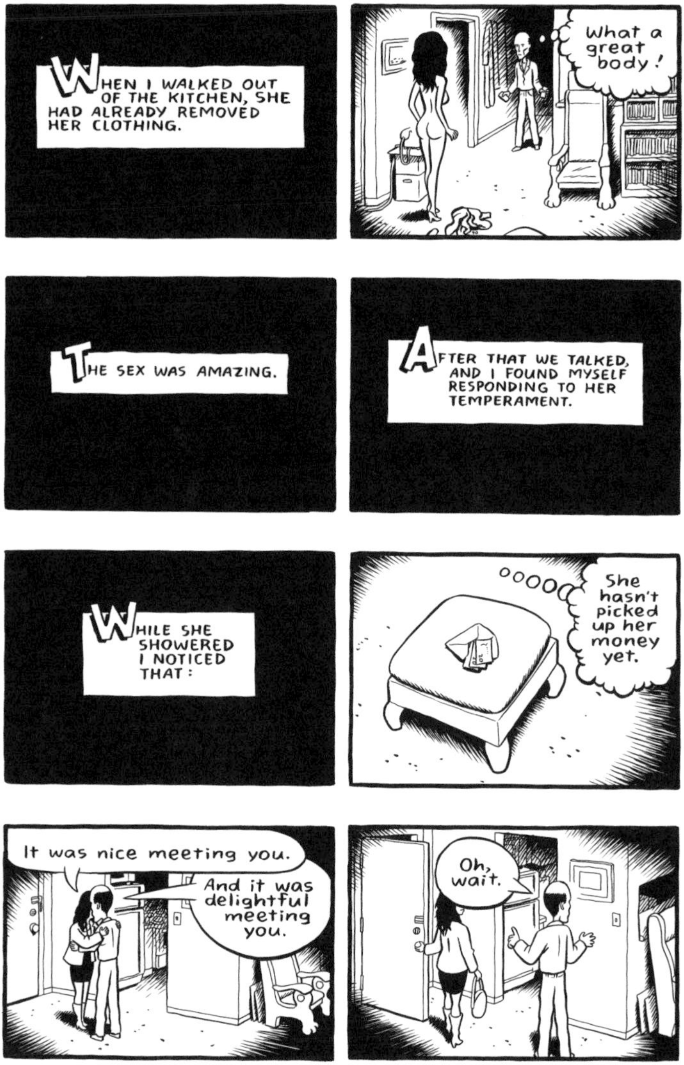
WHEN I WALKED OUT OF THE KITCHEN, SHE HAD ALREADY REMOVED HER CLOTHING.
What a great body!
THE SEX WAS AMAZING.
AFTER THAT WE TALKED, AND I FOUND MYSELF RESPONDING TO HER TEMPERAMENT.
WHILE SHE SHOWERED I NOTICED THAT:
She hasn't picked up her money yet.
It was nice meeting you.
And it was delightful meeting you.
Oh, wait.

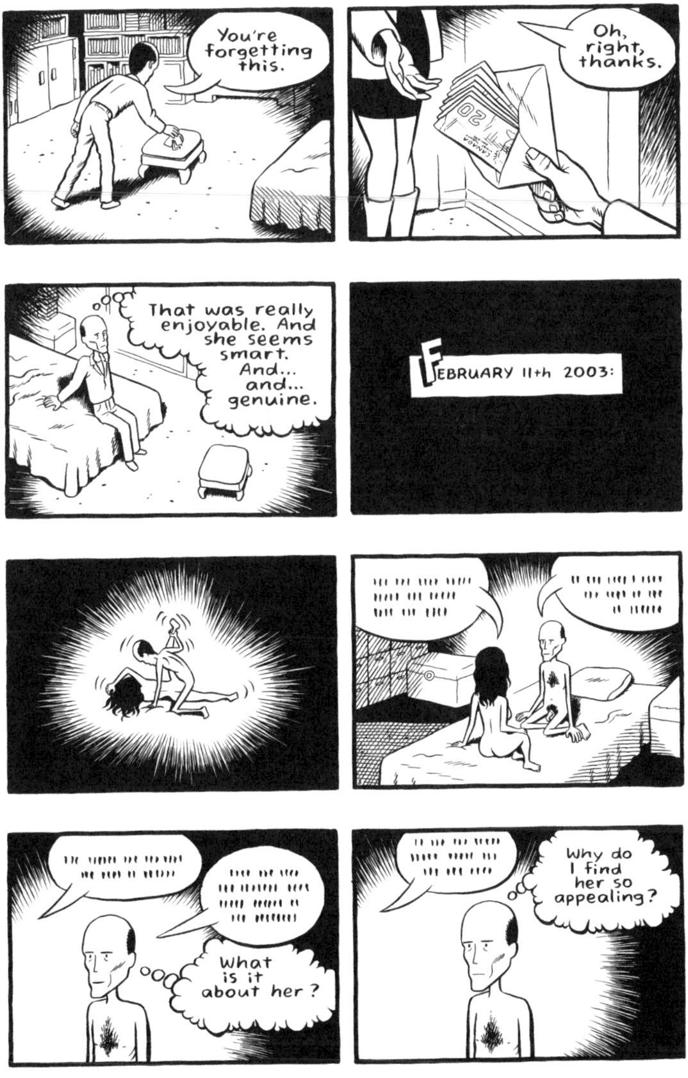
You're forgetting this.
Oh, right, thanks.
That was really enjoyable. And she seems smart. And... and... genuine.
FEBRUARY 11th 2003:
What is it about her?
Why do I find her so appealing?

CHAPTER 30

Many of the other prostitutes I've met have had good personalities, but something about this one goes beyond that.
I WAS WORKING ON MY BOOK ABOUT LOUIS RIEL, AND AS THE PUBLICATION DEADLINE LOOMED I BECAME TOO BUSY FOR SEX.
I'd like to see Denise again, but I can't right now.
A FEW MONTHS LATER:
Now I have no time to have sex because the Riel book's been published and I'm busy promoting it.

CHAPTER
31
—
NANCY

LATE OCTOBER 2003:

At last, the promotion for the book is winding down. I think I have time to get together with a prostitute.

I haven't had sex since I saw Denise back in February. I was thinking of seeing her again, but maybe I'll check to see who else is available.

AT AN INTERNET CAFÉ:

CHAPTER 31

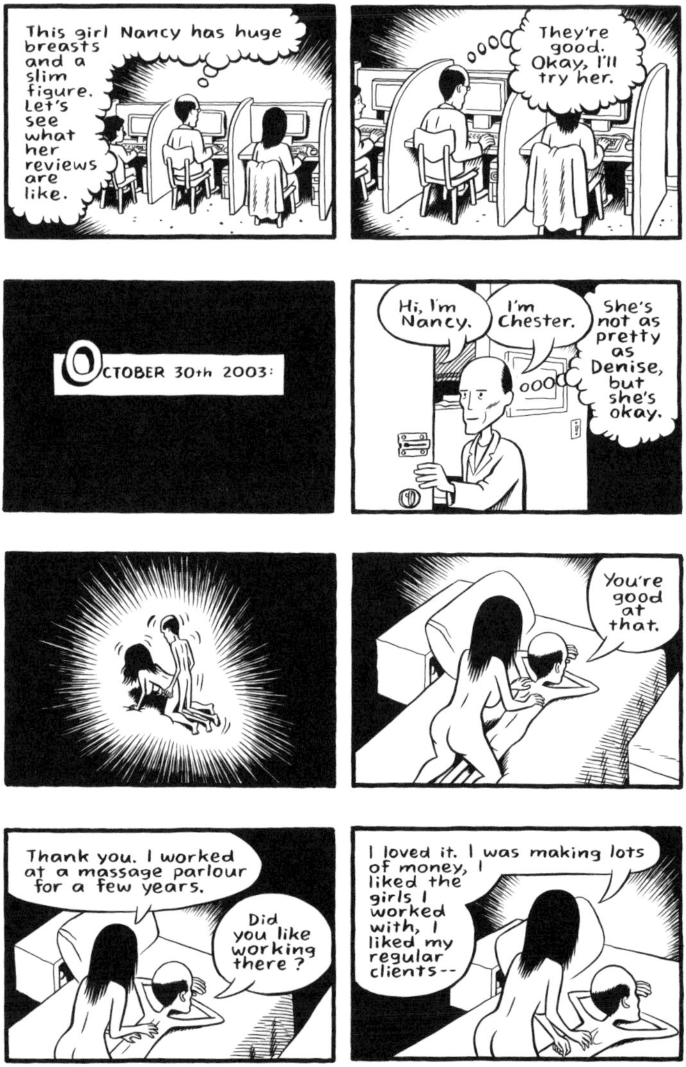

This girl Nancy has huge breasts and a slim figure. Let's see what her reviews are like.
They're good. Okay, I'll try her.
October 30th 2003:
Hi, I'm Nancy.
I'm Chester.
She's not as pretty as Denise, but she's okay.
You're good at that.
Thank you. I worked at a massage parlour for a few years.
Did you like working there?
I loved it. I was making lots of money, I liked the girls I worked with, I liked my regular clients--

--and I was comfortable with the work. I masturbated the guys -- I didn't have sex with them.

So why aren't you still working there?

The cops raided the place and arrested me. I vowed that I'd never be arrested again. I quit the massage parlour--

--and began working as an escort.

But you'd rather be working at the massage parlour?

Escorting's okay, but yes, I'd rather be back at the massage parlour.

215

CHAPTER 32
—
MILLIE

DECEMBER 2003:

Part of me wants to see Denise again, but this girl Millie has positive reviews, and her photos look good...

DECEMBER 27th 2003:

JACKPOT! She's even more beautiful than Gwendolyn! She's radiant!

Hi, I'm Chester.

CHAPTER 32

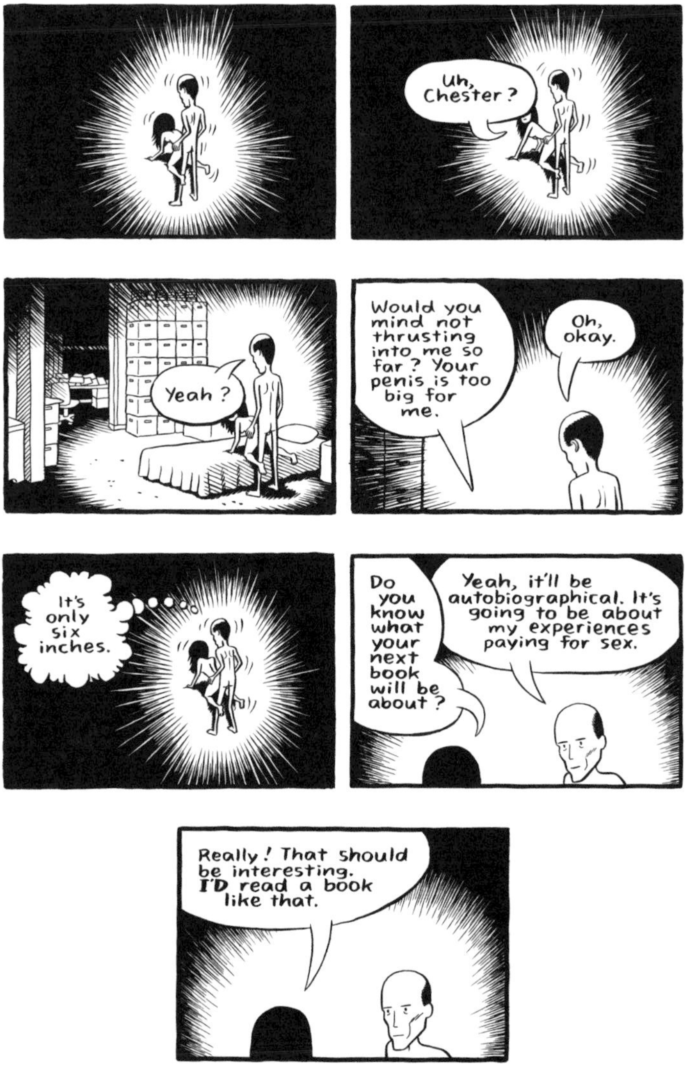
Uh, Chester?
Yeah?
Would you mind not thrusting into me so far? Your penis is too big for me.
Oh, okay.
It's only six inches.
Do you know what your next book will be about?
Yeah, it'll be autobiographical. It's going to be about my experiences paying for sex.
Really! That should be interesting. I'D read a book like that.

CHAPTER 33

BACK TO MONOGAMY

JANUARY 2004:
Should I see Millie or Denise next?
Millie's younger and more beautiful.
On the other hand, Denise is better in bed. And she IS pretty.

CHAPTER 33

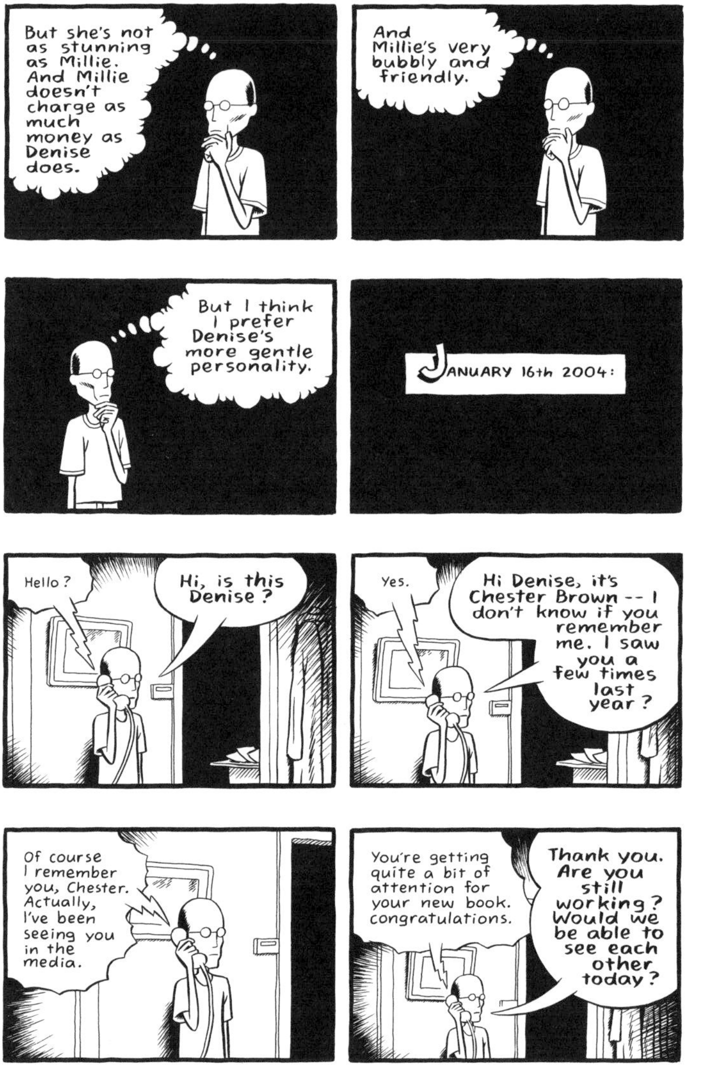

But she's not as stunning as Millie. And Millie doesn't charge as much money as Denise does.
And Millie's very bubbly and friendly.
But I think I prefer Denise's more gentle personality.
JANUARY 16th 2004:
Hello?
Hi, is this Denise?
Yes.
Hi Denise, it's Chester Brown -- I don't know if you remember me. I saw you a few times last year?
Of course I remember you, Chester. Actually, I've been seeing you in the media.
You're getting quite a bit of attention for your new book. congratulations.
Thank you. Are you still working? Would we be able to see each other today?

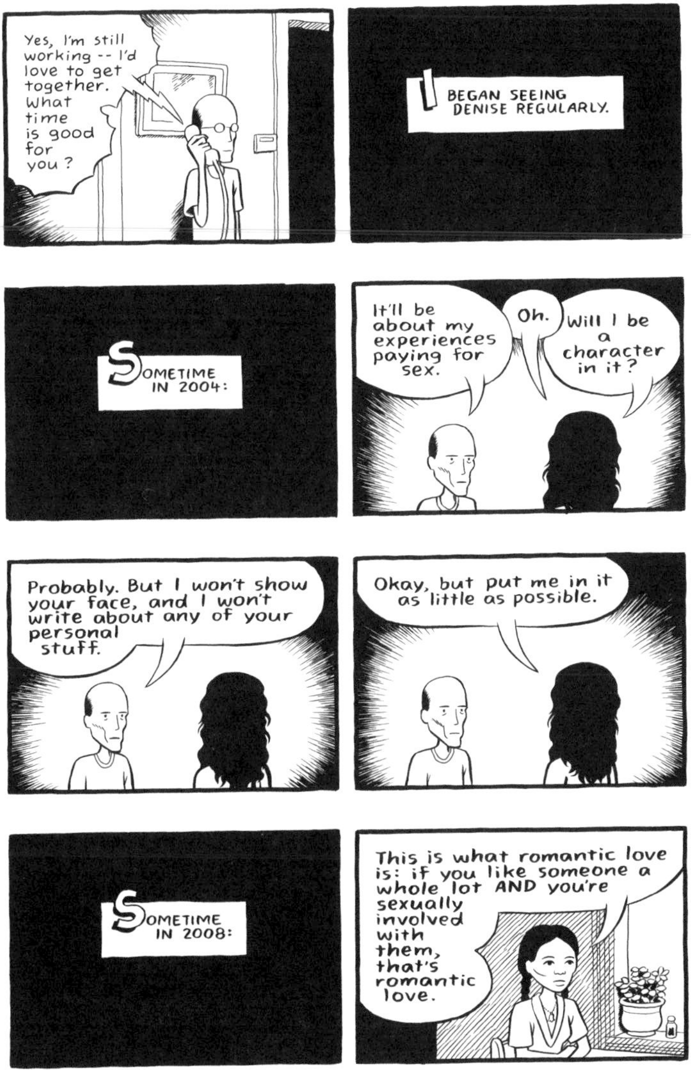
Yes, I'm still working -- I'd love to get together. What time is good for you?
I BEGAN SEEING DENISE REGULARLY.
SOMETIME IN 2004:
It'll be about my experiences paying for sex.
Oh.
Will I be a character in it?
Probably. But I won't show your face, and I won't write about any of your personal stuff.
Okay, but put me in it as little as possible.
SOMETIME IN 2008:
This is what romantic love is: if you like someone a whole lot AND you're sexually involved with them, that's romantic love.

CHAPTER 33

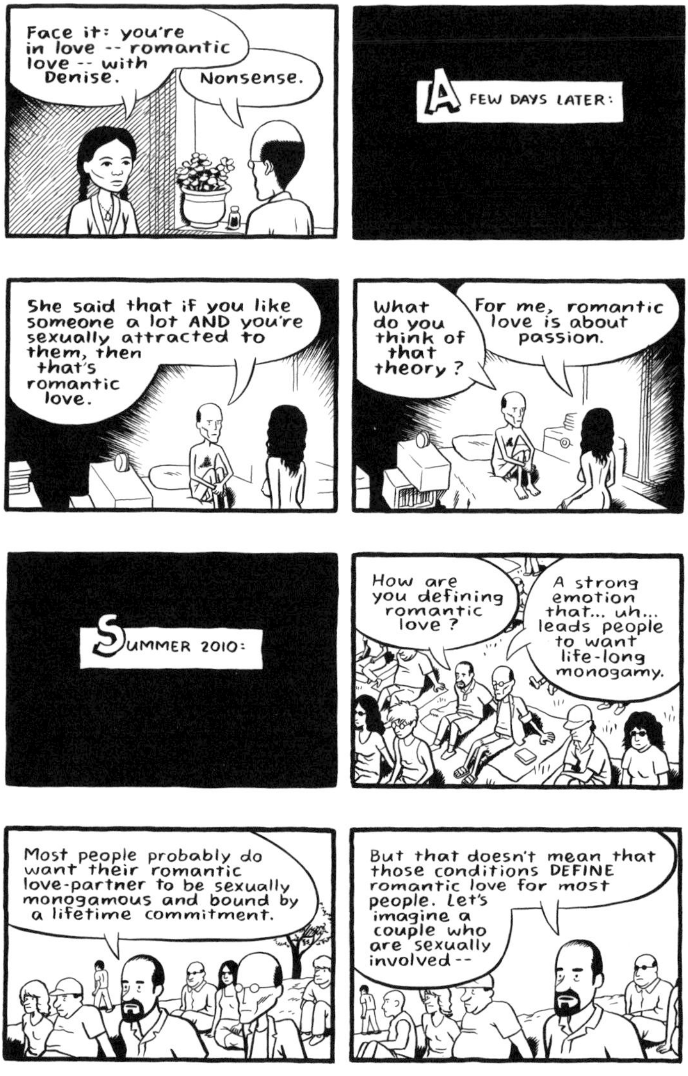

Face it: you're in love -- romantic love -- with Denise.
Nonsense.
A FEW DAYS LATER:
She said that if you like someone a lot AND you're sexually attracted to them, then that's romantic love.
What do you think of that theory?
For me, romantic love is about passion.
SUMMER 2010:
How are you defining romantic love?
A strong emotion that... uh... leads people to want life-long monogamy.
Most people probably do want their romantic love-partner to be sexually monogamous and bound by a lifetime commitment.
But that doesn't mean that those conditions DEFINE romantic love for most people. Let's imagine a couple who are sexually involved --

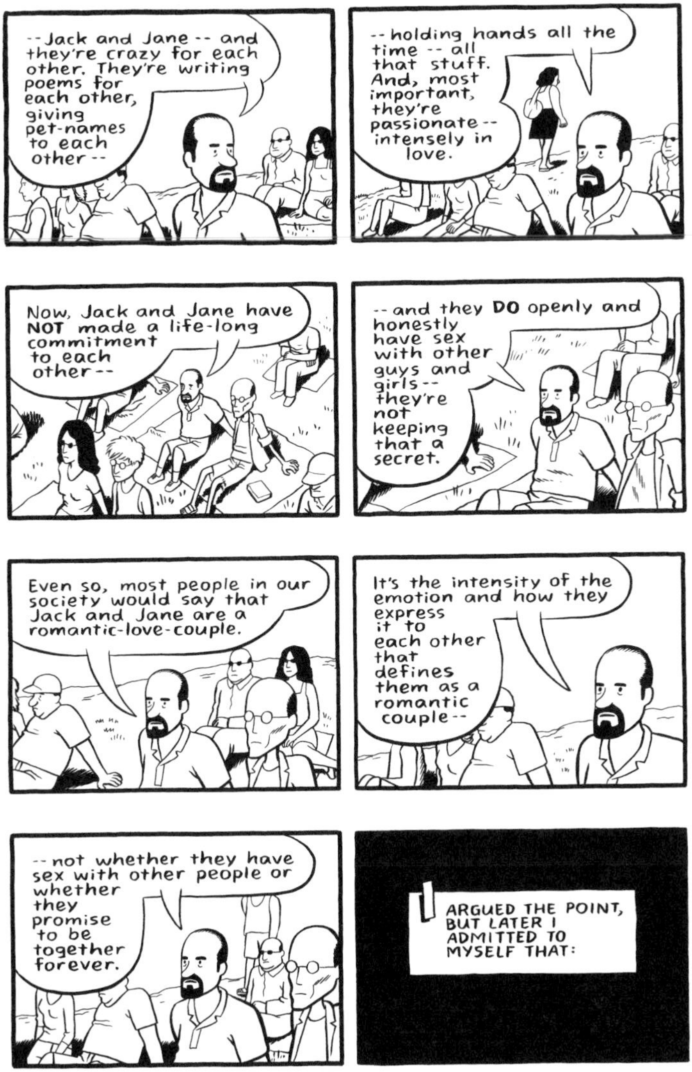

--Jack and Jane-- and they're crazy for each other. They're writing poems for each other, giving pet-names to each other--
--holding hands all the time-- all that stuff. And, most important, they're passionate-- intensely in love.
Now, Jack and Jane have NOT made a life-long commitment to each other--
--and they DO openly and honestly have sex with other guys and girls-- they're not keeping that a secret.
Even so, most people in our society would say that Jack and Jane are a romantic-love-couple.
It's the intensity of the emotion and how they express it to each other that defines them as a romantic couple--
--not whether they have sex with other people or whether they promise to be together forever.
I ARGUED THE POINT, BUT LATER I ADMITTED TO MYSELF THAT:

CHAPTER 33

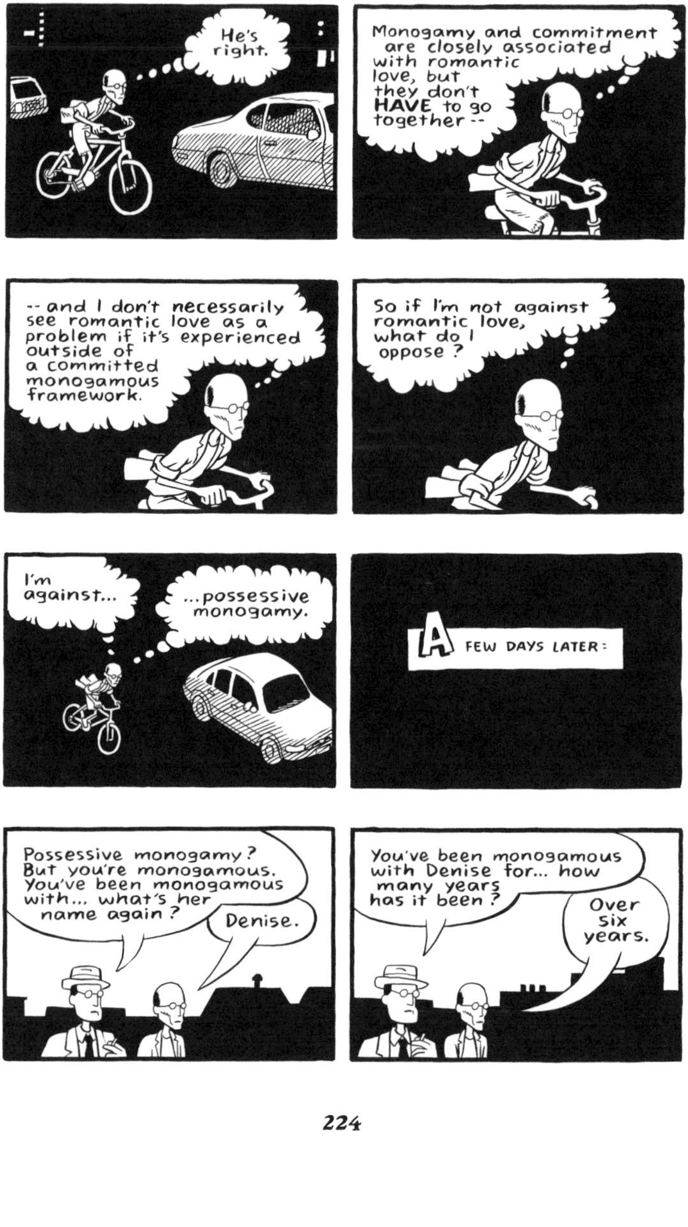
He's right.
Monogamy and commitment are closely associated with romantic love, but they don't **HAVE** to go together --
-- and I don't necessarily see romantic love as a problem if it's experienced outside of a committed monogamous framework.
So if I'm not against romantic love, what do I oppose?
I'm against...
...possessive monogamy.
A FEW DAYS LATER:
Possessive monogamy? But you're monogamous. You've been monogamous with... what's her name again?
Denise.
You've been monogamous with Denise for... how many years has it been?
Over six years.

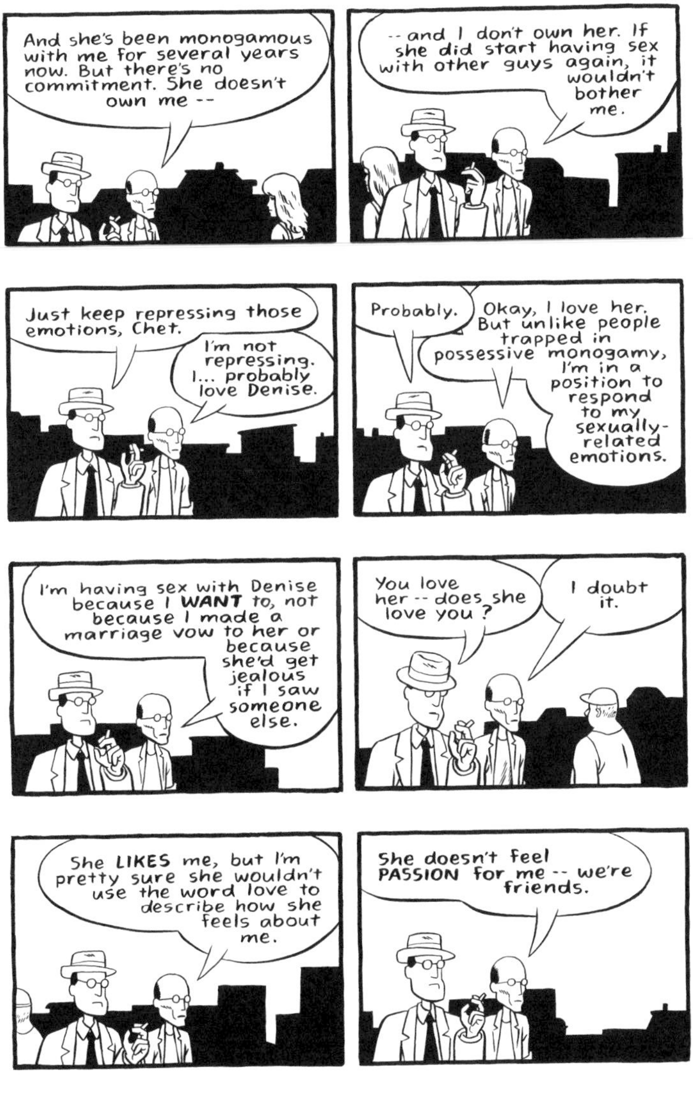
And she's been monogamous with me for several years now. But there's no commitment. She doesn't own me --
-- and I don't own her. If she did start having sex with other guys again, it wouldn't bother me.
Just keep repressing those emotions, Chet.
I'm not repressing. I... probably love Denise.
Probably.
Okay, I love her. But unlike people trapped in possessive monogamy, I'm in a position to respond to my sexually-related emotions.
I'm having sex with Denise because I **WANT** to, not because I made a marriage vow to her or because she'd get jealous if I saw someone else.
You love her -- does she love you?
I doubt it.
She **LIKES** me, but I'm pretty sure she wouldn't use the word love to describe how she feels about me.
She doesn't feel **PASSION** for me -- we're friends.

CHAPTER 33

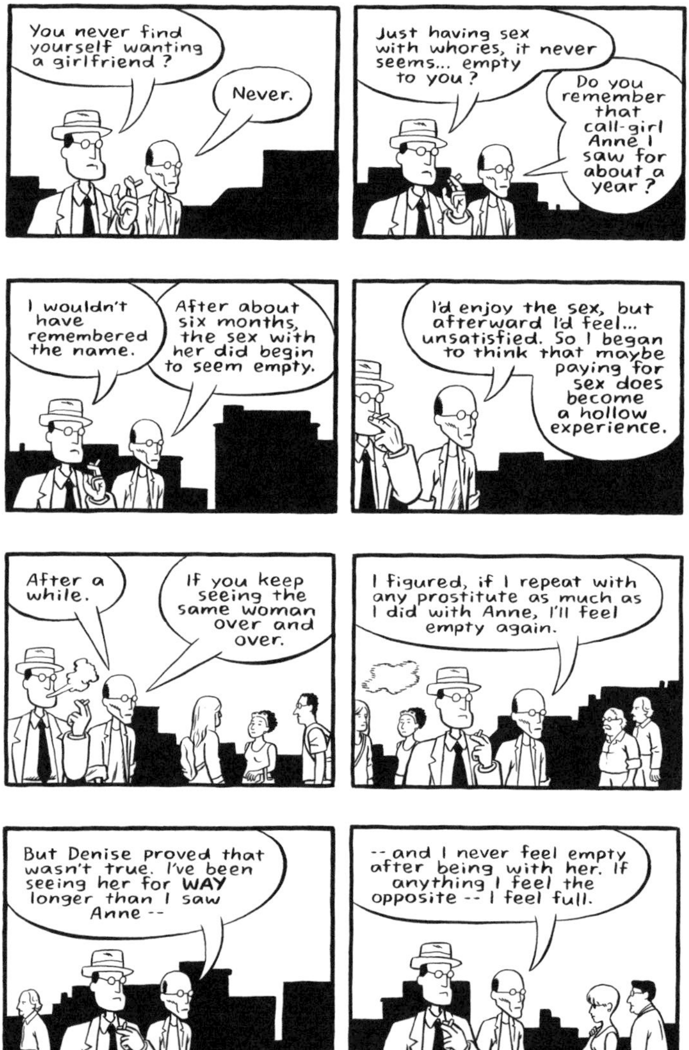

You never find yourself wanting a girlfriend?
Never.
Just having sex with whores, it never seems... empty to you?
Do you remember that call-girl Anne I saw for about a year?
I wouldn't have remembered the name.
After about six months, the sex with her did begin to seem empty.
I'd enjoy the sex, but afterward I'd feel... unsatisfied. So I began to think that maybe paying for sex does become a hollow experience.
After a while.
If you keep seeing the same woman over and over.
I figured, if I repeat with any prostitute as much as I did with Anne, I'll feel empty again.
But Denise proved that wasn't true. I've been seeing her for **WAY** longer than I saw Anne --
-- and I never feel empty after being with her. If anything I feel the opposite -- I feel full.

EMOTIONALLY full?
Uh... something like that. It's something beyond mere sexual satisfaction. Denise is an amazing person.
Anne fulfilled me sexually but not in other ways, even though she was pleasant and likeable.
So paying for sex isn't an empty experience if you're paying the right person for sex.
July 7th 2010
CWOB

AFTERWORD

In a recent conversation with a friend, I mentioned
that "Denise" is no longer a prostitute. He objected,
"What do you mean? Of course she's a prostitute --
you're paying her for sex." I pointed out that she's
monogamous with me and that prostitutes have sex
with multiple men. My friend countered, "That's not
the dictionary definition." I didn't know what the
dictionary definition would be, so I reached over to
my copy of the GAGE CANADIAN DICTIONARY. According to
that source, a prostitute is "a girl or woman who
accepts money to engage in sexual acts with men." I
emphasized the word "men" as I read the passage to
my friend. He conceded the point.

Later, I picked up my WEBSTER'S -- it defined a
prostitute as someone who has "promiscuous" sex for
money. Not all dictionaries agree -- the COLLINS CANAD-
IAN DICTIONARY and the CONCISE OXFORD ENGLISH DICTIONARY
both characterize a prostitute as someone who has sex
for payment, but neither specifies anything about
the number of sexual partners.

Is "Denise" still a prostitute? Am I still a john?

Two people are in a monogamous sexual relationship
that's lasted for years. They care for each other
(even if they wouldn't say they're "in love"). One of
the two assists the other financially. What do you
call such a relationship?

229

AFTERWORD

Ultimately, I don't care what you call us. The significant thing to me is that our relationship should not be against the law. We should be allowed to have sex, and I should be allowed to give her money.

"Denise" isn't the only person depicted in this book whom I love: My brother Gordon Brown lives in Quebec City and lived there throughout the years covered in these pages, which may explain why he's only in two scenes. (The first panel he's in is 57:2.) In 2000, the guy with the hat, Seth, moved to Guelph (a small city about an hour-and-a-half away from Toronto). He comes into the big city on occasion, so we still see each other pretty frequently. Joe Matt moved to Los Angeles in 2003, and Kris Nakamura moved to Vancouver in 2004, so I don't see them much, but I still talk to them on the phone quite often. (Kris's first panel is 8:5.) I'm glad that Sook-Yin Lee still lives in Toronto and that we get to spend a lot of time together.

When I finished drawing PAYING FOR IT, I let the above-mentioned six people read it. I was worried that some of them might want me to change things -- their actions, their dialogue, the way I drew them -- but none of the six asked me to alter a line or word. That doesn't mean they were all completely happy with their portrayals. I did tell them that I would give them space in the book to have their say. Only Seth took me up on that offer. His notes about the scenes he's in are in Appendix 23.

I called Justin Peroff to let him know that he's in the book and to ask him if he wanted to see his scenes. (He appears in panels 7:5 and 7:6.) He was fine with being a character in the story but said he wanted to experience the graphic-novel in its finished printed form.

Not all of my friends are characters in this memoir. The following friends helped me in some way in creating it: Mark Askwith, Peter Birkemoe, Antonella Brion, Robin Ganev, Jeet Heer, Jason Kieffer, Dave Lapp, Adam Litovitz, Catharine Liu, Nick Maandag, Marc Ngui, Magda Wojtyra, Ethan Rilly, Zach Worton, Dave Sim *, Tim Slater, Siu Ta, John Tran, James Turner, Colin Upton, and Tania Van Spyk. None of these people agree with all of the opinions I express in here and some disagree with most of what I say. These friends helped by being willing to discuss and debate the topics of love and prostitution with me. They also helped in various other ways -- pointing out important books to read, proofreading, making design suggestions, discussing approaches to drawing, and in many other ways. I thank them all.

And thanks to everyone at Drawn And Quarterly, particularly Chris Oliveros, Peggy Burns, and Tom Devlin.

APPENDIX 1
THE NORMALIZATION
OF PROSTITUTION

Prostitution is just a form of dating.

There is no regulatory or legal framework for unpaid dating. Nothing happens during paid dates that doesn't happen in unpaid dates. From a legal perspective they should be seen as identical. No regulatory or legal framework is necessary for paid dating.

What I hope we're moving toward is a time when giving and receiving money is part of the normal give-and-take of sexual activity. It won't be what everyone does, but it will become so common that no one will think it odd, disgusting, or unusual if one adult (male or female) pays another adult (male or female) for sex. It will be seen as normal.

I believe that, if prostitution is decriminalized, its normalization will happen relatively quickly -- within a few generations.

When I was born, in 1960, homosexuality was widely seen as "sick" and disgusting. It was illegal to engage in homosexual activity in this country (and probably all of the other "western" countries). In 1967, Pierre Trudeau decriminalized homosexuality in Canada. Other countries began to do the same thing.* The result, forty-something years later, is that homosexuality has become normalized for most people in "the west". It's no longer widely seen as sick or disgusting.

APPENDIX 2
SEXUAL RIGHTS

You've compared homosexuality to prostitution. Gays have a right to have gay sex because they're born gay.
You weren't born a john. Prostitutes aren't born prostitutes.
Prostitutes and johns don't have the sexual rights that gays have.

Hypothetically, let's say that in a few years geneticists will be able to point to a specific gene which causes people to sexually desire members of their own gender: a "gay gene".* Both sides in the nature-versus-nurture debate admit that both environment and in-born characteristics influence behaviour, so even if there is a gay gene which is responsible for most homosexual behaviour, there will probably be at least a few homosexuals who don't have the gene, who became gay through the influence of their environment. Let's say it turns out that 99 % of the homosexual population have the gene and 1 % don't. If gay rights are predicated on being <u>born</u> gay, what do we do if we discover that a few gays were not born gay? Do we say that they don't have the right to have gay sex? Do we force them to have heterosexual sex?

If a lesbian (who was born lesbian) is good friends with a gay man (who was born gay) and they decide to have sex together just to see what male-and-female coitus is like, are they doing something morally wrong? Is the lesbian <u>only</u> allowed to have sex with women? Is the guy <u>only</u> allowed to have sex with men? No, that lesbian and her gay male pal have every right to have sex together. Their in-born sexual orientations don't determine who they're allowed to have sex with -- those orientations don't limit their sexual rights.

Gay rights aren't predicated on being born gay or having the right gene. Gay rights are predicated on choice and consent. If you're a man and you can find another man who consents to have sex with you, it's that consent that gives you the right to have sex with him.

Genetics are irrelevant when it comes to sexual rights. Just as gay rights are based on choice and consent, so are prostitution rights. All sexual rights are based on choice and consent.

APPENDIX 3

MORE ON THE
NORMALIZATION OF PROSTITUTION

It may be difficult for people who haven't given the matter much thought to picture what I'm talking about.

Let's say that prostitution is decriminalized in ten years. Now let's jump ahead to the year 2080. A young woman works in a hat shop -- let's call her Mary. A young man who also works there decides to ask Mary out on a date. They've known each other several months and she likes him, so she says yes, adding that, if he wants to have sex with her, it'll cost an amount of money that she specifies. He doesn't find this shocking -- it's a common request in a situation like this. They go out to dinner and then have sex at either his apartment or hers. He pays her the specified price. The next day, Mary tells her friends about the date. They all have sex for money too, so none of them are shocked. Mary tells her mother. She's not shocked either -- she still gets paid for sex herself. Most people in this future society have paid-sex at least occasionally. There are still a few people who believe in possessive monogamy and only have sex if they fall in love with someone, but most people in 2080 see that as weird, old-fashioned behaviour. A middle-aged guy who also works at the hat shop approaches Mary and suggests a date. She's not interested in older men, so she politely declines. There's no expectation that she has to have sex with anyone who has money. If Mary acquires enough friends-who-pay-for-sex, maybe she'll be able to quit the hat shop job, but until then, the money she makes from sex nicely supplements her income. No one would see Mary as a slut for having multiple sex-partners -- it's seen as normal to have multiple sex-partners.

What about love ? Mary may develop loving feelings

for one, some, or all of her friends-who-pay-for-sex. (Being paid for sex doesn't preclude the possibility that one could love the person paying.) Or she might have a sexual friend she loves who doesn't pay her for sex. Maybe she pays him. (It's common for women to pay men for sex in this society.) Or maybe no money changes hands at all in that particular relationship.

Because it's normal and nothing is secretive about it, Mary can have paid-sex with people she knows -- there isn't the same need to search for strangers who might buy or sell sex. This takes a good deal of the risk out of the activity. Perhaps in this predicted world of 2080 there will still be streetwalkers and brothel-workers who have paid-sex with strangers, but most people will want to have some prior connection with the individuals they get into bed with, just as most people liked that back in 2011.

When young people are told that back in 2011 having sex for money was seen as a shameful thing, it will seem bizarre to them. "It was illegal? Why? It's so... normal."

How likely is it that this will be the way things are in 2080? Not likely at all because governments aren't about to decriminalize prostitution.

APPENDIX 4

YOU OWN YOUR BODY

Your body is your property. Just as you own property like books and clothes, you own your body. You should have the right to do whatever you want with your body (and any other property you own) as long as you respect the property rights of others. (By which I mean: you don't harm or steal anyone else's property, or use fraud or threats of force to acquire it, and you don't use physical force to make someone do something they don't want to do.)

If you respect the property rights of others and treat them with courtesy, you're living a moral life.

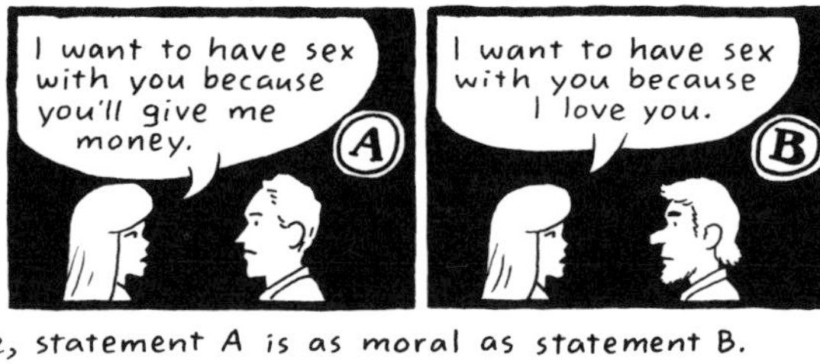
I want to have sex with you because you'll give me money.
A
I want to have sex with you because I love you.
B

To me, statement A is as moral as statement B.

APPENDIX 5
JOHNS DON'T BUY WOMEN

Johns buy women. No man should have the right to buy a woman.

When I buy something -- say, a book -- I take it home and get to keep it for as long as I want. I <u>own</u> it. When I had an appointment with a prostitute, I did not buy her. I paid to have sex with her. Afterward, we'd part company. I didn't get to keep her -- I didn't own her.

APPENDIX 6
POWER

Prostitution is wrong because it gives a man sexual power over a woman. The john gets to dictate what happens.

Just as male prostitutes do, female prostitutes have their rules -- what they will and won't do with clients. Some will have vaginal sex but won't give oral. Others only fellate.* Some let johns perform cunnilingus on them, others don't. Some kiss, some won't. Etcetera. And it's not just about rules -- prostitutes do have sexual power in their interactions with their clients. Sexual desirability is power. When a man thinks a woman is attractive, he wants to please her. Also, sex-workers can and do speak up if they don't like what's happening. "Millie's" request in panel 218:4 is an example. I remember a similar incident with "Anne":

Chester, my legs are getting tired. Could we change positions?

Of course.

A few months ago "Denise" told me that I was being a bit too aggressive sexually, so I toned down what I was doing.

Are there jerky johns who would disregard a prostitute's mid-coital request or suggestion? I'm sure there are. But there are also guys who ignore similar requests and suggestions in unpaid sexual situations, so if we criminalize paid sex because some guys are boorish in bed, we should criminalize unpaid sex for the same reason.

Here's a sex-worker on the subject:

> My clients are invariably polite. [...] I control what I wish to do and set my limits, which are always respected. [... I]n four years at various agencies, I can remember only once having to slap a man who was too insistent. (He was immediatly pushed out the door [.)**]

Prostitutes aren't passive puppets, and most johns aren't dictators.

APPENDIX 7

MONEY'S INFLUENCE

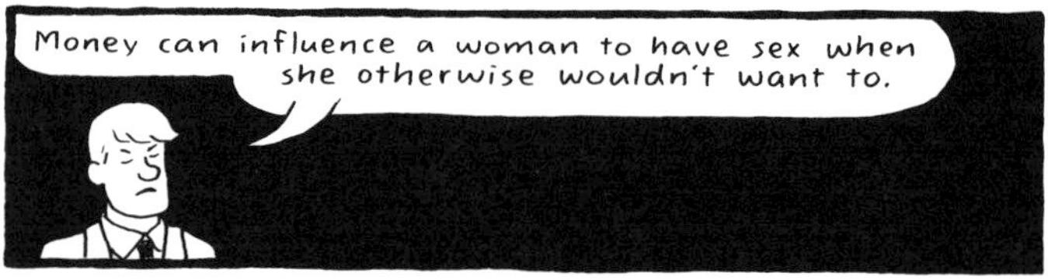
Money can influence a woman to have sex when she otherwise wouldn't want to.

If that means that the influence of money is bad, then it also means that romantic love is bad. Many people in love relationships have sex they don't want to have.

I don't want to have sex with this guy, but I need the money, so I will.

I don't want to have sex right now, but he's my boyfriend, and I love him, so I will.

I no longer feel desire for my husband, but for the sake of our marriage I'll have sex with him.

There is no moral difference between the above three circumstances.

APPENDIX 8
SELF-RESPECT

Prostitution should be illegal because it destroys the self-respect of prostitutes.

Many gays prior to the sexual revolution experienced shame, depression, guilt, and disgust about being gay. That doesn't mean that homosexuality is wrong, it means that, at a certain point in time, homosexuality was reviled, and many gays internalized the gay-negative values of the culture they lived in. Today, many prostitutes internalize the whoring-is-bad attitude of the culture we live in. That doesn't mean that sex-work is bad, it means we have to do for it what we did for homosexuality: decriminalize it.

Not all prostitutes internalize the negative cultural values regarding paid sex -- many claim to like the work, and even that it improved their self-esteem.

Phyllis Luman Metal wrote:

> When I first charged for it, I had much more self respect and self worth than I ever had before. I felt appreciated.[*]

According to Jane of New York:

237

Before I started escorting, I had a few boy-friends [....] They weren't shy about flat out telling me that I didn't look good because I was too tall and too thin. [... M]ost of [my clients] helped me learn two very important things: that I am beautiful just the way I am, and that my pleasure is important too. When I started working, I met all these [clients] who thought I was gorgeous, model-like, even. They loved my small breasts and impossibly long legs. They told me I was beautiful over and over again until I understood it. [* *]

AnaNicole of Berkeley, California, addresses a particular john:

Through my sessions with you, I have acquired invaluable self-esteem in regards to my body, sex appeal, and service. I have grown as a sexual being not only in my profession, but in my real life as well. [* *]

Veronica Monét contends that:

Sex work has been empowering and liberating for me. My self-esteem has improved drastic-ally in the last six years since I entered the sex industry. [...] I am not degraded by sex. I am not a resource or property that can be devalued through use. I am not hurt by such terms as "slut" or "whore." I proudly assert that I am both. [*ı*]

APPENDIX 9
CHOICE

When they confront female sex-workers who claim to have freely chosen their profession, anti-prostitutionists (who are often feminists) are put in the position of looking like they're trying to restrict the freedom of a group of women. Several of these anti-prostitutionists have decided that the way out of this quandary is to assert that choice is not possible when it comes to sex-work.

Sheila Jeffreys, a feminist, argues this in her book THE IDEA OF PROSTITUTION:

The word <u>choice</u> is not appropriate for a woman whose "choice" is between low-paid service work which does not fit in with child-care, and the chance of a better income with more flexible hours through the violation of her body. [Jeffreys, pp. 155, 156.]

This hypothetical woman may not feel that prostitution is a violation. Some women would, others wouldn't. More to the point, if it's not possible for an attractive single mom to choose between low-pay work and prostitution, then why are there attractive single mothers who work at minimum-wage jobs? Some women can't stomach the thought of having paid-sex with strangers, so they choose the drudgery of working for low pay. Meanwhile, there are other moms who choose sex-work over low wages and are happy to be able to improve the material circumstances that their children live in. If two people face the same problem and make two different decisions about how to solve that problem, then choices are being made. That doesn't mean the choices are easy, but a difficult choice is still a choice.

When girls have been sexually abused in childhood, as prostituted women often have, it is hard to see them as having a really free choice. [Jeffreys, p. 153.]

I think we're stepping into dangerous territory when we start saying that certain adults are not allowed to make choices because they had bad childhoods. If women-who-were-abused-in-childhood aren't competent to make the choice to engage in paid-sex, then are they competent to make other sexual choices? Regardless of what happened to them in childhood, adults should have the right to make sexual choices, including choices that Sheila Jeffreys would disapprove of.

When prostituted women themselves use the language of "choice", they can be seen to be engaging in what deviancy sociologists call "neutralising techniques". Sociologists use this term to describe the way in which socially despised and marginalised groups create rationalisations which enable them to survive their marginal condition. Such techniques may be employed because the only alternative may be the painful one of self-contempt. [Jeffreys, p. 137]

Let's contrast that opinion with the following items written by two women who are or were sex-workers.

I can say for the first time in my life that I love my job. It's the least exploited I have ever been

239

at work, for adequate money this time. [...] I'm even able to enjoy the work itself, not just its fruits, and have come to appreciate all body types as long as they're clean and kind [.*]

It has all come down to choice for me. I chose to see some clients and I chose not to see others. I chose what sexual activities I was willing to engage in for pay and I chose what was not "on the menu." I asserted my boundaries and I honored the unique sexuality of individuals. [**]

Jeffreys says that prostitutes like these are rationalizing and that they actually feel self-contempt. Unless Jeffreys is alleging that she has psychic powers, she can't know if a particular prostitute feels self-contempt. When you have to resort to claiming to know what your ideological opponents are secretly feeling, you've run out of good arguments.

To see how desperate Jeffreys can get, read the following:

Oppression cannot effectively be gauged according to the degree of "consent", since even in slavery there was some consent if consent is defined as inability to see, or feel entitled to, any alternative. [Jeffreys, p. 135.]

Jeffreys is surely the only person on the planet who defines consent this way.

A person is bound in heavy iron chains. In that moment there is no alternative to being bound by chains, but that does not mean that the person is consenting to being bound. Not having an alternative to a situation does not mean that you are choosing to be in that situation. You face choices when you have alternatives (like the one between a low-wage job and prostitution). Slaves didn't choose to be slaves.

Feminists have accepted that choice is possible when it comes to a different, difficult subject: abortion. The feminist position (and I agree with it) is that women own their bodies and therefore each woman has the right to choose to get an abortion if she gets pregnant. This is called being "pro-choice". Feminists should be consistent on the subject of choice. If a woman has the right to choose to have an abortion, she should also have the right to choose to have sex for money. It's her body, it's her right.

240

APPENDIX 10
VIOLENCE

Jeffreys and some other feminists contend that the relationship between a prostitute and a john is always a violent one. Jeffreys quotes Evelina Giobbe:

> Prostitution is sexual abuse because prostitutes are subjected to any number of sexual acts that in any other context, acted against any other woman, would be labelled assaultive or, at the very least, unwanted and coerced.[*]

It's my impression, reading accounts by johns and prostitutes, that paid-sex is usually pretty much the same as unpaid-sex. Certainly I never did anything sexual with a prostitute that I hadn't done with my girlfriends. The things I like sexually are (as far as I can gather) pretty normal and not at all kinky. (Not that I think that kinky sex between consenting adults is wrong.) My girlfriends didn't experience sex with me as abusive or assaultive, so it's not true that the sex I had with prostitutes would, "in any other context, [with] any other woman, [...] be labelled assaultive". Did prostitutes like having sex with me the way my girlfriends did ? No, probably not. ** But that's not Jeffreys' and Giobbe's point. Even if that was their point, it would be a leap to say that, because someone isn't enjoying a sexual encounter, they're therefore experiencing it as assaultive or coercive.

Jeffreys sees sexual harassment as a form of sexual violence.*¹* She gives examples of sexual harassment:

> [...] leering, menacing, staring and sexual gestures [...] whistles, use of innuendo and gossip, sexual joking, propositioning [...] unwanted proximity [... Jeffreys, p. 264.]

Looking at that list, it becomes clear how Jeffreys can think that prostitution is a form of violence. She doesn't use the word "violence" the way other people do. If you know that by standing close to someone you're making them uncomfortable, then it's inconsiderate and rude to continue to stand in their proximity. Still, that doesn't make "unwanted proximity" violent. Sexual jokes can be insensitive, but jokes aren't a form of violence.

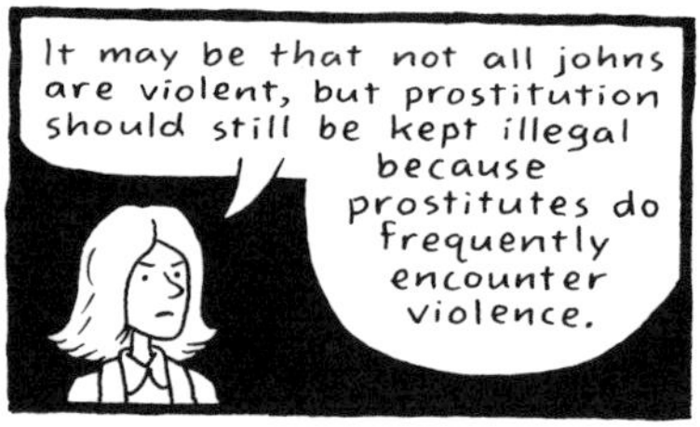
It may be that not all johns are violent, but prostitution should still be kept illegal because prostitutes do frequently encounter violence.

Not all prostitutes encounter violence * but, yes, many do. That doesn't mean that prostitution should be illegal. When a taxi driver is stabbed or shot, no one advocates that driving a cab should be criminalized. Each person should have the right to determine for him-or-herself the amount of risk he-or-she is willing to take for a particular job.

Also, keeping prostitution illegal makes the problem worse, not better.

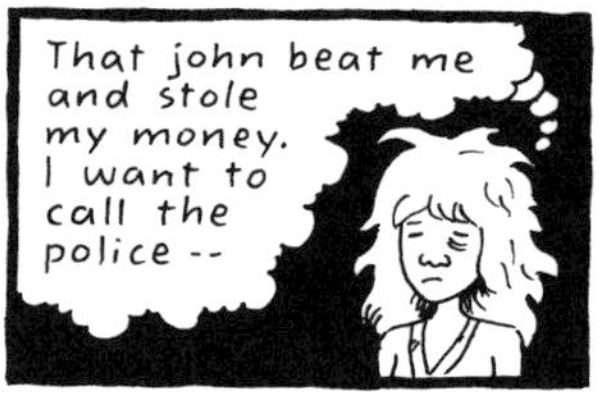
That john beat me and stole my money. I want to call the police --

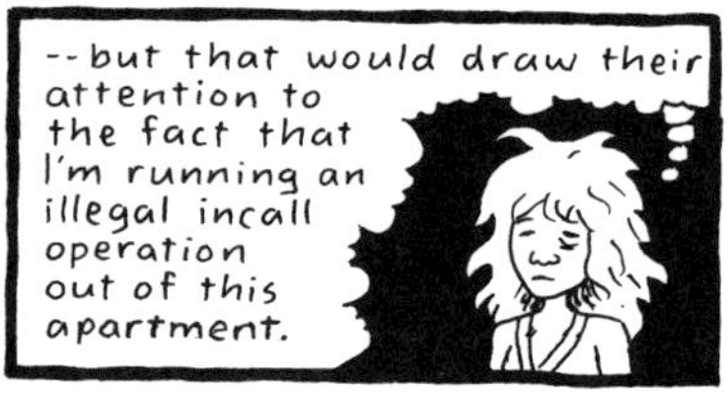
--but that would draw their attention to the fact that I'm running an illegal incall operation out of this apartment.

Decriminalizing prostitution will make it more likely that a sex-worker would report this sort of crime. Of course decriminalization won't completely irradicate violence against prostitutes, but it will give them an option to deal with that violence.

APPENDIX 11

SEXUAL OBJECTIFICATION

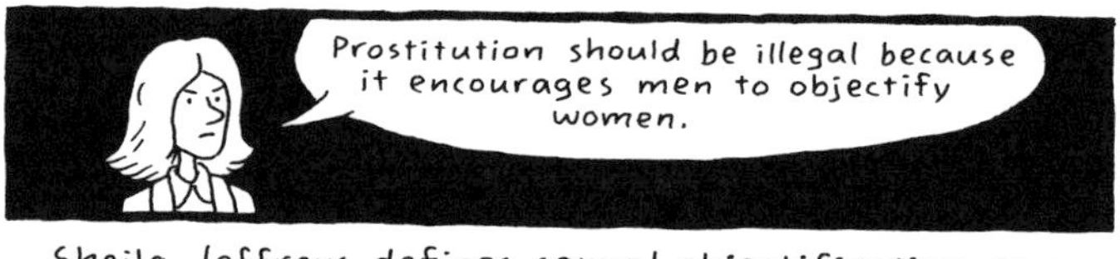
Prostitution should be illegal because it encourages men to objectify women.

Sheila Jeffreys defines sexual objectification as a form of emotional indifference.* Is it wrong for people who are emotionally indifferent to each other to have sex? Should we make unpaid one-night-stands illegal?

I actually don't think prostitution does encourage emotional indifference. Any time a john starts to forget that he's dealing with real people, an incident happens like the one I show in panels 60:8 to 66:2 which brings

the guy back to the realization that he's in bed with
someone whose feelings he has to take into account.
There may be some insensitive johns who fail to recognize that responsibility, but I don't think it's paying for
sex that <u>causes</u> them to be insensitive.
   I felt a variety of emotional responses to the sex-
workers I saw. I was never completely emotionally
indifferent to any of them. I was less concerned about
what they felt when they didn't seem to care what I
felt. "Yvette" (Chapter 17) would be an example, but I
still didn't want her to feel badly about our encounter.
Most of the prostitutes I was with I felt at least some
affection for. Several of them I really liked. A few of
them I genuinely respected. With "Denise", emotional
indifference is the opposite of what I feel. If paying
for sex causes a man to feel increasingly emotionally
indifferent to the women he's having sex with, then
by the time I started seeing "Denise", I shouldn't have
been able to have any emotional response to her.
   I think it might be possible that paying for sex could
lead a man to greater emotional sensitivity, at least
for some johns -- those who are open to the possibility
that they might have things they could be learning from
encounters with sex-workers.

APPENDIX 12
HUMAN TRAFFICKING
AND SEX-SLAVES

   There seems to be some confusion about the term "human
trafficking". When I originally heard it several years ago,
it referred to transporting migrants across borders illegally.
Lately I've heard and seen the expression used interchangeably with "pimping" as if they mean the same thing. There
are times when certain traffickers do things that are
similar to what pimps do, but I see no reason to blur the
distinctions, so I'm going to hold to the original meaning
of human trafficking for this appendix.
   Most people who are trafficked <u>want</u> to be trafficked.
They're from poor countries and want to come to richer
countries either for the economic opportunities or because
they want to travel. Some of them have bad experiences
while being trafficked -- others don't and are happy
that there's a way to get to where they want to go.*
In the majority of cases, human trafficking has nothing to do with prostitution. (According to one source,
"just 4 percent [of trafficking] involves the sex
industry".**) In the cases where prostitution is
involved, many of the women choose to be trafficked
knowing they'll be working as prostitutes in the country
they'll be taken to. Some do not make that choice and

are forced to work as prostitutes against their will. For the sake of clarity I'm going to use the term "sex-slave" to refer to trafficked females who are forced to have paid-sex.

To judge by accents, four of the prostitutes I saw were not born in Canada: "Angelina" (Chapter 3), "Amanda" (Chapter 7), "Arlene" (Chapter 27), and "Laura" (Chapter 29). (I consider whether any of these women were sex-slaves in the notes section.) The last of the four was "Laura" -- I saw her on December 12th 2002. I wasn't aware of the existence of sex-slavery in Canada until I heard an interview about the subject on C·B·C Radio on December 16th 2003,*¹* so it never even occurred to me to wonder if "Angelina", "Amanda", "Arlene", and "Laura" were sex-slaves. If I ever do find myself with a foreign-born prostitute again, I'm sure I'll ask myself if she's been forced to do the work. If I have strong reasons to suspect that she has been, I'll ask if there's anything I can do to help her and will offer to call the police on her behalf. As a john who's not married and is open and "out" about paying for sex I probably have more options about how I could help in such situations. Many johns, worried about their wives finding out, wouldn't want to phone the cops.

Men who pay for sex are creating a demand for sex-slaves.

In order to stop that demand we have to criminalize paying for sex. It should be illegal to be a john.

Let's say a certain shoe company uses slave labour to manufacture its shoes -- should we criminalize the wearing of shoes in order to stem the demand for slave-made shoes? No, wearing shoes and creating a demand for shoes is not in itself wrong, and manufacturing shoes is not wrong when free adults consent to do it. This hypothetical shoe company would probably contract out the work -- those contractors and anyone at the company who was aware of the slavery should be the people held legally responsible for the problem, not purchasers of the shoes, who wouldn't know about the slaves.

I don't want to have sex with sex-slaves. When I hire a prostitute I hope that she's a free person who has chosen the work. If I found out that a prostitute I had hired was a sex-slave, I would be willing to try to help her. Most johns don't want to hire sex-slaves. There is no significant consumer demand for sex-slaves. Punishing johns for something we don't want and don't knowingly participate in is misplacing the blame -- especially when, in Canada, the majority of prostitutes are not sex-slaves, so that johns can be reasonably certain that most of the time we're with sex-workers who have chosen the profession.

A further point: if we criminalize the purchase of sexual services, then police resources will go into tracking down and identifying johns. Those resources would be better utilized in tracking down sex-slavers and freeing sex-slaves.

If we licence female prostitutes, we'll be able to make sure that only women-who-have-the-legal-right-to-work-in-Canada work as prostitutes.

We'll be able to identify who the sex-slaves are.

Licence-checking officials would go into legal brothels and check the licences of the sex-workers.

The sex-slaves at the brothels wouldn't have licences, so they'd be easily identified and easily saved.

People who make this argument are ignoring a big complicating factor: the black market. If prostitutes are licenced, most Canadian-born prostitutes will choose to work in the black market without licences. (Prostitutes have strong reasons for protecting their privacy, particularly from the government, which has NEVER worked in their best interests.) The black market would become huge -- too large to be controlled. Sex-slaves would be forced to work in the black market, not in legal brothels. Nevertheless, the majority of prostitutes in the black market would be free Canadians who choose the work. Identifying which prostitutes in the black market are citizens and which are illegal-immigrants-who-might-be-sex-slaves would be a never-ending and very expensive task for the authorities. Licencing would make it no easier to identify sex-slaves than it is now.

On top of that, as I've argued elsewhere in this book, the idea of licencing consensual sex between adults is an offensive restriction on our sexual civil rights. Two consenting adults should not need to acquire a government-issued document to have sex. Freeing sex-slaves should be a priority for our law enforcement officers, but in attempting to do so they should have to operate within parameters that respect the civil rights of the citizenry (just as the police have to operate within those parameters when they deal with other crimes).

APPENDIX 13
PIMPING

Why are you only defining foreign-born women as sex-slaves?

Canadian women who are forced by pimps to have paid-sex are also sex-slaves.

It's widely recognized that when a pimp wants to lure a woman into prostitution, he doesn't use force -- he romances her. If he's successful, she sees him as her boyfriend. This isn't slavery, it's a voluntary relationship. I don't have a problem with voluntary relationships between adults. If a pimp beats a prostitute, I hope she would choose to leave the guy and get the police to arrest him for assault, but I also think she has the right to stay with him if she wants to.

Canadian women are rarely kidnapped and forced into prostitution the way some female illegal immigrants are. This is in large part because it's easier for Canadian women to escape. A Canadian woman who was kidnapped and forced into prostitution within Canada probably wouldn't hesitate to call the Canadian police if she got her hands on a phone -- every sympathetic john with a cell-phone would be an escape opportunity. (I don't have a cell-phone, but the sex-workers who came to my apartment would frequently ask if they could use my phone, and I always let them.) On the other hand, an illegal immigrant might worry that the police in Canada are as corrupt as the ones back in her home country. She could have concerns about being deported. She might not even know that the emergency number is 9-1-1. A Canadian woman could probably also call family or friends for help. An illegal immigrant's family and friends are probably on another continent. As for Canadian women being kidnapped in a foreign country -- it could happen in a country like Somalia where _every_ "western" person would be at risk, but it rarely if ever happens in countries with any kind of tourist industry. The authorities there don't want those tourist dollars going away. Bad things occasionally happen to Canadian

246

tourists in foreign places, but if Canadian women were regularly and systematically being kidnapped in a particular country, it would be noticed and our government and media would start warning people to avoid that area of the world.

Johns can be reasonably certain that if a prostitute has a Canadian accent, she is not a sex-slave.

How many of the sex-workers I saw had pimps? Five of them told me enough about their lives in enough detail that I was convinced they didn't have pimps. As for the rest, I don't know. It's worth noting that many prostitutes work without pimps, and that incall and outcall workers are less likely than streetwalkers to have pimps.

APPENDIX 14
EXPLOITATION

Maybe not all prostitutes are slaves, but they are all exploited.

People are exploited when they're not fairly compensated for the work they do. Yes, some prostitutes are exploited when most or all of their money is taken by pimps, but not all prostitutes are exploited.

"Denise" began working as a prostitute when she was an adult. She chose to do so -- no pimp or trafficker forced her. She charged over $200 an hour. The money she earned was hers alone -- she didn't have to split it with anyone. After a few years, when she decided she wanted to quit prostitution, nobody forced her to continue to work -- the decision was hers alone to make. I don't see how anyone could look at those facts and conclude that her condition was similar to slavery or that she was exploited. She was and is a free person, making choices that make sense to her.

APPENDIX 15
THE COMMERCIALIZATION
OF THE SACRED

Sex is sacred. It shouldn't be commercialized.

If commercialization of the sacred is wrong, then you'd better tell churches to stop passing the collection plate and bookstores to stop selling the Bible. Speaking of bookstores, I love reading -- I see the transmission of knowledge and wisdom in print as a sacred activity. I'm glad that we've commercialized the production and distribution of books and made them easy to acquire. It's because I do see sex as sacred and potentially spiritual that I believe in commercializing it and making this potentially holy experience more easily available to all. Commercialization is not something disgusting that contaminates. It's just a way of making goods and services easily available, whether those goods and services are religious, sexual, or both at the same time.

APPENDIX 16
NEVADA

The profession is legal and regulated in Nevada. Sex-workers are licenced and have to work in brothels. My hostility to licencing and regulating prostitution grew stronger while I read Alexa Albert's BROTHEL: MUSTANG RANCH AND ITS WOMEN. She did her research in Nevada back in the 1990s, but I doubt that the kind of control the state's prostitutes have to put up with is much different now.

The mobility of the sex-workers at the Mustang Ranch was limited -- for the amount of time they were on schedule (which could be days or weeks) they had to sleep at the brothel. They were not allowed to go home at the end of a shift. (Albert, p. 45.) They often wouldn't see their children for weeks at a time. (Albert, p. 45.)

> Brothel management and law enforcement [...] try to limit prostitutes' contact with local communities. Mustang Ranch, for example, required a runner, or escort, to accompany prostitutes on errands to town at the women's own expense -- $5 - $10 per errand or stop. [Albert, pp. 46, 47.]

> Each bedroom was equipped with a hidden intercom system that cashiers used to eavesdrop on women's negotiations [. Albert, p. 47.]

APPENDICES

> [M]anagement conducted unannounced room
> searches [. Albert, p. 47.]

> When a woman refused a customer willing to pay
> the house minimum, management expected a
> reasonable excuse (e.g., that he refused to wear a
> condom). While [a prostitute] would negotiate her
> own deals and could raise her prices to deter
> unappealing customers, management would raise
> its eyebrows if she did this too often.
> [Albert, p. 49.]

Openly reading a book while waiting for clients to show
up was not allowed. (Albert, p. 150.) Telephone use was
restricted. (Albert, p. 78.)*

When I read Albert's book I was already seeing
"Denise", and I ended up knowing quite a bit about
her life. I couldn't help but contrast "Denise's" freedom with the restricted lives of the Nevada
sex-workers.

I don't want to reveal whether or not "Denise" has kids,
but IF she does, she would have been able to live with them
during the years she worked as a prostitute. At the end of
the day she got to sleep in her own bed (or whatever other
bed she chose to sleep in). She had the mobility of a regular
Canadian citizen -- she didn't need a "runner" to accompany
her when she went shopping, or went to a movie, or whatever. Her negotiations with her clients were their business
alone -- no one was listening in on them. No one conducted
unannounced searches of her home. She could (and did)
refuse to see clients if she wanted to. She didn't need to
explain or justify her reasons to management -- there was
no management. Between clients she could read a book. No
one restricted her access to the telephone.

Conditions at other Nevada brothels could be even worse
than the ones at the Mustang:

> For example, the owner of a brothel in southern
> Nevada allegedly confiscated women's personal supplies
> (condoms, lubricants, nylons) and required them to
> repurchase everything directly from the brothel at
> inflated prices, like sharecroppers or miners buying
> from the company store. And "his" working girls had to
> buy their meals à la carte from the brothel kitchen,
> where slabs of tomato cost $2, a box of frozen vege-
> tables $5, and a hamburger $7 [...]. "The owner took
> advantage of the fact we were confined to his
> brothel," one prostitute divulged to me. "Nothing was
> free. Everything was overpriced. [" Albert, p. 62.]

Those who tout the advantages of the Nevada licencing

system haven't really thought about the difference between living in an oppressive situation and living in freedom.

Prostitutes should be allowed to set up brothels, but the Nevada system is evil. Any government scheme to licence sex would be evil.

APPENDIX 17
DRUGS

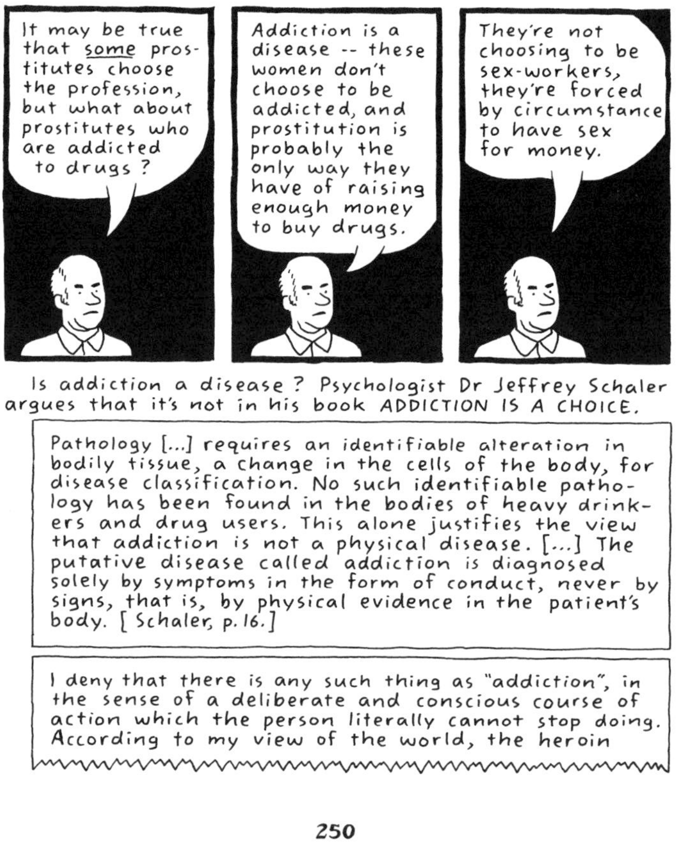
It may be true that some prostitutes choose the profession, but what about prostitutes who are addicted to drugs?
Addiction is a disease -- these women don't choose to be addicted, and prostitution is probably the only way they have of raising enough money to buy drugs.
They're not choosing to be sex-workers, they're forced by circumstance to have sex for money.

Is addiction a disease? Psychologist Dr Jeffrey Schaler argues that it's not in his book ADDICTION IS A CHOICE.

> Pathology [...] requires an identifiable alteration in bodily tissue, a change in the cells of the body, for disease classification. No such identifiable pathology has been found in the bodies of heavy drinkers and drug users. This alone justifies the view that addiction is not a physical disease. [...] The putative disease called addiction is diagnosed solely by symptoms in the form of conduct, never by signs, that is, by physical evidence in the patient's body. [Schaler, p. 16.]

> I deny that there is any such thing as "addiction", in the sense of a deliberate and conscious course of action which the person literally cannot stop doing. According to my view of the world, the heroin

addict can stop injecting himself with heroin, the
alcohol addict can stop himself from swallowing
whiskey, and so forth. People are responsible for
their deliberate and conscious behavior.
[Schaler, p. XV.]

Schaler points out that many people are able to quit
supposedly addictive drugs, but rather than see this
as evidence that people can choose to do or not do
these drugs, proponents of (what Schaler calls) "the
'involuntary addiction' ideology" claim that those who
continue to do the drugs are the ones who have the
disease of addiction.

Notice that according to this way of thinking, individuals demonstrate their inability to make a choice
simply by making the "wrong" choice, the one we
wish they hadn't made. [Schaler, p. XV.]

It's probably bad for your body if you choose to smoke
crack or inject heroin, but it's your body and you should
have the right to do what you want with it (including
unhealthy things) so long as you respect the property
rights of others.

APPENDIX 18
MARRIAGE

Prostitution weakens the institution of marriage.

Yes, it probably does. I don't have a problem with that
since I think marriage is an evil institution. I hope that
fewer people will see possessive monogamy as an ideal.
You should be in a sexual relationship with a particular
person, not because you made a vow at some point in
the past, but because right-now-in-the-present you _want_
to be in a sexual relationship with that person.

What about children ? We need marriage because we need a social structure in which children can be raised.

Even if marriage and sexual fidelity disappear from human society, people would still want to have children, and most parents would love their children, just as most parents do now. If marriage collapses, new social and legal structures will arise. Perhaps, instead of a marriage contract, prospective parents would sign a child-raising contract that would spell out what sort of support and care each would provide for the kid.

APPENDIX 19
TAXATION

Prostitutes should pay taxes.

I have an extreme take on Trudeau's famous statement that "The state has no place in the bedrooms of the nation" * (as long as the people in those bedrooms are consenting adults). It's not just the Justice Department and law enforcement that shouldn't be in there, NO branch of government should be in those bedrooms -- that includes the Tax Department. Income earned from sexual activities should not be taxed. Sex is too intimate, too sacred -- people should not have to expose their bed-lives to the prying eyes of tax-collecting bureaucrats.

Prostitution is a business -- businesses are taxed.

Religious organizations get tax breaks despite the fact that they generate income. We see their business identities as secondary to their primary sacred identities. Prostitution should be seen as primarily sacred and only secondarily as a business. Indeed, perhaps we shouldn't see it as a business at all. Perhaps we should see the money given to prostitutes as gifts, not payments.

APPENDIX 20

STREETWALKING

I think that when people are on private property they should be free from government interference and regulation as long as they're respecting the property rights of others. But on public property (streets, sidewalks, public parks, etc.) I do think that a greater degree of regulation is justified. For example, I see nothing wrong with compelling people to obey traffic-signals. More relevant to the topic at hand is where you can engage in business. Obviously I don't think it's wrong for a business-person to sell things on private property (typically a storefront either owned or rented by the business-person). But selling things on public property is different. If we let anyone set up sales-stands or tables on public property, there would be all sorts of problems. For one thing, the sidewalks would quickly fill up with business-people looking to avoid the cost of owning or renting storefronts, and all of their tables and stands would get in the way of pedestrians. For another, without the clearly defined ownership of property that the private property system provides, there would be turf-wars.

Hey! I always set up my table on this corner!
Sorry, pal! This is public property -- you don't own this spot, and I got here first today!
Fuckin' bastard!
Hey! Ow!

That said, I do think that people who have a "mobile" business that can be conducted on two legs, with no stands or tables, should be allowed to sell goods or services on the street. The Toronto writer Crad Kilodney sold his books on the street for many years without inconveniencing anyone.* To me, these are the relevant questions regarding streetwalkers:

① "Should we let prostitutes walk or stand on sidewalks?" Well, of course -- everyone who's not in jail or under house arrest should be allowed to use sidewalks.

② "Should they be allowed to talk to people?" Well, of course -- it's a simple matter of free speech.

Prostitutes shouldn't have the right to verbally harass people.

Being asked if I want a blow-job for twenty bucks is not harassment, it's just a question. If a prostitute won't take no for an answer and follows me down the street, repeatedly offering her services, that's harass-ment, but it's not a common problem.

Allowing street solicitation will make prostitution more visible.

That's the price of living in a free society. You have to be tolerant of other people as long as they're not harming anyone and are going about their business in a reasonably civil and polite way. In the past, the sight of two men holding hands or kissing in public would have been upsetting to many people. Now that gay rights are widely accepted, homophobes have to tolerate seeing gay behaviour in public. Homophobes don't like it, but that's the price of living in a free society.

APPENDIX 21
MALE PROSTITUTION

Anti-prostitutionists are focused on why women shouldn't be prostitutes. They ignore the existence of male prostitutes largely because anti-prostitution argu-ments would sound ridiculous if applied to men. As a culture we see men as being in control of their sexuality, so we accept that men can choose sex-work. We're not worried that a man is putting himself in a potentially risky situation because we accept that men do that.

Anti-prostitutionists have a paternalistic attitude toward women.

APPENDIX 22
LICENCING AND WORKING AT HOME

I've already made points similar to the following ones -- I apologize for sounding repetitious, but I want to empha-size why it's wrong to constrain a prostitute's choices.

If we make it mandatory for prostitutes to have licences to work, not all of them will bother to acquire those licences. If something bad happens to an unlicenced sex-worker (like, if a john beats him-or-her) he-or-she will be less likely to call the police because he-or-she won't want to admit to working without a licence.

Sex-workers should also have the right to work out of their homes for the same reason. It's probably safer for prostitutes to work collectively in brothels, but if we make that the only legal option, there <u>will</u> be sex-workers who choose to work out of their homes, and if they get beat up, they'll be less likely to call the cops because they won't want to report that they're working illegally at home.

I want <u>every</u> prostitute who is the victim of a crime to be able to call the police without fearing that there might be negative consequences for not having the right paper-work or for working in the "wrong" place.

APPENDIX 23
SETH'S NOTES

As I mentioned in the afterword, Seth has written notes regarding some of the scenes he's in.

PANELS 10:3, 4   I may have believed Chet was repressing the expected emotions back then, but my opinion has altered over the years. I often jokingly refer to Chet as "the robot". In posing a question to him I might quip, "Perhaps I should ask a person who has actual human emotions instead." The truth is, Chester seems to have a very limited emotional range compared to most people. There does seem to be something wrong with him. He's definitely an oddball. That said, he is also the kindest, gentlest and most deeply thoughtful oddball I know. Perhaps he is missing something in his emotional makeup, perhaps not. Who can say what is natural and what is learned behaviour? I'll say this -- he <u>really</u> doesn't appear to be suffering. You can't argue with that.

87:5 - 88:6   Chet's pretty hard on the idea of romantic relationships. I agree with him that for the most part they are difficult to maintain. Look around the culture and you will see that people have a hard time finding meaningful and positive long term romantic relationships. That said, I'm not so cynical as he. Chet, I suspect, thinks it is essentially impossible. While the odds are certainly against most couples, there are plenty of examples of long lasting good pairings. If you ask me, it is more a problem of human nature than romantic love. People just can't get along with each other in general. Why should romance or marriage be any different? For that matter, most people can't maintain long lasting friendships either. Chet and I have hashed this out more than a few times. He maintains it is the sexual element that mostly causes the trouble. I disagree.

124:5 I don't recall the specific exchange, but I probably did make this remark -- I say a lot of unfounded and mean things. Still, I doubt Chet was actually having a mid-life crisis. Robots don't have mid-life crises.

181:8 - 184:4 I'm not in this scene, but I can't resist noting that the idea of Chester Brown and Joe Matt discussing the nature of romantic love is not unlike two blind men painting a sunset.

191:3 - 197:2 First off -- where is this conversation taking place, Chet? I'm guessing the lobby of a hotel.

Secondly, I suspect Chet is letting me off lightly here. The quality of my argument was probably even feebler than what he's reported in these pages. I wouldn't have had well grounded opinions on these matters back then. And I doubt my opinions today would be much better informed. That said, I do think Chet comes off a little better here than he probably would in real life. He's definitely the "voice of reason" on these pages, and I have my doubts that most people would come away with that opinion if they'd ever had a good solid argument with Chester in the real world. He's certainly set in his ways -- he's thought his position out well, and he's committed to it. No doubt about that. But often his opinion is a little too dogmatic for my tastes -- a little too tied to the libertarian party-line about the sanctity of property rights. It's a bit of a broken record listening to these arguments over and over again. I gotta say, it tires me out. I really couldn't give a shit about most of these issues. I'm busy moping about the past, folks -- I don't have time to read every new book on the ethics of prostitution. Cut some slack if I come off looking ill-informed here! And yes, backed into a rhetorical corner I likely did utter that stupid line about smoking.

227:3 | Who knows? Maybe he's right.

Knowing Chet has been a learning curve for me. He's forced me to consider many unconventional positions I would not have given much thought to otherwise. Disputing issues with him has helped me to think more critically. It's been good for me. It's taught me to question my own assumptions. I suspect that if I had a better memory I would be embarrassed by the many knee-jerk, reactionary comments I have undoubtedly made to him over the years regarding love and prostitution. The truth is, if I had a problem with Chet's involvement with prostitutes in the past I have certainly gotten over it. Prostitution may not work for every man, but it works for him.

The funny thing about Chester is that out of all the men I know he's quite possibly the one I think would make the most considerate boyfriend or husband for a woman... and yet he is the one who picked the whoring. It's a funny world.

NOTES

COVER My publishers wanted this book to be called
PAYING FOR IT. I don't like the title -- there's an implied
double-meaning. It suggests that not only am I paying
for sex but I'm also paying for being a john in some
non-monetary way. Many would think that there's an
emotional cost -- that johns are sad and lonely. There's
a potential health cost if one contracts a sexually
transmitted disease. There's a legal cost if one is
arrested. If one is "outed", then one could lose one's
job and also suffer the social cost of losing one's
friends and family. I haven't been "paying for it" in
any of those ways. I'm very far from being sad or
lonely, I haven't caught an S-T-D, I haven't been
arrested, I haven't lost my career, and my friends and
family haven't rejected me (although I should admit
that I still haven't told my step-mom).
   So far, I've been paying in only the one sense. (Since
this is a memoir, "so far" is all that's relevant.)
   But let me be clear that my publishers did not
force the title on me. I chose to give in to what they
wanted. If I had insisted, they would have allowed
me to put whatever words I wanted on the cover. I
love and respect Chris and Peggy and realize that
this is a difficult book to market.

NOTES

PANEL 9:5 Jealousy is natural, but that doesn't mean that not feeling jealous is not natural. It's probably better to frame the matter in relation to maturity. It's immature to be jealous, it's mature to not feel jealous.

Although I can't really defend the position that jealousy is learned, I do think our culture encourages the reaction. An example of a culture that discourages it is the Moso culture of Himalayan China. In Cai Hua's book about the Moso (A SOCIETY WITHOUT FATHERS OR HUSBANDS), he reports a conversation he had with two young men:

> ["W]e don't know how to be jealous."
> "He's right!" his friend interjected. And to explain himself he added: "Girls belong to everyone. Whoever wants can visit them. There is nothing to be jealous about." [Hua, p. 213.]

From Yang Erche Namu's memoir about growing up as a Moso girl (LEAVING MOTHER LAKE):

> Although we feel such passions, we must repress jealousy and envy [....] In Moso eyes, no one is more ridiculous than a jealous lover [...., N]obody in Moso country today can recall [...] a truly ugly fight between [...] jilted lovers. [Yang, p. 69.]

Having brought up the subject, I should explain that Moso sexual partners don't usually live together. At night the men go visit their girlfriends (who live with their mothers). In the morning, the men return home. (The men also live with their mothers.) According to Christine Mathieu (who co-wrote LEAVING MOTHER LAKE):

> [T]hey have discarded marriage. [...] The Moso advocate [their] maternal way of life as the best possible, and the most likely to foster happiness and harmony. Visiting relationships, they say, keep relations between men and women pure and joyful, and people who live in large maternal houses do not fight like married people do. We can trust that they are speaking from experience, because many Moso have tried marriage, under pressure from the Communist authorities, and most gave up. [Yang, p. 280.]

For those of you who are interested in learning about this culture, the more readable of the two

260

NOTES

above-mentioned books is LEAVING MOTHER LAKE. Actually, it's more than readable -- I found it really involving.

18:8 - 23:3 We were attending the big San Diego comic-book convention. I don't depict them, but also sharing the hotel room with us were fellow cartoonists Joe Sacco, Adrian Tomine, and Chris Oliveros. (Chris is also one of the publishers of this book.) I don't think there were more than two beds in the room. (I don't remember who slept with whom.)

20:3 I think Ms Baggett was charging $50 for those signed polaroids, but I'm not 100 percent certain.

25:2 - 26:4 Savage, p. 60.

26:6 Escort print ads in Toronto in 1999 didn't have photos. Some on-line ads probably did, but I wasn't aware of their existence yet. When I did discover them a short while later, they weren't convenient. It could take five minutes or more for one photo to appear, and the computer would often crash as it struggled to put the image together. It was a few years before browsing on-line escort ads became easy.

30:6 I've never heard of the police doing anything like this. My paranoia is on display here.

31:6 I'm certainly capable of finding women who are older than 28 attractive. (Without giving her exact age, "Denise" is several years beyond 28.) My thinking here was that, since I couldn't see photos of the prostitutes, my odds of finding someone attractive were greater if I saw younger women. There are women who are fifty who are beautiful, but they're a small percentage of the whole females-who-are-fifty population -- there are more good-looking women in the females-who-are-twenty population.

34:8 I apologize to anyone named Steve McDougal.

35:4,5 No, they weren't watching me. Johns will apparently sometimes make appointments and never show up. Prostitutes who work incall want to give their location to as few people as possible -- they only want to give the address to guys who are really going to show up. If a john was calling from a pay-phone that was close to the incall, it increased the odds that he would actually arrive since at least he was in the neighborhood. (This practice was common at the time. I would guess that johns are now expected to use their cell-phones.)

44:4 I'm breaking Dan Savage's rule here: "let her lead". Even though I didn't want a massage, I should have let "Carla" give me one. That was probably her way of easing into physical intimacy with as little awkwardness as possible.

44:5 Yes, that's what I really said.

47:6-8 Tipping: I ended up usually giving a $30 tip when I was happy with a prostitute's service. ("Denise" tells me that many johns didn't tip her, but those who did typically gave $10 or $20. It may seem like an insignificant amount, but she appreciated even the $10 tips.)

Because independent sex-workers get to keep all of the money, while escorts-who-work-for-an-agency have to give "anywhere from 35 to 50 per cent" of the fee to the agency (McLaren, p. 52), some johns have made the argument that agency-escorts should be tipped, but not independents. This reasoning ignores the fact that independents have expenses that agency-escorts don't have. Also, as self-employed business-people, independents have time-consuming duties to deal with. (And time is money.) Depending on various factors, independents may or may not make more money, but tipping shouldn't be about trying to equalize things between different sorts of sex-workers -- it's a gesture that lets an individual prostitute know that you enjoyed the time you spent together.

48:8 - 49:2 I figured that most readers would understand, at least in a general way, what I meant by "the burden" here, but Sook-Yin has told me that she's puzzled by these panels, and since there's no reason to be coy or mysterious, I'll explain.

Every time I saw an attractive woman, I wanted to walk up to her and try to initiate some sort of interaction. I usually lacked the confidence to do so.

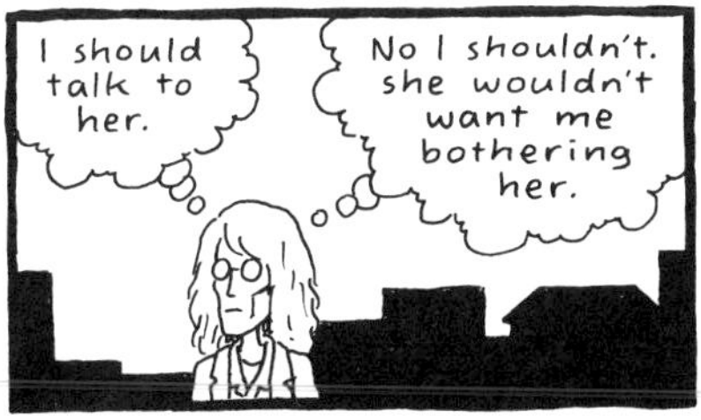
I should talk to her.
No I shouldn't. she wouldn't want me bothering her.

Those frequent inner battles led to a lot of tension. I rarely acted, which added to the burden because I'd condemn myself for failing to do anything and for missing potential opportunities. Further adding to the burden was the fact that sometimes attractive women (often complete strangers) would flirt with me or try even more direct means to get my attention. There was the young woman who yelled at me on the street, "You're cute!" and then hid behind her friend, and the one who asked me in a record store what my favorite band was, and the one in the subway who wanted to know about the book I was reading -- I could give many more examples. That sort of thing happened to me quite often when I was younger. Because I was socially awkward I usually said the wrong thing (or nothing at all) and nothing of significance would happen. I'd condemn myself for blowing all those opportunities, and I obsessed about them.

I wasn't even aware that all of that felt like a burden until I walked out of that brothel and saw an attractive woman on the street and realized I felt no inner tension about whether or not I should talk to her. Of course I shouldn't -- she was a stranger. Why would I worry that I was missing an opportunity to potentially have sex? Suddenly, sex with beautiful women was easy to get. Suddenly, it didn't matter that, years before, a beautiful young woman had yelled at me, "You're cute!" and I'd just kept walking without talking to her. Suddenly those sorts of memories weren't memories of missed opportunities -- they were things that could have gone wrong. What if I'd talked to that "You're cute!" girl, and we'd ended up in a miserable marriage, and I'd stayed unhappily faithful to her, and I'd never visited the brothel that I'd just walked out of? In that moment I wasn't condemning any past actions or failures to act, and I wasn't worrying about whether or not to talk to any of the beautiful women walking by me on the sidewalk. Instead I was looking forward to a future of sexual satisfaction.

NOTES

And, as I wrote: The burden has never returned.

51:2 There are two weekly newspapers in Toronto that
print escort ads, NOW and EYE. Although I mention
only NOW in the comic-strip, I also regularly perused
the ads in EYE.

52:2 Joe would like me to note that, while he is
cheap, that's not why he isn't a john. He wouldn't
pay for sex even if he was rich, because, despite his
reputation, he's very romantic. Which is true -- my
portrayal of Joe doesn't properly convey his romantic
side.

55:6-8 My bedroom looks different here than the
way it looks in Chapter 1. That's because it was
different. In the fall of 1998, Sook-Yin and I moved
from an apartment to a small house that she bought.

65:7 Just to make it clear -- she was refusing the
tip, not the fee for the half-hour.

69:1 - 76:8, 81:1 - 84:3 Was "Angelina" a sex-slave? She
worked in an incall brothel -- this is the preferred
working venue for sex-slavers because it gives them
the most control over the sex-slaves. (Perrin, pp. 45,
46.) "Angelina's" hesitation about getting up when I
chose her (73:7 - 74:6) is suggestive -- she was acting
the way one would expect a sex-slave to act: reluc-
tantly. On the other hand, it's possible she wasn't reluc-
tant but just confused since she didn't speak English.
And many prostitutes who choose the work also choose
to work in brothels since they're seen as being safer
than working on the streets, or out of one's home, or
doing outcalls.
     There are two other factors to consider: "Tina"
and the "monster in a mini-skirt" from Chapter 5,
who I'm going to call "Angelina II". Imagine you're a
sex-slaver who's running a brothel and you have
some unattractive women working for you and
some beautiful women. (As I mention in panel 73:6,
there were two good-looking ladies in the place the
first time I visited. The second time, I saw yet a
third beauty there.) Sex-slavers presumably care
about making money, not about the feelings of the
sex-slaves. If you wanted to maximize your profits,
who would you use to greet johns at the door:
unattractive sex-slaves or beautiful ones? If you use
the unattractive ones, there's a good chance the
guys will leave without even walking in, so obviously you'd use the attractive women to lure the men

inside. Yet that wasn't what happened. The first time I was there, plain-and-dumpy "Tina" answered the door, and the second time it was "Angelina II", who was flat-out ugly. It's hard to be sure based on only two experiences, but it looks like the place was being run by someone with an egalitarian bent -- they were letting the unattractive women have an equal shot at getting clients. Actually, forget the who-got-to-answer-the-door issue -- I can't imagine that sex-slavers would have bothered to kidnap "Angelina II". She wasn't someone who might have been attractive at one point -- she had clearly always been very difficult-to-look-at. None of this proves that the place was not run by sex-slavers, but it seems unlikely that it was, since whoever-ran-the-brothel doesn't seem to have thought of money as their only consideration.

| 84:1, 2 | It may seem odd that I hadn't noticed "Angelina's" inability to speak English during our first session. As you see on pages 74 to 76, most of my attempts to talk to her were met with the two-word reply, "It's okay." I took that as an indication that she didn't want to talk. I try to be sensitive to the cues that each sex-worker gives. I'll make an effort to start a conversation, but if a woman doesn't seem to want to chat, I'll shut up.

While "Angelina" seemed uncomfortable during our first session, she was very sweet and loving the second time despite her obvious lack of sexual excitement. I wish I'd been able to see her more.

| 86:6 | I used my real name with prostitutes from this point on.

My graphic novel LOUIS RIEL was serialized in ten 24-page "comic book" pamphlets before it was released as a book in 2003. This was the first of the pamphlets -- it was published in June 1999.

| 86:7 | The right pronunciation is LOO-ee ree-EL.

| 91:1 - 92:7 | "Amanda" spoke with a foreign accent. Was she a sex-slave? When I phoned her to ask if we could get together, she didn't automatically say yes. When I said I'd already seen "Anne", "Amanda" made me wait while she consulted with her work-mate. Only after "Anne" had said I was okay did the appointment get booked. The impression I get is that sex-slaves are not allowed to be that picky about their clients and wouldn't get to book their own appointments. And I don't see why sex-slavers would set her up in the sort of incall situation she was in with "Anne", who

was not trafficked. ("Anne" said she was born here and certainly seemed and sounded completely Canadian.) I would think that sex-slavers would want to isolate sex-slaves away from Canadian prostitutes, who might, through regular interaction, develop sympathy for the foreign girls and, as a result, might want to help them.

100:1 - 101:8 The web-site in question is terb.ca. It's a valuable source of information for johns who live in Toronto or visit it.

These review-sites are controversial for prostitutes. SPREAD MAGAZINE, which is written by sex-workers, ran pro and con pieces on the subject in their summer 2009 issue. (Vol. 5, issue 1.) Kelly of Washington, DC wrote:

> Any businessperson knows there's no better advertisement than word of mouth, and [...] these sites are wonderful outlets for exactly that type of free advertising. [...] I don't even pay for advertising anymore, since I get new clients every time someone writes a new review. [P. 20.]

Natalie of San Francisco had a very different opinion:

> Seeing the intimate details of my encounter with a client makes me feel disgusting, no matter how positively he rates the experience.

She instituted a no-review policy.

> Without allowing reviews, I find I am better able to offer a unique, special experience to each client I come in contact with. I don't have specific things to live up to, and am able to relax, enjoy myself, and ultimately offer a better time to both parties. While it's true that I don't get as high a volume as I did [when I allowed reviews], I much prefer spending my time with the few men who will take a chance. [P. 21.]

Both women had more to say on the subject -- I'm just printing these excerpts to give a sense of the debate.

By the way, SPREAD is worth checking out whether you're selling sex or buying it. I'm always happy to see a new issue. The web-site is spreadmagazine.org.

100:8 The expression is actually "bare-back blow-job", so Joe was close. He's now embarrassed that he didn't guess correctly, but I don't think he should be. He got the right meaning, if not the exact wording, and I'd been puzzling over the initials for at least fifteen minutes with no success, while Joe was able to come up with his suggestion immediately.

107:8 – 108:1 This was how I broached the topic of her age, but there were other reasons why I thought she was older. She had told me various details about her life, and some of those details seemed improbable unless she was older than eighteen.

127:1 – 129:7 This scene takes place in the same brothel that "Carla" (Chapter 2) worked in. "Jolene" (Chapter 15) and "Myra" (Chapter 22) also worked there.

128:8, 129:1 "Diane" did not have a hairy mole. She had a problem that I'm going to be deliberately vague about (just as I was vague about the location of the non-existent mole). Let's just say that this problem was hindering my ability to find her sexually attractive, and she could easily have dealt with the problem so that it wouldn't have been as noticeable as it was.

135:2 That was the best blow-job of my life until I met "Denise".

149:4 I always carry a book with me, and this was the book I was reading at the time. I do remember that "Susan/Alexis" asked a question that indicated a knowledge of American history beyond what your average person would know, but I don't remember what the question was.

150:6 – 151:2 Why didn't I recognize her? She had a different hair-style. More significantly, she was acting differently. The first time I saw her, although she was polite, she was also detached and distant. The second time she was much more friendly.
    This chapter is set in the same brothel that "Danielle" (Chapter 14) worked in.

155:4 I'd read a book which claimed that "half and half" is a common expression in the world of prostitution. This was my first and last attempt to use the expression.

159:3 – 160:1 Sook-Yin would like me to make it clear that it was Steve who was concerned about my presence in the house, and he asked her to suggest that I find another place to live. Steve's a good guy and I understand why he was uncomfortable with the idea of having an ex-boyfriend of Sook-Yin's living with the two of them.

167:3, 4 "Gwendolyn" and I did get back in touch a few years later through terb.ca. (There's a private message system on the site.) She hoped I'd be willing to start seeing her again. I would have been eager to do so, but by that time I was seeing "Denise" and felt committed to her. So, with some regret, I told "Gwendolyn" that I couldn't see her.

(Yes, I used the word "committed" there. I do feel committed to "Denise". But <u>feeling</u> committed is different from having a formally stated commitment or promise. That feeling might change with time, or it might not -- I don't know. I recognize that emotions aren't necessarily permanent. The relationship I have with "Denise" will continue for as long as we both want it to continue.)

170:1 None of the incall-girls kissed me on the mouth, most of the outcall-girls did. I don't know why there was a difference.

170:3 Similarly, I never got the impression that any of the incall-girls I saw would have been willing to give me a condomless blow-job, while at least three of the outcall-girls would have done so if I hadn't stopped them. (The other two were "Kitty" and "Larissa".)

173:2 Kris complained that it wasn't clear why I never saw "Jenna" again. The explanation is in this panel -- she was too expensive. At $300 an hour, she was the most costly prostitute I saw. I was <u>really</u> happy with her service, but I couldn't afford it on a regular basis. It's also worth noting that I was just as happy during my later encounters with "Larissa", "Edith", and "Denise", even though they all charged less. My best sexual experiences with prostitutes were with those four young women. (The sex continues to be great with "Denise".)

173:4 I'm not wearing glasses in this panel. I bought contact-lenses a short while before seeing "Kitty" and began wearing them when I was with prostitutes. I did write and draw a few panels to show this, but I edited them out.

186:3 - 188:3   Was "Arlene" a sex-slave ? She didn't seem like one -- she was very cheerful and attentive. Also, sex-slaves are less likely to be sent on outcalls. In his book INVISIBLE CHAINS, Benjamin Perrin explains why:

> [Outcall e]scort services may provide the women with a measure of temporary freedom, increasing the risk that they may flee [. Perrin, pp. 45, 46.]

While Perrin does give an example of an outcall in which the prostitute was a sex-slave, she was accompanied to the john's hotel room "by a couple of burly men." (P. 154.) No burly men accompanied "Arlene".

191:3 - 197:2   In his notes (Appendix 23), Seth asks where this conversation took place. The dialogue in this scene is actually based on my memories of two conversations we had that I've mashed together as one. I can't remember when the first conversation happened, but I remember where : The Keg Restaurant on Church Street. Seth's wife Tania was with us, and she also took part in the discussion. The second conversation took place on March 30th 2007. Chris Ware was visiting and gave a talk at the University Of Toronto. The school put up Chris in a house on campus. Seth and I were hanging out with Chris in the living-room of this house. He left to do something -- perhaps unpack -- and Seth and I got into the second conversation. The setting in these panels is based on my (probably inaccurate) memory of what that living-room looked like. Chris rejoined us at some point but didn't participate in the exchange until we switched topics.

193:4, 5　This is how I _wish_ I'd responded to Seth's statement in panel 193:3. The rest of the word-balloons I wrote for myself in this scene reflect the way I remember the actual conversations going. Still, what Seth writes in Appendix 23 is valid: "Chet comes off a little better here than he probably would in real life." I'm sure I expressed my points more awkwardly in the real discussions. And those discussions would have been more like debates -- Seth would have been more forceful in opposing what I was saying.

196:8 - 197:2　While Seth said this, he wasn't actually smoking when he said it. (But he probably lit up within twenty minutes.)

198:2 -8　A further point about the exclusionary nature of possessive monogamy: it causes resentment. If you're in a possessive monogamy relationship and you find yourself sexually attracted to someone-other-than-your-romantic-partner at a party (or work, or wherever), and you find yourself wishing you could act on this attraction, but you can't because you're in a monogamous relationship, you're likely to feel resentment. That resentment builds up and results in the sort of melodramatic fights that are common in possessive monogamy. Those sorts of intense, heavily emotional fights are rare between friends, and one of the reasons is because there's less resentment between friends. That's because you can have as many friends as you want -- it's not an exclusive relationship. If the social code said you could have only one friend, resentments between friends would increase. (This is a general tendency. I'm sure there are emotionally mature people who know how to defuse their resentments or who never feel the emotion to begin with. And people who have difficulty getting laid might feel less resentment in monogamous relationships than people who don't have that difficulty.)

199:7　It may seem like I was being cruel by forcing "Edith" to admit that she was having sex with all of her clients and that therefore, by implication, she actually was a prostitute. The thing is, given the argument she made, I didn't know what her answer would be. I actually did think that maybe she wasn't having sex with all her clients.

201:8　The Cathar heresy, a pacifist brand of Christianity embracing tolerance and poverty, rose to prominence in the middle of the twelfth century [. O'Shea, p. 7.]

For the Cathars, the world was not the handi-
work of a good god. It was wholly the creation of
a force of darkness, immanent in all things. Matter
was corrupt, therefore irrelevant to salvation.
Little if any attention had to be paid to the elabo-
rate systems set up to bully people into obeying
the man with the sharpest sword, the fattest
wallet, or the biggest stick of incense. Worldly
authority was a fraud, and worldly authority
based on some divine sanction, such as the
Church claimed, was outright hypocrisy.
    The god deserving of Cathar worship was a
god of light, who ruled the invisible, the ethereal,
the spiritual domain; this god, unconcerned with
the material, simply didn't care if you got into
bed before getting married, had a Jew or
Muslim for a friend, treated men and women as
equals, or did anything else contrary to the teach-
ings of the medieval Church. It was up to the individual (man or woman) to decide whether he or
she was willing to renounce the material for a
life of self-denial. If not, one would keep retur-
ning to this world -- that is, be reincarnated --
until ready to embrace a life sufficiently spotless
to allow accession, at death, to the same blissful
state one had experienced as an angel prior to
having been tempted out of heaven at the beginning of time. To be saved, then, meant becoming
a saint. To be damned was to live, again and
again, on this corrupt Earth. Hell was here, not
in some horrific afterlife dreamed up by Rome
to scare people out of their wits.
[O'Shea, pp. 10, 11.]

In 1208, the Catholic church declared a crusade
against the Cathars. The heresy was finally crushed in
1244.

202:2, 3   Rougemont, Book II, Chapters 6-10.
    Was there a connection between the troubadours
and the Cathars ? I'm not well-versed enough in the
subjects to say with confidence whether Rougemont
was right or wrong on this matter.

202:5   While courtly love was important in the devel-
opment of the concept of romantic love, probably just
as important was the influence of what C. Stephen
Jaeger calls "ennobling love" in his book of the same
title. He defines it as "a spiritualized love that
responds to the 'virtue,' the 'majesty,' the charisma, the
saintliness, of the beloved, to some inner force of auth-

ority or amiability or sanctity." (Jaeger, p. 4.) This was
a form of love that men expressed for other men. Prior to
the 12th century, it was commonly believed that "the love
of men for women could not ennoble, since sexuality
was its natural fulfillment. Love and friendship of men
for women that claimed 'virtue' and innocence inevita-
bly roused suspicion." (Jaeger, p. 7,) Jaeger points out
that expressions of intense friendship-love between men
were very common from ancient times up until the devel-
opment of courtly love. Although these friendships were
not sexual, the expression of this form of love was so
effusive that it resembled what we call romantic love.
Jaeger contends that, in her letters to Abelard, Heloise
(ca. A-D 1090 - 1163) was the first to apply "ennobling
love" to a sexual relationship between a man and a
woman.

> The defense of passionate love is a creation of
> Heloise. [...] She constructed a virtuous sexual
> passion of the elements of ennobling love: self-
> lessness, purity of intention, love of merit, purity
> of love, mutuality, complete self-abandonment.
> She is the architect of a higher law of pure love
> sanctioning sexuality [. Jaeger, p. 169.]

(Heloise was defending the pre-marital sex that she
and Abelard had enjoyed. She had not wanted to
marry Abelard because she was afraid that marriage
would destroy their love. She was right.) The
letters of Abelard and Heloise became famous, and
when combined with the popularity of courtly love-
poetry, influenced men and women to relate to each
other in a different way. (This, in turn, influenced
how men related to each other. According to Jaeger,
expressions of "ennobling love" between men died off
as male-and-female love-literature became fashionable.)
    This doesn't mean that regular people started
marrying for love immediately. The idea percolated in
European literature for the next few centuries, and
people became gradually more receptive to it. Personally, I think what really began the popularity of marrying for love was the rise of the romantic novel in
the 18th century (beginning with the success across
Europe of Samuel Richardson's PAMELA, published in
1740).

> By the end of the 1700s personal choice of partners
> had replaced arranged marriage as a social ideal,
> and individuals were encouraged to marry for
> love. [Coontz, pp. 145 - 146.]

> The new norms of the love-based, intimate marriage did not fall into place all at once but were adopted at different rates in various regions and social groups. In England, the celebration of the love match reached a fever pitch as early as the 1760s and 1770s, while the French were still commenting on the novelty of "marriage by fascination" in the mid-1800s. Many working-class families did not adopt the new norms of marital intimacy until the twentieth century.
> [Coontz, p. 147.]

Marrying for love started to gain widespread acceptance in the 18th century. I don't think it was a coincidence that at the same time our modern concept of "the prostitute" was forming. From Laura María Agustín's SEX AT THE MARGINS:

> [T]here was no word or concept which signified exclusively the sale of sexual services until the [late 18th century]. "Whoring" referred to sexual relations out of marriage and connoted immorality or promiscuity without the involvement of money, and the word whore was used to brand any woman who stepped outside current boundaries of respectability. [Agustín, p. 101.]

Money was not a defining characteristic of prostitution in the pre-modern era. Reading Agustín's book I began to wonder if it's a modern idea to separate "trade" aspects of a sexual relationship from "non-trade" aspects and if, in attempting to do so, we aren't drawing arbitrary boundaries. It looks obvious to us in the 21st century that prostitution is a form of commercial trade and that romantic love and marriage have nothing to do with trade. But prior to the 18th century, one rarely married for love -- it was much more common to marry for money.

> In Europe, from the early Middle Ages through the eighteenth century, the dowry a wife brought with her at marriage was often the biggest infusion of cash, goods, or land a man would ever acquire. Finding a husband was usually the most important investment a woman could make in her economic future.
> [Coontz, p. 6.]

Of course, many people still marry for money -- it's just taboo to openly admit it now. Even when it's not the primary reason for marriage, most people entering into matrimony do consider the financial situation of the person they're marrying.

It's also worth pointing out that, aside from rape (which is about taking without giving anything), sex is always about trade: "I want to give you physical pleasure because I want physical pleasure in return", or, "I'll have sex with you because I want affection", or, "You can fuck me for 200 dollars." It's all trade.

> **203:7** Antiquity has left no record of an experience akin to the love of Tristan and Iseult. It is well known that the Greeks and Romans looked on love as a sickness [...] whenever it went, no matter how little, beyond the sensual pleasure which was considered to be its natural expression. Plutarch calls love "a frenzy". "Some have believed it was a madness.... Thus those who are in love must be forgiven as though ill." [Rougemont, p.60.]

203:8 - 204:1 Cartoonist Eric Shanower has been retelling the story of the Trojan War as a series of graphic-novels. According to the first volume, AGE OF BRONZE: A THOUSAND SHIPS, Odysseus had wanted to marry Helen but instead was given her cousin, Penelope, as a sort of consolation prize. I trust that Shanower is basing that on some ancient version of the tale, or at least isn't contradicting the original sources. (The book isn't paginated. If the first page that starts the story is page one, then the relevant passages regarding Odysseus and Penelope are on pages 126 and 135.)

Incidently, I've been enjoying the AGE OF BRONZE series. I hope Shanower manages to finish it.

> **204:3** We find isolated records of passionate love experienced by spouses among the ancient Hebrews, Greeks, and Romans. But since arranged marriages, rather than love marriages, were the norm in premodern times, brides and grooms did not enter marriage with the expectation of "loving" each other as we understand the term. [Yalom, p. xvi.]

204:4 I believed for a while that there are no pre-12th-century literary works that contain characters who first fall in love and _then_ get married. This is <u>almost</u> true, but not quite. Reading THE SEVEN BASIC PLOTS by Christopher Booker, I came across a reference to the ancient Greek novel DAPHNIS AND CHLOE by Longus (ca. the 2nd or 3rd century A·D). Booker's description indicates that it's about a couple who marry because

they've fallen in love. I went out and picked up an
English translation -- Booker is right. According to the
introduction in my copy of DAPHNIS AND CHLOE, there are
other similar Greek and Latin works from this period.
[Longus, p. x.] It seems that they didn't persuade people
in any significant numbers to put marriage-for-love
into practice.

207:2 - 208:1   Was "Laura" a sex-slave? During our
post-coital conversation, "Laura" told me about a trip
she'd just taken back to her homeland and how she'd
visited her family while there. That indicates to me a
greater degree of mobility and freedom than one
would expect a sex-slave to have.

209:3   I'm not a teetotaller, but it's rare that I drink
any kind of alcohol, so I never have any at home.

210:6 - 211:2   "Denise" doesn't remember this happening.
After she read the book, she asked, "Really? I forgot to
pick up the money that first time?" Yes, she did.
Mistakes like that can happen. A few years later I
forgot to put the money out, which led to mutual
embarrassment. She was embarrassed to have to ask
for it, and I was embarrassed because I didn't want
her to think that I'd been trying to get away with not
paying. I now have a check-list of things to remember
to do before "Denise" arrives -- at the top of the list it
says, "money out".

212:2, 3   It may seem hard to believe that I was working so hard that I couldn't spare an hour or two a
month to see a prostitute. All I can say is, that was
the head-space I was in. Yes, I could have paid for sex
a few more times in 2003 and still have made the
publication deadline for LOUIS RIEL and completed all of
my promotional duties, but I was in such a panicked
state that I felt like I didn't have an extra minute.
   I'm in a similar panicked state as I finish this book.
The only reason why I'm having sex during this
deadline-crunch is because my relationship with
"Denise" is too firmly established in my life.

221:8   When I first met Sook-Yin, she braided her hair
like this most of the time. Over the years she gradually
stopped doing so. By 2008 she would not have worn her
hair in this style.

222:8 - 223:7   I remember the point Gord made in this
conversation, but not exactly how he expressed it. He

did not use an imaginary couple named Jack and Jane to clarify what he was saying.
(By the way, my brother is not himself in an open Jack-and-Jane situation. He's in a committed, monogamous relationship.)

225:3, 4 I've failed to convey how amused Seth was when I admitted that I love "Denise". Seth and I were actually sitting in a restaurant on Queen Street at the time -- Terroni.

226:2 - 227:3 This part of the conversation never happened. When I drew these panels I had only told "Denise" about feeling that emptiness.

227:3 The date at the bottom of this panel -- June 7th 2010 -- is when I thought I was finished drawing the book. A few days later I read the whole work through and I wasn't happy with the result. I had more to do -- editing out panels and drawing new ones. By September 9th I had a version of the story that I was happier with.

AFTERWORD * Fellow cartoonist Dave Sim stopped regarding me as a friend in 2008 because I refused to sign an internet petition that he set up that reads, "Dave Sim is not a misogynist." I don't agree with his opinion that women are intellectually inferior to men, but my affection and respect for him remain unchanged.

APPENDIX 1 * The way I've phrased this might seem to imply that other countries followed Canada's lead in decriminalizing homosexuality. Canada was actually following England's lead. (Gudgeon, p. 197.)

A. 2 * I have no strong opinion on the connection between genes and sexual preference. It wouldn't surprise me if there is a "gay gene", and it wouldn't surprise me if there isn't one.

A. 6 * If you're wondering why I didn't encounter any prostitutes who only gave oral, it's because they made it clear in their ads what the nature of their service was. I knew I wanted more than a blow-job, so I didn't call the oral-only sex-workers.

A. 6 ** Amy, "A `Professional Lover' Speaks", NATIO-NAL POST, July 15th 2006.

NOTES

I should admit that I rearranged the order of the quote -- the "[I]n four years" section appears before the "My clients" section in Amy's essay.

A. 8 *   Delacoste, p. 120.

A. 8 **   Jane and AnaNicole, "Dear John", SPREAD, Winter 2008, p. 18.

A. 8 *I*   Monét, p. 221.

A. 9 *   Name withheld, "Letters", EYE WEEKLY (Toronto), March 1st 2007, p. 5.

A. 9 **   Monét, p. 220.

A. 10 *   Jeffreys, pp. 260, 261.
Jeffreys is quoting from page 159 of a 1991 publication, RAPE AND SEXUAL ASSAULT III : A RESEARCH HANDBOOK, edited by Ann Wolpert Burgess.

A. 10 **   "Denise" tells me that she enjoys having sex with me. Many of you reading this will think that she's being less than honest with me. Personally, I believe her, but I realize that she probably enjoys sex with me less than she has enjoyed it with the non-paying sexual partners she's had and that, if I wasn't paying her, she wouldn't continue to go to bed with me.

A. 10 *I*   Feminist work on the effects upon women of sexual violence, such as rape, incest, sexual harassment and marital rape, can be usefully applied to the effects of prostitution.
[Jeffreys, p. 268.]

A. 10 *   Many prostitutes have developed screening systems that successfully filter out violent customers. For instance, one independent Toronto call-girl requires that "New clients must provide either a real name and work phone number or two references from other respected call girls." (McLaren, p. 56.)

A. 11 *   Here's the context in which Sheila Jeffreys associated sexual objectification with emotional indifference. This is her definition of prostitution:

> Male sexual behaviour characterized by three
> elements variously combined: barter, promiscuity,
> emotional indifference. Any man is a prostitution
> abuser who, for the purposes of his sexual satis-
> faction, habitually or intermittently reduces
> another human being to a sexual object by the
> use of money or other mercenary considerations.
> [Jeffreys, p. 4.]

"Prostitution abuser" is a term she uses interchangeably
with "john".
　　Jeffreys is Australian -- does the word "barter" have
a different meaning in Australia ? Here in Canada it
refers to trade <u>without</u> money.

A. 12 ＊　　The best book I've read about trafficking
and sex-work is Laura María Agustín's SEX AT THE
MARGINS. She recognizes that most trafficked people
don't see themselves as helpless victims. Regarding
their debt-bondage, she quotes a Columbian
trafficked into Spain:

> I never considered it to be a debt. For me it was
> like a favour that they did for me.
> [Agustin, p. 34.]

A. 12 ＊＊　　Andrew Rosetta, review of SEX TRAFFICKING,
edited by Siddharth Kara, SPREAD, Fall 2009, p. 59.
　　The statistic comes from Kara, who sees
prostitution as a form of exploitation.

A. 12 ＊I＊　　The show was SOUNDS LIKE CANADA, hosted by
Shelagh Rogers. The interview subjects were Benjamin
Perrin and Detective Gordon McCulloch.

A. 16 ＊　　I'm sure that in most ways the licenced prostitutes of Nevada are similarly controlled now, but in
a time when almost everyone has a cell-phone I wonder
if telephone use in the Nevada brothels is restricted
the way it was in the 1990s.

A. 19 ＊　　Then came the breakthrough that marked
[Pierre] Trudeau's public emergence as the [...]
charismatic figure that a traumatized Canada
was seeking. Early in December [1967] -- only days
after [Canadian Prime Minister] Lester Pearson
had formally announced his retirement at last --

NOTES

Trudeau brought before the House of Commons a divorce reform bill and several amendments to the Criminal Code liberalizing laws on abortion and homosexuality. This overhaul of social legislation had been under way in the Justice Department for years. But Trudeau made the changes his own by telling the television cameras outside the House, "The state has no place in the bedrooms of the nation." That this idea was borrowed directly from an editorial written by Martin O'Malley that week for THE GLOBE AND MAIL went unnoticed. Delivered by a minister of the Crown wearing a leather coat and sporting a Caesar haircut, it had an electrifying effect on the public imagination. It expressed a widely felt need to bring Canada up to date in a way that everybody could understand. Here was a man who was willing to declare himself in opposition to the established order, a man who was saying that Canada did not have to be a Victorian backwater, a museum of outmoded ideas.
[Clarkson, pp. 107, 108.]

Trudeau was then the minister of justice. This is what he actually said to the above-mentioned television cameras on December 21st 1967:

Take this thing on homosexuality. I think the view we take here is that there's no place for the state in the bedrooms of the nation. I think that what's done in private between adults doesn't concern the Criminal Code. When it becomes public this is a different matter, or when it relates to minors this is a different matter.
[Gudgeon, p. 199.]

He became the prime minister in 1968.

A. 20 *   I highly recommend Crad Kilodney's autobiographical novels EXCREMENT (Charnel House, 1988) and PUTRID SCUM (Charnel House, 1991). Unfortunately they're both out of print, but perhaps you can find used copies.

BIBLIOGRAPHY

Agustín, Laura María. SEX AT THE MARGINS: MIGRATION, LABOUR MARKETS AND THE RESCUE INDUSTRY. London: Zed, 2007.
Albert, Alexa. BROTHEL: MUSTANG RANCH AND ITS WOMEN.

2001. New York: Ballantine, 2002.

Booker, Christopher. THE SEVEN BASIC PLOTS: WHY WE TELL STORIES. 2004. London: Continuum, 2007.

Clarkson, Stephen, and Christina McCall. TRUDEAU AND OUR TIMES: VOLUME I: THE MAGNIFICENT OBSESSION. 1990. Toronto: McClelland & Stewart, 1997.

Coontz, Stephanie. MARRIAGE, A HISTORY: FROM OBEDIENCE TO INTIMACY. New York: Viking, 2005.

Delacoste, Frédérique, and Priscilla Alexander, eds. SEX WORK: WRITINGS BY WOMEN IN THE SEX INDUSTRY. Second edition. San Francisco: Cleis, 1998.

Gudgeon, Chris. THE NAKED TRUTH: THE UNTOLD STORY OF SEX IN CANADA. Vancouver: Greystone, 2003.

Hua, Cai. A SOCIETY WITHOUT FATHERS OR HUSBANDS: THE NA OF CHINA. Trans. Asti Hustvedt. New York: Zone, 2001.

Jaeger, C. Stephen. ENNOBLING LOVE: IN SEARCH OF A LOST SENSIBILITY. Philadelphia: Univ. Of Pennsylvania, 1999.

Jeffreys, Sheila. THE IDEA OF PROSTITUTION. Melbourne: Spinifex, 1997.

Longus. DAPHNIS AND CHLOE. Trans. and intro. Ronald McCail. 2002. Oxford: Oxford Univ., 2009

McLaren, Leah. "The Happiest Hooker." TORONTO LIFE, December 2010.

Monêt, Veronica. "Sedition." WHORES AND OTHER FEMINISTS. Ed. Jill Nagle. New York: Routledge, 1997.

O'Shea, Stephen. THE PERFECT HERESY: THE REVOLUTIONARY LIFE AND DEATH OF THE MEDIEVAL CATHARS. 2000. Vancouver: Douglas & McIntyre, 2001.

Perrin, Benjamin. INVISIBLE CHAINS: CANADA'S UNDER-GROUND WORLD OF HUMAN TRAFFICKING. Toronto: Viking, 2010.

Rougemont, Denis de. LOVE IN THE WESTERN WORLD. Trans. Montgomery Belgion. 1940. Princeton: Princeton Univ., 1983.

Savage, Dan. SAVAGE LOVE: STRAIGHT ANSWERS FROM AMERICA'S MOST POPULAR SEX COLUMNIST. New York: Plume, 1998.

Schaler, Jeffrey A. ADDICTION IS A CHOICE. Chicago: Open Court, 2000.

Yalom, Marilyn. A HISTORY OF THE WIFE. 2001. New York: Perennial, 2002.

Yang Erche Namu, and Christine Mathieu. LEAVING MOTHER LAKE: A GIRLHOOD AT THE EDGE OF THE WORLD. 2003. New York: Back Bay, 2004.

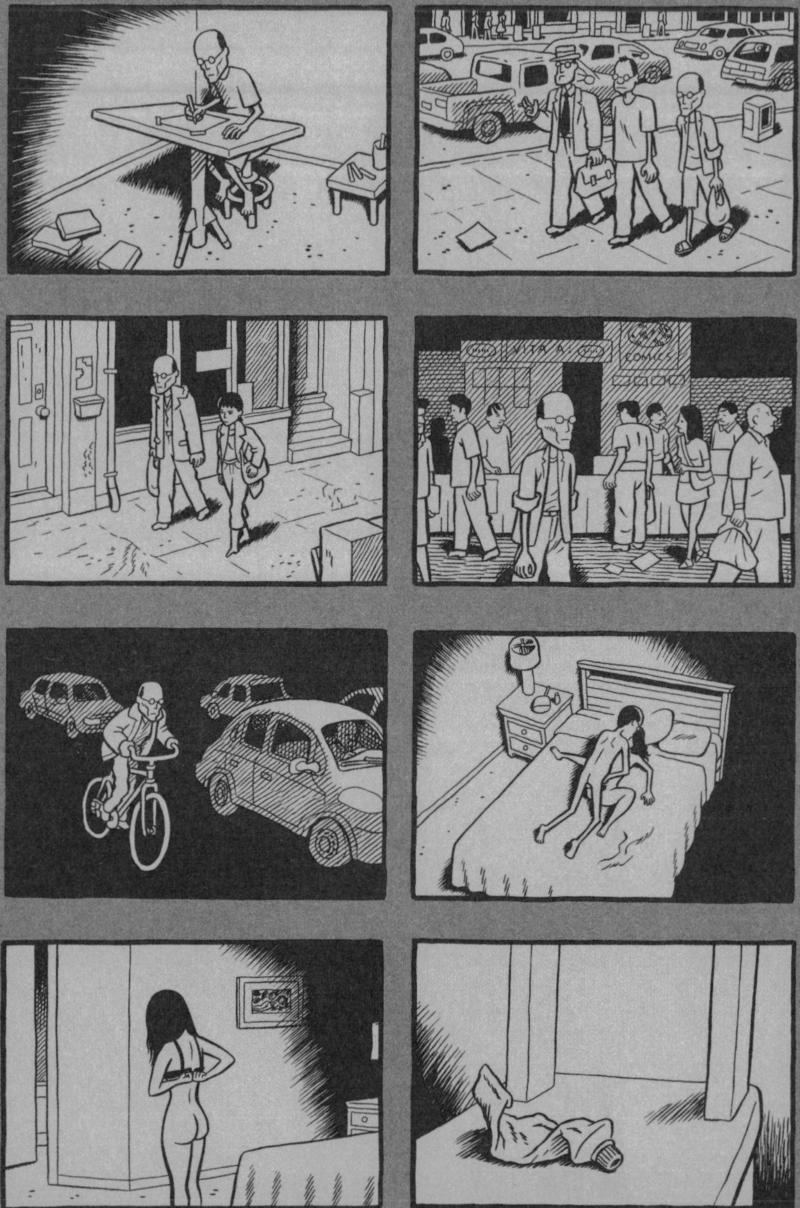
VITA A.
COMICS